Basic Cinematography
A Creative Guide to Visual Storytelling

by Kurt Lancaster

First edition published 2019
by Routledge
52 Vanderbilt Avenue, New York, NY 10017
and by Routledge
2 Park Square, Milton Park, Abingdon, Oxon OX14 4RN
Routledge is an imprint of the Taylor & Francis Group, an informa business

©2019 Taylor & Francis

The right of Kurt Lancaster to be identified as author of this work has been asserted by him in accordance with sections 77 and 78 of the Copyright, Designs and Patents Act 1988.

All rights reserved. No part of this book may be reprinted or reproduced or utilised in any form or by any electronic, mechanical, or other means, now known or hereafter invented, including photocopying and recording, or in any information storage or retrieval system, without permission in writing from the publishers. Printed in Canada.

Notices
Knowledge and best practice in this field are constantly changing. As new research and experience broaden our understanding, changes in research methods, professional practices, or medical treatment may become necessary.

Practitioners and researchers must always rely on their own experience and knowledge in evaluating and using any information, methods, compounds, or experiments described herein. In using such information or methods they should be mindful of their own safety and the safety of others, including parties for whom they have a professional responsibility.

Product or corporate names may be trademarks or registered trademarks, and are used only for identification and explanation without intent to infringe.

Library of Congress Cataloging in Publication Data

Names: Lancaster, Kurt, 1967– author.
Title: Basic cinematography : a creative guide to visual storytelling / Kurt Lancaster.
Description: London ; New York : Routledge, 2019] | Includes bibliographical references and index.
Identifiers: LCCN 2018052081| ISBN 9780815396444 (hardback : alk. paper) | ISBN 9780815396451 (pbk. : alk. paper) | ISBN 9781351182126 (e-book)
Subjects: LCSH: Cinematography. | Motion pictures--Technique.
Classification: LCC TR850 .L34 2019 | DDC 777--dc23
LC record available at https://lccn.loc.gov/2018052081

Contents

FOREWORD by Manuel Billeter vii
ACKNOWLEDGMENTS ix
INTRODUCTION The Foundation of Visual Storytelling xiii
CHAPTER 1 Visual Storytelling Through Blocking 1
   Section 1: Think like a director 2
   Section 2: Visual storytelling through the blocking of subtext 8
   Section 3: Hitchcock's key rules of filmmaking 14
   Section 4: Body language and blocking in *Girl with a Pearl Earing* 20
   Section 5: Discovering dramatic action through script analysis in
      Ozu's *Tokyo Twilight* 26
   Section 6: Visualizing subtext through blocking and body language in
      Ozu's *Tokyo Twilight* 31
   Section 7: Body language and subtext in documentary 40
CHAPTER 2 Visual Storytelling Through Lenses and Composition 51
   Section 1: Ten tools of composition 53
      1. Shot size and lenses: 56
      2. Camera height and angle: 61
      3. Camera motion: 63
      4. Focal depth of field: 66
      5. Light and dark: 70
      6. Line and linear perspective: 71
      7. Layers: 73
      8. Weight: 74
      9. Color: 76
      10. Texture: 78
   Section 2: Shooting for the edit 83
      1. Coverage: 83
      2. Eye lines: 83
      3. Point of view and cutaways: 84
      4. 180 degree rule: 84
      5. Jump cuts: 86
      6. Kuleshov effect: 88
   Section 3: Case study in lenses and composition from *Jessica Jones*
      with DP Manuel Billeter 95
   Section 4: Case study in lenses and composition from *Chef's Table*
      with DP Adam Bricker 98
   Section 5: Case study in lenses and composition from Ozu's
      Tokyo Twilight class reinterpretation 102

CHAPTER 3 Visual Storytelling Through Lighting ... 119

Section 1: The psychology of lighting ... 120
1. Foundation: 120
2. Light placement terminology: 122
3. Six elements of lighting: 123
   1. Quality: 123
   2. Intensity: 126
   3. Direction: 128
   4. Texture: 129
   5. Contrast: 136
   6. Color temperature: 141

Section 2: Some basic tools of exposure ... 144
1. The zone system: 144
2. Histogram: 148
3. Waveform: 150
4. Aperture and ISO: 152
5. ND filters: 154
6. Shutter angle and frame rates: 154
7. Lighting modifiers: 155

Section 3: Indoor day and outdoor day setup examples from "Fragments" ... 156

Section 4: Outdoor night case study from *Jessica Jones* with DP Manuel Billeter ... 162

Section 5: Indoor night case study from Ozu's *Tokyo Twilight* class project reinterpretation ... 166

Section 6: Documentary lighting case study from *Chef's Table* with DP Adam Bricker ... 176

CHAPTER 4 Visual Storytelling with Camera Log, RAW, and LUTs ... 191
Section 1: An overview of a dozen key camera features ... 193
Section 2: Shooting in log ... 205
Section 3: Shooting in RAW ... 211
Section 4: Shooting with LUTs ... 216

CHAPTER 5 Workflow Tools for the Beginning Cinematographer ... 221
Section 1: Preproduction for cinematographers ... 221
Section 2: Production for cinematographers ... 235
Section 3: Postproduction for cinematographers ... 236

CONCLUSION ... 260
INDEX ... 277

FOREWORD

Manuel Billeter, DP of *Jessica Jones, The Punisher, Luke Cage*

Filmmaking is a highly subjective endeavor. Filmmaking is also a collaborative endeavor. This apparent contradiction lays bare that there is no formula or equation that could explain or solve all the decisions to be made when approaching the visual translation from script to images. Where should we begin? I have always considered image-making an expression of non-verbal writing, of finding what's between the written lines, and composing it into a visual language that supports the underlying ideas of story, character, and setting—representing the script with evocative images.

The most basic building block to the visual language is the single shot, or take. That is "Basic Cinematography," if you will. But from my own experience, early during my own learning about cinema while in Berlin, I learned a curious linguistic fact about the term "shot" in German: *Einstellung*. Beyond the technical settings of lens, aperture, height, or movement, it also means attitude—or opinion, approach, perspective. In that sense, a shot not only technically reproduces the reality it captures, but more importantly, it also conveys an idea, an emotion, a tone.

In that sense, the "shot" has a much bigger responsibility than to merely capture a fact. Inspired by the narrative of the script, the characters, and the movement of the plot, as cinematographers it is our mission to write this vision down in images that echo what is inherent in the blueprint of the script, and also what it is only hinted at. In collaboration with the director and all the creative forces present during the preparation of the shoot, and then on set, all the minds and hands come together in creating images and emotions that continue to attract and fascinate audiences around the world. Shaping these images with composition, movement, lighting, color, and texture is one of our roles as cinematographers.

Writing with a sequence of images that are shaped to support the narrative almost becomes a musical or lyrical act. The pairing of colors, the play of contrast, the framing of the settings and landscapes, the sensuality of the light, the texture of materials—they all interact and create an additional layer of meaning to the material at hand.

A good eye is more important than the most advanced or "best" camera equipment. There are many tools that are given to us, and most of them lay outside the confines of the equipment list. Getting to know all the functions of our given instruments cannot possibly be experienced in a book. Nothing can really replace hands-on, immersive experience. But a book can summarize some ideas and categorize many aspects of what can help find conscious and thoughtful decisions when "writing with images." Reading before doing can be a simple and inspirational process.

Lancaster's book, *Basic Cinematography*, provides a strong foundation to do just this, offering tools that will help you become a better visual storyteller.

Manuel Billeter
15 October 2018

ACKNOWLEDGMENTS

Many thanks to Emily McCloskey for accepting the idea for this book during lunch at NAB a couple of years ago. Sheni Kruger has adeptly taken over the book and shepherded it to Sarah Pickles, who has kept me on schedule, as well as my production editor, Kris Siosyte. I also want to thank Simon Jacobs and John Makowski. Susan Leaper and Victoria Kelly are eagle-eye proofreaders and I thank them for the detailed task of finding and pointing out errors. The team at Focal Press/Routledge all rock!

Thanks to all of the manufacturers, artists, and photographers—too many to name individually—for permission to use their images in this book. Without the pictures, it would have just been words, which would just not have been as exciting.

Furthermore, much appreciation for the critical eyes of peer reviewers. Their thoughts made this book better.

Manuel Billeter and Adam Bricker are *tour de force* with cameras and lighting. Their cinematography is top notch and I'm privileged that they wanted to be a part of this book. Italian cinematographer Matteo Bertoli stressed the importance of cinematographers taking as much control of postproduction as possible.

I also wish to thank my colleagues at the School of Communication at Northern Arizona University, who provided moral support during the writing of this manuscript as I held down a full teaching load: Bill Carter, Toni DeAztlan-Smith, Paul Helford, Janna Jones, Anka Malatynska, Harun Mehmedinovic, Mark Neumann, Jon Torn, and Xin Yi. I also want to thank my dean, Karen Pugliesi.

In addition, I thank my cinematography, directing, and documentary students, who inspire me to do even better work—both in teaching and shooting. The inspiration of this book was drawn from them.

I also want to thank my friend Beau L'Amour, who always expresses deep insights on filmmaking. The section on the psychology of lenses and camera movement would not be the same without his insights.

My brother and sister-in-law, William and Dalia Mattison, and my niece, Nora let me hang out in New Jersey as I did the final proofreading of this book. Yummy food! They're the best! Finally, special thanks to my wife, Stephanie, who has supported this project since day one as well as to my stepson, Morgan. And, of course, to my mother, Judy Bennett, who always opens up her home in Maine for us in the dead cold of winter or during the balmy summers!

This book is dedicated to my students who went with me and my wife, Stephanie, to Bologna, Italy to shoot documentaries in June 2018:

- Kyle Bagdonas
- Marisol Elias
- Joshua Feygin
- Haydon Hoffman
- Brian Kibbee
- Kassandra Kraus
- Daniel Brown Muñoz
- David Niehaus
- Alexis Parks
- Alejandrin Zubia

You all made it fun! Keep shooting movies!

Still from *Chef's Table* "Francis Mallmann." DP: Will Basanta. (Image ©2015 Netflix.)

INTRODUCTION

THE FOUNDATION OF VISUAL STORYTELLING

The number one piece of advice I've heard at every film talk I've been to, when given by professional, working cinematographers, revolved first and foremost around the importance of storytelling—not the type of camera, or sensor size chosen, nor the brand of lights used. Technical skills and lights are important, but that's not what makes good films and it is not the focus of this book. Most cinematography books tend to be highly technical, so another technical book isn't needed. Rather, my focus entails the storytelling aspects of cinematography, a key element not found—or simply covered only in a cursory way—in other cinematography books. The storytelling aspects of filmmaking should be the foundation of cinematography training.

The first step in the cinematographer's job involves discovering emotions found in a story and translating them physically to the screen with a camera. It begins with the script. Filmmakers need to analyze the script for ways to visualize the story in order to reveal the emotional intent of the film, then utilize the tools of blocking, lenses, composition, camera movement, lighting, and sound design in order to make those emotions visible to an audience.

Some cinematographers may simply adhere to what the director wants without offering any creative input, but that's not the premise of this book. This book bridges the realm of the director, as well as the cinematographer, in order to give beginning filmmakers strong guiding tools for visual storytelling.

Many film schools force students to specialize in producing, screenwriting, cinematography, directing, editing, sound design, among others. At Northern Arizona University, we focus on independent filmmaking and train students to do most aspects of writing, production, and postproduction. We teach cinematography and directing at the same time and with the same cohort of students, focusing on visual storytelling. This holistic approach is important if we want cinematographers and directors to do better work.

Theater knowledge is important to visual storytelling in film. I've seen too many student films (and even some professional films) where actors stand around and *talk* rather than *do*. Aristotle, in his lecture notes on Greek drama (*Poetics*), says that characters are defined by the actions they take. I studied theater at the Master's level with my mentor and friend, Tom Mikotowicz, at the University of Maine and later with faculty—such as Richard Schechner—at New York University's Department of Performance Studies. While at NYU I took a summer film course at their film school—a six-week boot camp using 16mm film. After graduating from NYU with a PhD, I taught classes at the Massachusetts Institute of Technology and was asked to direct a production with MIT's Shakespeare Club.

> I've seen too many student films (and even some professional films) where actors stand around and *talk* rather than *do*. Aristotle, in his lecture notes on Greek drama, says that characters are defined by the actions they take.

Although I had a working and theoretical knowledge of what it meant to be a director in theater and film, it wasn't until I sat in the audience of MIT Shakespeare Club's production of *A Midsummer Night's Dream* that I understood the link between script, body language, and blocking as the foundation for visual storytelling in theater and film. It all came in an instant—Shakespeare's text is poetic and beautiful, and you can read it all day just to enjoy the language. It's what we did in high school English classes. I've seen many Shakespeare productions where the actors would stand around, performing the beautiful poetry, but it bored me—the actors were not *doing*, not embodying the text in body language and actions—the visual story (the emotional intent) occurring beneath the words spoken. There was too much telling instead of showing. Show. Don't tell. Reading is fine because we imagine what the characters are doing, but if, as an audience, we watch a film or a play and little *doing* happens, we get bored fast.

Not so in this production of *A Midsummer Night's Dream* I saw at MIT. It *moved*. Every intent of every actor expressed a purpose, visually telling the story beyond performing words. It was exciting to watch. A film—like a play—needs to physicalize the text in actions.[1] Look at most films that tend to bore us. The director failed to express the dramatic needs of the characters in a physical way, and good cinematography—slick camera moves and expressive lighting—cannot fix it. It simply glosses over the fundamental problem, the lack of visual storytelling.

The shots may look good, they may even be poetically beautiful, but if the story emotions contained in the script fail to materialize in a moment-to-moment manifestation through the blocking and body language of the actors, then the composition, camera movement, and lighting will unlikely serve the story.

Once that link is made—where the composition, lens, and lighting express, enhance, and reveal the underlying emotions and subtext of a scene—then the cinematography fulfills the needs of the story. Anything less fails the film.

> Once that link is made—where the composition, lens, and lighting express, enhance, and reveal the underlying emotions and subtext of a scene—then the cinematography fulfills the needs of the story. Anything less fails the film.

And this is why I wrote this book, because nothing quite like it exits. There are several really good books on cinematography, such as Blain Brown's *Cinematography: Theory and Practice: Image Making for Cinematographers and Directors* (Focal Press, 2016), now in its third edition. It's a great book, containing a lot of technical information. I've used it in my cinematography class, but it's too detailed for students who are still learning to shoot at an intermediate level.

You cannot ignore such classic cinematography books such as Joseph Mascelli's *The Five C's of Cinematography: Motion Picture Filming Techniques* (Silma-James Press, 1998, republished from the 1965 text). This book covers key concepts of

---

[1] I'm not asserting that theater and a film are the same thing. I'm talking about how the underlying dramatic action of characters in a story are similar.

camera angles, continuity, cutting, close-ups, and composition. And of course, John Alton's *Painting with Light* (University of California Press, 2013, republished from the 1949 text), presents an exhaustive overview of different shooting techniques with practical examples. David Stump's *Digital Cinematography: Fundamentals, Tools, Techniques, and Workflows* (Focal Press, 2014) is written by a member of the American Society of Cinematographers (ASC). This encyclopedic book comes in at nearly 500 pages and it provides intricate detail of technical knowledge needed in today's world of digital cinematography. It's an indispensible reference text needed for today's working professionals and advanced students.

And there's several great books focused just on lighting, such as David Landau's *Lighting for Cinematography: A Practical Guide to the Art and Craft of Lighting for the Moving Image* (Bloomsbury Academic, 2014, reprint edition). A good book that focuses on lighting in a solid way with clear examples. And you cannot dig into a solid understanding of visual storytelling in cinema without reading Bruce Block's foundational text, *The Visual Story: Creating the Visual Structure of Film, TV, and Digital Media* (Focal Press, 2007, 2nd edition). It examines the principles of visual images, including the ideas of contrast and affinity, space, line and shape, tone, color, movement, and visual rhythm, using examples from contemporary films.

I recommend all of these books for learning better filmmaking techniques, whether as students or as working professionals who want to deepen their craft. As I said at the beginning of this introduction, these books are mainly focused on the technical craft of cinematography—a good thing—but there's that missing element in all of them, the foundational concepts of visual storytelling,[2] the practical relationship between the visual story and technique that I feel is an essential foundation for students and beginning filmmakers since nearly all decisions in the production process—from documentaries, music videos, and shorts to feature narratives—need some understanding of story.[3]

---

[2] Bruce Block's book, *The Visual Story*, provides a strong foundation of the visual structure along with how to engage these elements in story, but he doesn't necessarily link it to the embodiment of the story through performances.

[3] As of this writing, I have not read Tania Hoser's *Introduction to Cinematography: Learning Through Practice* (Routledge/Focal Press, 2019), since it had not yet been released. The table of contents look solid and it addresses the role of the cinematographer as a working professional, along with storytelling and lighting, but other than that, I cannot speak to how it relates to visual storytelling.

The Foundation of Visual Storytelling   INTRODUCTION

Basic Cinematography fills this gap. It shows, in practical ways, how to apply composition, lenses, and lighting to story choices by linking concepts of storytelling to foundational elements of cinematography. I feel that this book is a strong precursor or supplement to technical cinematography books. It is written for beginning and intermediate filmmakers who want to take their cinematography to the next level of visual storytelling.

Good storytelling, of course, begins with a good script. The director must envision the script as a film that an audience watches. The cinematographer's job is to translate the ideas and emotions contained in the script into something that can be physically seen and felt onscreen. Some directors will know what kind of shots they want. Others will know what kind of emotions they want the camera and lighting to express in their story. In either case, the cinematographer will use lights, cameras, lenses, and composition to execute that vision for the story into concrete visual images. A lot of films, however, tend to focus on the *style* of visual storytelling—making shots look technically cool—without applying the substance of storytelling to the cinematographer's techniques. If directors are not attuned to visual storytelling, the cinematographer must fill in the gap and offer ideas that enhance a story, visually.

Therefore, the premise of this book is to help train cinematographers as visual storytellers.

> The cinematographer's job is to translate the ideas and emotions contained in the script into something that can be physically seen and felt onscreen.

CHAPTER SUMMARIES

Many students and beginning filmmakers need storytelling knowledge first before they can accurately apply technical aspects of filmmaking to the stories they create. Story analysis is the first step in this process, so the first chapter shows how to take a scene from a script, ask the right questions to discover the dramatic needs of the scene, then visualize it on paper by writing out visual blocking notes for the characters. In the second chapter, I address lenses and composition as the means by which cinematographers frame these actions. And in the third chapter, I continue this analysis by adding lighting as another tool to make visible the emotional intent of a story. The fourth chapter entails the importance of understanding what lies beneath the hood of a camera—from the sensor to color bit depth—as well as exploring the differences between shooting in log, RAW, and with LUTs. The fifth and final chapter provides an overview of a variety of planning tools that can be used during preproduction, production, and postproduction, including the tools of color grading.

In *Chapter 1 Visual Storytelling Through Blocking*, I examine approaches to the psychological motivations of characters, a form pioneered by the great Russian theater director, Konstantin Stanislavski. Instead of just writing a quick summary of what blocking is and why it's important to filmmakers, I go deep into this analysis in order to show how Stanislavski shaped the stage into a form of realistic drama never seen before, and how his concepts on blocking and body language can be applied to filmmaking. Even though cinematographers do not work with actors, they must understand the role of the actor and director in order to visualize acting, blocking, and subtext in their compositions. It helps them communicate and envision shots that are linked to the story, rather than just coming up with "cool" visual images. This chapter is as much for the beginning director as it is for the cinematographer and it provides the foundation of what follows in the subsequent chapters.

The first chapter includes seven sections

1. *Think like a director*. The role of the cinematographer as the conduit of visual storytelling.
2. *Visual storytelling through the blocking of subtext*. A historical overview of Stanislavski's vision for his famous production of Chekhov's *The Seagull* at the Moscow Art Theatre, placing it in context with late 19th-century theater and why what he did changed theater forever. It shows, in practical ways, how to creating subtext through an analysis of Stanislavski's psychological approach to blocking in his notes, something every filmmaker should study closely.
3. *Hitchcock's key rules of filmmaking*. Whatever is *said* instead of being *shown* is lost upon the viewerl It includes an examination of how Hitchcock used visual storytelling through body language of performers, making their films visual.
4. *Body language and blocking in Girl with a Pearl Earring*. An example of a short scene in how the director changed the script to meet the needs of visual storytelling, and the blocking and body language informing the types of shots used.

5. *Discovering dramatic action through script analysis in Ozu's* Tokyo Twilight. This section includes the fundamental questions to ask when interpreting the story in a script, using a transcribed scene from Yasujiro Ozu's *Tokyo Twilight* (1957) as a case study in discovering the subtext and making it visible.

6. *Visualizing subtext through blocking and body language in Ozu's* Tokyo Twilight. This section continues the analysis of Ozu's *Tokyo Twilight*, now interpreting the dramatic meaning and subtext through visual blocking and body language. It also includes an example of how the blocking and body language of the actors must change when making a different interpretation of the story.

7. *Body language and subtext in documentary.* How can the concept of blocking as a form of visual storytelling be used in documentary work? This section examines work by photo- and video-journalist Travis Fox, as well as a scene from the Francis Mallmann episode of Netflix's *Chef's Table*. The approach is certainly different in documentary work, but the principles of observing and filming human behavior is the same.

Once you've gained a strong sense of how visual storytelling plays out through the blocking of the actor, then you can apply lens choices and composition to the story, the subject of **Chapter 2 Visual Storytelling Through Lenses and Composition**. This brings home the interpretation and application of the storytelling concepts explored in Chapter 1. This is where the application of cinematography begins, as composition and lenses are the foundation of the cinematographer's tools (as well as lighting, which is covered in the third chapter). I segment this chapter into the following five topics:

1. *Ten tools of composition.* Using the opening sequence from the Netflix series *Godless* (episode 1) as a case study in defining ten composition tools used by cinematographers, I explore and describe the practical and psychological impact on the story through:
   - Shot sizes and lenses
   - Camera height and angle
   - Camera motion
   - Focal depth of field
   - Light and dark
   - Line and linear perspective
   - Layers
   - Weight
   - Color
   - Texture

2. *Shooting for the Edit.* This section examines the visual storytelling aspects of such important filmmaking elements as:
    - Coverage
    - Eye lines
    - Point of view and cutaways
    - 180 degree rule
    - Jump cuts
    - Kuleshov effect

    Contemporary and historical film and television examples show practically how each of these are used, including a scene from Netflix's *Jessica Jones*, Ozu's *Late Spring*, the Netflix series, *The Crown*, as well as David MacDougall's classic observational documentary, *To Live with Herds* (1972). I place such material in this chapter, because often shoots must be planned around the edit.

3. *Case study in lenses and composition from* Jessica Jones *with DP Manuel Billeter.* Applying the concepts explored in the previous section, I examine a scene from the first episode of *Jessica Jones* and include interview material from the show's DP, Manuel Billeter, discussing why he made certain choices.

4. *Case study in lenses and composition from* Chef's Table *with DP Adam Bricker.* In this section, I examine the Dominique Crenn episode of *Chef's Table*, including an interview with one of the show's DP's, Adam Bricker.

5. *Case Study in lenses and composition from Ozu's* Tokyo Twilight *class project reinterpretation.* This last section of the chapter includes the script analysis began in Chapter 1, but now adds story justifications for lens choices, as well as including selected shots from a classroom exercise that shows the use of different lens choices designed to help reinforce the story visually.

In **Chapter 3 Visual Storytelling Through Lighting**, I examine the following six areas of lighting:

1. *The psychology of lighting* is about the psychological impact of different forms of lighting; a definition of key lighting terms; as well as a close examination of the six elements of lighting—light quality, intensity, direction, texture, contrast, and color temperature. Throughout this section, I include examples from *Blade Runner* (1982), *Blade Runner 2049* (2017), *Casablanca* (1942), and *THX 1138* (1971) as a means to define and explore the use of lighting as a storytelling tool.

2. *Some basic tools of exposure* provides technical details and examples for using the zone system, histogram, waveform, aperture and depth of field, ISO, ND filters, shutter angle and frame rate, and lighting modifiers.

3. *Indoor day and outdoor day setup examples* includes shots from Joe Simon's "Fragments," a short film showing some of the tools he used to shape light—including images of the setup and screen grabs of what the resulting shots looks like.

4. *Outdoor night case study from* Jessica Jones *with DP Manuel Billeter* is an examination of the opening scene of the first episode of the series as Billeter explains how he made certain choices to build the visual story as Jones spies on a couple in a seductive rendezvous.

5. *Indoor night case study from Ozu's* Tokyo Twilight *class project reinterpretation*. In a different scene from Ozu's film, I continue the case study used as an in-class exercise, but now focusing on lighting choices. The script analysis includes notes on blocking and the justification for lens choices, as well as notes on lighting, along with a floor plan showing the lighting setup.

6. *Documentary Lighting Case Study from* Chef's Table *with DP Adam Bricker*. In the final section of this chapter, DP Adam Bricker explains how he uses three different lighting setups for different styles of shooting in the series, including the use of natural lighting in *vérité* scenes, lighting used for interviews, and lighting used for food symphony sequences of the food displays.

Chapter 4 Visual Storytelling with Camera Log, RAW, and LUTs provides an overview of some of the key features of a camera and the tools the cinematographer can use to help shape a look in-camera (or at least prepare a look for post). Although not as important as which camera a filmmaker uses, knowing the key features and the different modes of shooting will help filmmakers understand the limits and capabilities of their camera. This chapter includes the following four sections:

1. *An overview of a dozen key camera features.* A look under the "hood" of cameras and learning what these technical features are, including the lens mount, sensor type, sensor size, resolution, dynamic range, frame rate, shutter angle or speed, color space and color gamut, compression and bit depth, chroma subsampling, and audio quality.

2. *Shooting in log.* An examination of log recording, exploring what it is, what it does, when to use it, and when not to use it.
3. *Shooting in RAW.* What are the advantages of shooting in RAW? This section defines and explores RAW shooting, which is the most powerful way to render an image for post, since, if it is uncompressed at 12-bit, it will contain the deepest color depth and tonal range. With uncompressed RAW, the image can be manipulated during post into different levels of exposure and with different types of color that compressed images can never deliver.
4. *Shooting with LUTs.* Look up tables (LUTs) are tools used by cinematographers to help see what the end result of an image may look like after recording an image in the camera. This is especially important when shooting in log or RAW, since the image needs to be processed in camera in order to provide an accurate rendition of the image onscreen. The footage will, of course, be brought into post, where it can be manipulated into the same image used with the in-camera LUT or a different one may be applied.

Chapter 5 Workflow and Tools for the Beginning Cinematographer summarizes some of the key elements of the book and provide tables and charts for beginning filmmakers to plan and execute their film throughout the production cycle. It also includes a brief overview of some of the apps for preproduction and production, as well as providing an overview of the main tools for creating the final look in postproduction.

1. *Preproduction* features a Dramatic analysis chart (designed for directors and cinematographers), a tool for script analysis. It includes places to write notes about a character's needs and wants, scene objectives, conflict, and visual notes. In addition, the chapter contains a Scene composition chart, mapping both the setup of a scene (the normal state of affairs at the beginning) and a place to write notes about what happens when the scene shifts (the change of state occurring in the scene), along with the ten tools of composition and lens choices, examined in Chapter 2.

It also includes the tables provided in Chapter 2 on the Psychological impact of camera movement, Psychological impact of lenses, and Emotional distance and intimacy in shot sizes.

As part of the preproduction process, this chapter also explains the importance of testing your camera throughout the entire production cycle, shooting tests for exposure and dynamic range, the use of LUTs, log, and/or RAW (if camera capable), color tests, and postproduction tests for contrast, color correction, and the application of LUTs to see what the final look of the film would look like through these choices.

Another aspect of preproduction for cinematographers includes the use of a Technical scout location form, allowing cinematographers to take note of existing lights, windows, and electricity in a specific location. Finally, I list a series of apps that cinematographers can use to help them plan their shoots, from Magic ViewFinder to a digital slate.

2. *Production* lays out some simple definitions of the roles of different people in the camera department, light department, and grip department. There are really no tools or charts in this section, since the preproduction is where the planning occurs and during production, the execution must happen based on those plans. This book does not go into "how-to" aspects of setting up lights or cameras, for example, since the intent is to plan the visual story, and other books and online tutorials provide setup explanations.

3. *Postproduction.* Since the final look of a film is made in postproduction, it's important that cinematographers understand the tools of postproduction color correction and grading so they can communicate with professional colorists or learn to color on their own when working on smaller projects. The tools of the colorist for reading color and exposure in an image include the use of scopes (such as the waveform monitor, RGB parade, vectorscope, and histogram). The tools to manipulate color and exposure include color wheels, curves, HSL qualifier (for adjusting elements of hue, saturation, and luminance in specific parts of an image), as well as the use of windows to select and manipulate part(s) of an image. I also include a Color and exposure data table, allowing the cinematographer to log the ISO, f/stop, shutter angle, color space, LUT, and the visual reference scopes of particular shots recorded during the production—notes useful during color correction in post.

The *Conclusion* reinforces the main concepts of the book by examining how students apply cinematography and directing to documentary work they did in Bologna, Italy, as well as a classroom exercise from a *Blade Runner* scene for a lesson in night cinematography.

Ultimately, the book is meant to provide beginning filmmakers an understanding of how visual storytelling impacts a script, and that the tools of the cinematographer must serve the underlying emotions contained in a story. It is not meant to be an exhaustive book or a "how-to" platform for learning how to execute the technical craft of cinematography—there are many books and online tutorials that do this. By focusing on how to apply the tools of cinematography to the story—rather than just creating cool looking shots without thinking about how those shots serve the story—I'm hoping that beginning filmmakers will begin to create more compelling films.

Image from Netflix's *The Crown*, "Beryl," DP: Adriano Goldman. (Image ©2017 Left Bank Pictures.)

"[I]n every physical action, unless it is purely mechanical, there is concealed some inner action, some feelings."
—Konstantin Stanislavski (cited in Mitter, 1992: 23)

CHAPTER 1

VISUAL STORYTELLING THROUGH BLOCKING

OVERVIEW

Too many young directors and cinematographers (and, yes, even some who should know better) tend to focus on style over substance in filmmaking—shots that are considered "cool," "hip," and "slick," shots that often do not necessarily support the story being told. On the other hand, shots that support visual storytelling—making physical the underlying emotions of a scene (the subtext)—offer deeper purpose, since they're designed to support the story.

Subtext is defined simply as the thoughts of characters manifesting in physical behavior. As stage director (and actor) Konstantin Stanislavski said, "It is the subtext that makes us say the words we do in a play" (Jones, 1986: 108). In film it's made visible through the blocking (the movement and body language of performers), which is captured visibly by the composition (lens choice and camera placement), along with camera movement (the way cinematographers move the composition in a shot), as well as by lighting (and eventually with sound design). To create subtext, we must explore a combination of psychology, behavior, emotions, thoughts, and motivations of characters—the material implied beneath the surface text of a script—and then find ways to make them physical, and visible to an audience.

Still from Truffaut's *The 400 Blows* (1959). A lesson in blocking and body language.
(Image ©1959 Les Films du Carrosse and Sédif Productions.)

Contemporary filmmakers and students of filmmaking tend to take for granted realistic, psychologically-motivated acting, but early experiments in filmmaking favored pictorial realism over narrative structure or the quality of realistic acting, and usually engaged in exaggerated forms of performances found in 19th-century acting styles. Naturalistic acting and the use of subtext as an outcome of blocking (or staging) and body language of performers, was crafted in the theater, pioneered primarily and successfully on the stage in 1898 at the Moscow Art Theater by Stanislavski.

So, I'll begin an examination of visual storytelling with Stanislavski, then move on to Alfred Hitchcock, whose concept of "pure cinema" reverberates with elements from Stanislavski, and then follow this with practical visual examples from Hitchcock's *Strangers on a Train* (1951), French New Wave director François Truffaut's *The 400 Blows* (1959), and Peter Webber's *Girl with a Pearl Earring* (2003). I show how these latter films embodied both the key elements of Stanislavski and Hitchcock's pure cinema. Later, I'll apply these principles to an updated adaptation of a scene from Ozu's *Tokyo Twilight*, offering an analysis of its dramatic structure in order to show how to make the emotions of a story physical through blocking.

The chapter is organized around the following seven topics:
1. Think like a director
2. Visual storytelling through the blocking of subtext
3. Hitchcock's key rules of filmmaking
4. Body language and blocking in *Girl with a Pearl Earring*
5. Discovering dramatic action through script analysis in Ozu's *Tokyo Twilight*
6. Visualizing subtext through blocking and body language in Ozu's *Tokyo Twilight*
7. Body language and subtext in documentary

SECTION 1: THINK LIKE A DIRECTOR

I want to address the issue of why we're covering the basics of visual storytelling through blocking and body language in a text on cinematography. One, cinematographers must communicate with directors, and to some extent, think like a director in order to anticipate a director's needs. Composition, camera movement, and lighting are all fundamental tools cinematographers use to tell the story, so knowing how to make the emotional intent of a scene (the subtextual inner life of characters) visible to an audience must be the first step before picking up a camera and shooting a scene. Without this foundation, then what are filmmakers really shooting? Two, most students and independent filmmakers want (or need) this foundation in visual storytelling in order to create better films.

> **Cinematographers must understand blocking in order to discover and execute the subtext through their camera and lighting work.**

It must be stressed that blocking, the staging of the action, and the body language of performers, clearly falls under the purview of the director. But we're examining how cinematographers must understand blocking in order to discover and execute the subtext through their camera and lighting work, so the first chapter begins, here.

Fundamentally, exploring the subtext is the first step that a director—and by extension—the cinematographer must think about when starting to visualize her story. Cinematographers must be able to communicate with the director and share inspiration they may have about the blocking in a scene as it relates to visual storytelling occurring through the lens. For example, in a scene from *Crazy/Beautiful* (2001), where Carlos comes into the photo classroom to talk to Nicole, who is being kicked out of school, the original blocking set Nicole unpacking her locker. Carlos enters, stops, and sees her, then walks towards her. But Shane Hurlbut, ASC, the DP for this film,[1] writes how he came up with a more visual concept that matched the story intent, and convinced the director, John Stockwell to make the change:

> After watching the first couple of blocking rehearsals, I turned to John Stockwell pitching the idea of her being on her knees and when Carlos comes in, all he would see would be a head over the top of the table. To me, this made her character feel more damaged and vulnerable to the world around her. It created an emotional perspective for Carlos as we establish him surveying the location at first glance. After pitching that, John looked to me said, "I LOVE IT!" (Hurlbut, 2017) (See Figure 1.1, p. 4.)

---

[1] Shane Hurlbut, ASC, the DP on such films as *Swing Vote* (2008), *Terminator Salvation* (2009), *Act of Valor* (2009), *Need for Speed* (2014), *Fathers and Daughters* (2015), as well as the television series, *Into the Badlands* (2015), among others.

Although cinematographers don't focus on blocking, Hurlbut says he finds "blocking to be beneficial" because "it helps you figure out camera placement, light placement, what lens will best emote the scene, where we might run into trouble, [...]." He defines blocking as the moment when:

> the director, director of photography, and the script supervisor get together one-on-one with the talent to break the scene down into beats. Essentially, we are taking the written action in the script and bringing it to life on location, figuring out shots, and vetting any problem-spots along the way. It's important for this to happen because it creates a foundation for creativity, and a direction in which to guide the rest of the crew.

While Hurlbut admits that some directors simply let the actors come up with their own blocking, it's more important to have it than not—and this is the fundamental principle of this chapter—for at the very least it'll save time and budget if there's a sense of where the camera and lighting setups need to go. But it's even more important to figure out the visual story from this blocking, because through such knowledge the cinematographer will create stronger work, enhancing the vision of the director, and of the film itself.

In addition, many independent documentary filmmakers and in some cases independent fiction directors—as well as many student filmmakers—shoot their own stories, which is another reason why cinematographers need to study staging and blocking as the first step in visual storytelling.

FIGURE 1.1
Shane Hurlbut, ASC conceived of a blocking change for this scene from *Crazy/Beautiful*, where Nicole is more vulnerably staged sitting low behind the table as she packs her things. Carlos enters to confront her. (Images ©2001 Touchstone Pictures.)

Let's go back 120 years—right after the birth of cinema—and look at a particular stage production. Konstantin Stanislavski's staging for Anton Chekhov's *The Seagull* (performed during the 1898–1899 season at the Moscow Art Theater), reveals the beginnings of his method in the development of psychological realism on stage.[2] It wouldn't appear in film until decades later in the 1930s.[3] Stanislavski created an extensive detailed plan for a production of *The Seagull*, a play about an emotionally tortured young man who wants to create a new art form and puts on a play for his family and neighbors. It is not received well. He wants emotional approval from his mother and from the actress in his play, Nina—both whom don't give him what he wants—leading to a tragic ending.

Ultimately, *The Seagull* is a naturalistic drama examining the ennui of summer life by an upper class family in pre-Revolutionary Russia. Up to this point (with a few exceptions), most playwrights defined and expressed their characters in plays through dialogue and soliloquies, not through suppressed internal psychology (Jones, 1986: 17). In the dramas of ancient Greece, the Renaissance, including Shakespeare, and into the late 19th century, dialogue in plays tended to reveal characters' intentions and propel the plot.

Chekhov did something different. His characters didn't always say what was on their minds. They spoke plenty of dialogue, but their true feelings were often suppressed and what they were really thinking was not necessarily reflected in the dialogue. A different layer of dialogue occurred internally, in the characters' heads, and actors had to find a new approach to engage in such work. What Stanislavski attempted to do—a "conscious articulation of subtextual psychology"—is now essential and even necessary in contemporary acting (Jones, 1986: 38).[4] This subtext could be perceived by an audience through the behavior and body language of the actors.

---

[2] Stanislavski would not develop his famous "system" of acting until 1906, but the work he developed, here, is an important foundation for his system and it holds promise for beginning filmmakers as inspiration to develop their own ideas for a physical interpretation of emotions that need to be captured through cinematography. This Chekhov production was co-directed by Stanislavski's Moscow Art Theater partner, Vladimir Nemirovich-Danchenko, who is the one that talked him into doing Chekhov's play in the first place.

[3] Scholar Cynthia Baron describes how films became more popular than Broadway plays in the 1930s, forcing many actors to move into film. These theater performers, including those trained at the dd, applied their knowledge of script analysis and character development to film, a process developed before Stanislavski (see Baron, 2014; and McTeague, 1993).

[4] This would eventually reach heightened awareness in film: "Film acting, because of the inexorable realism of its medium, has furthered this development [...] raising modernist internality to an extraordinary pitch" (Jones, 1986: 38).

As Chekhov scholar David Allen articulates: "A new form of drama demanded new methods of acting" (1998: 7). Chekhov purposely wrote a play that would oppose the melodrama and exaggerated acting that accompanied such plays on much of the 19th-century stage: "where—in streets and houses—do you see people tearing about, leaping up and down, and clutching their heads? [...] Subtle inner feelings, [...] must be subtly expressed in an external form" (Allen, 1998: 7).

Stanislavski was one of these pioneers in directing and acting as he attempted (and succeeded) to create a strong sense of behavioral and psychological "truth" on the stage. It would be Stanislavski's Moscow Art Theater tours in the United States in 1923 and 1924 that would influence a more naturalized style of acting training in theater and film, complementing the work already being done at the American Academy of Dramatic Arts (founded in 1884 in New York City).[5] And with the introduction of sync sound in 1928, acting in film started to become more natural (even though some of the exaggerated style still continued into the 1930s).

Even in such a masterpiece of silent-era cinema as Fritz Lang's *Metropolis* (Germany, 1927)—despite a strong scenic design and visual storytelling utilized in the film—the acting is exaggerated. In one scene, nearly an hour into the film, we see such silent era techniques as actors overtly physicalizing their performances, causing, in some cases, laughable moments, as some felt the need to engage in large gestures in order to communicate their emotions, an extension of 19th-century theater acting. As can be observed in this scene from *Metropolis*, a consistent style of subtle film acting had not yet worked its way into cinema. (See Figure 1.2.)

Although not a direct correlation to theater, we imagine this scene from *Metropolis* as being similar to what occurred on many 19th-century European stages—a form Stanislavski attempted to change with his 1898 production of *The Seagull*.

Section review
1. What are two reasons why cinematographers should think like directors?
2. How did the blocking note Shane Hurlbut, ASC, gave to the director help visualize the scene better in *Crazy/Beautiful*?
3. What techniques did theater director Stanislavski develop to help revolutionize acting?

---
[5] Like Stanislavski, the "Academy actor was taught to trust instinct, cultivate imagination, focus on the character's motive and objective, concentrate, and to think *as* the character" (McTeague, 1993: 92).

VISUAL STORYTELLING THROUGH BLOCKING   CHAPTER 1   7

FIGURE 1.2
We can see an exaggerated, overly dramatic acting style by Gustav Fröhlich and Brigitte Helm in Fritz Lang's *Metropolis* (1927). This type of acting was typical of the 19th-century stage Stanislavski challenged at the Moscow Art Theater. Modern acting techniques wouldn't appear in film until the 1930s, after the introduction of talkies. (Scene read top to bottom, left to right.)
(Images ©1927 Universum Film.)

SECTION 2: VISUAL STORYTELLING THROUGH THE BLOCKING OF SUBTEXT

In his production of *The Seagull*, Stanislavski's notes on the character of Konstantin reveal his inner psychology and motivations of behavior as physicalized through blocking, something rarely done in theater up to that time, and this becomes a fascinating case study for filmmakers to examine closely.

As described by Jones, Konstantin begins with high energy and the psychological impulses of his character were externalized, "strongly phrased in the physical" (Jones, 1986: 25). For example, when his uncle, Sorin, asked him about why his mother was in a bad mood, Stanislavski had the character of Konstantin "fiddling with cigarettes and matches, reaching down for a flower and plucking off its petals." His physical behavior included sitting up, swinging his leg over the bench, getting up and pacing, sitting back down, then back up again, and lighting cigarettes. He would lay down on the bench next to his uncle, but when he heard Nina approach, he jumped back up again. "This is an extraordinary sequence," Jones writes, "with a rationale in character analysis" (Jones, 1986: 25). In Stanislavski's description, Jones notes:

> The performance of [Konstantin's] play is to him an event that is of decisive importance to his future career. It is not for nothing that he is in such a nervous state after its failure. The more jumpy and agitated he is now, the stronger will his mood of despair be after the failure of his play. (Jones, 1986: 25)

By beginning with character analysis—interpreting it through his own imagination and sensibilities—Stanislavski's approach becomes a textbook manual for modern theater and a good model to begin our understanding of how to create visual storytelling in film, especially as it relates to the arc of the character in a story. The physical blocking, here, rooted in the dramatic (and psychological need) of this character, gets more interesting as Jones describes how Konstantin evolves over the course of the play. In continuation of Stanislavski's analysis of his story arc through physical behavior, Jones writes:

> Stanislavski consistently emphasized Konstantin's high energy, making him an ardent lover of Nina, a nervously fussy director on first night, an explosively angry son when his mother interrupted the play, and a hysterically active man in despair. By the end of the act he was forcefully pushing Masha out of his way and 'waving his arms in great agitation.' The actor's score began on such an energetic note so that he might slowly,

carefully descend into almost catatonic shock by the end of the play. The character's life thus curved gradually but inexorably toward silence, immobility, and despair. (Jones, 1986: 25)

The blocking—the physical behavior of Konstantin—visualizes his internal conflict. "[P]hysical activity can express character, indicate phrasing of material, and point to crucial moments," Jones writes in his incisive analysis of Stanislavski's approach (1986: 25). As Stanislavski would note years later in one of his books on acting, *Creating a Role*: "the actors are to discover emotions in their bodies, for 'in every *physical action*, unless it is purely mechanical, there is concealed some *inner action*, some feelings" (cited in Mitter, 192: 23). Jones asks us to look at how Stanislavski interprets the tone of this moment through blocking, which is "insistent, repetitive, passionate," and foreshadows the moment when Konstantin stops his play "because its reception is less than ideal, then to his later attempts to stop his imperfect life" (Jones, 1986: 25). It contains the kernel that propels Stanislavski's interpretation of Konstantin's character arc.

Stanislavski's approach becomes a textbook manual for modern theater and a good model to begin our understanding of how to create visual storytelling in film, especially as it relates to the arc of the character in a story.

When his uncle asks Konstantin about his nephew's passion for the theater, Konstantin says: "What we want is new forms, uncle. New forms. We must have new forms. If we can't get them, I'd much rather have nothing at all." In Stanislavski's blocking notes, he writes:

In disgust, [Konstantin] slaps his leg nervously, gets up and bends over Sorin, trying to convince him. Even beats his breast in agitation. Waves his hand, swings himself over the plank of the rocking bench and begins to pace nervously up and down the stage. A pause five seconds. After pacing up and down, Konstantin calms down a little, walks up to the place he occupied before, looks at his watch, and sits down astride the bench. (Stanislavski, 1952: 147)

Konstantin engages in this action as he speaks a fairly long monologue about how her mother is a famous actress, how he dropped out of university during his third year and lacks money, how other actors and writers are judging him as "insignificant." During this monologue, Stanislavski writes:

> Konstantin jumps up again, paces the stage again a few times, impetuously, along the whole length of the stage, then takes out a cigarette and goes to Sorin to ask him for a light or for his cigarette with which to light his own.

This shows his energy and nervousness in anticipation of the play he's about to show his family and friends on the estate. It also foreshadows his desire for Nina, who will perform in his play. Sorin asks about the novelist Konstantin's mother is dating. He replies how he's "intelligent" and "decent." Stanislavski notes:

> Konstantin delivers the whole of his speech while smoking, taking the cigarette out of his mouth, replacing it, inhaling the smoke, and so on.

Konstantin doesn't really care for his mother's boyfriend since he takes the attention off of him, her son. At the end of this reply, Stanislavski writes:

> A pause. Konstantin lies down again. Sorin speaks after the pause (which he fills in with whistling or humming).

Sorin adds that in his past he wanted to marry and be a writer, but failed at both. During this moment, Stanislavski works in another pause. "Sorin yawns contentedly." Konstantin interrupts him as he hears the approach of Nina's footsteps. Stanislavski notes: "Konstantin sits up with a start, then jumps up quickly with his feet on the plank, shaking it so violently that Sorin almost loses his balance. Konstantin listens."

For this moment, as he hears Nina's footsteps, Chekhov writes that he "*Embraces his uncle*" and follows this with: "Oh, I can't live without her! Even the sound of her footsteps is beautiful! Oh, I'm so happy, so deliriously happy!" Stanislavski adds these blocking notes:

> Konstantin jumps down from the plank. Sorin has scarcely time to recover from the jolt, when Konstantin hurls himself upon him and embraces him impetuously. The hat falls off Sorin's head and, not knowing what it is all about, he gets up from the bench, smooths his hair, then hooks his hat with his cane, trying to pick it up. Konstantin has meanwhile run off to meet Nina on the bridge.

Chekhov writes in his play: "(*Goes quickly to meet NINA who enters*")", while Konstantin says, "My darling! My dearest ...". During this, Stanislavski notes:

"Konstantin kisses Nina's hand ardently, and, as they walk, helps her off with her cloak, shakes it, folds it up, and puts it on the table." Nina replies, "I hope I'm not late. I'm not late, am I?" And Stanislavski adds: "Speaks pantingly, breathlessly, taking off her hat and smoothing her hair." (All quotes above from Stanislavski, 1952: 148–151.)

The behavior of these characters—their body language as mapped out by Stanislavski—reflects his desire that actors embody characters who reflect the contradictory nature of inner and outer behavior as observed in the subtext of real life. Decades later, Russian filmmaker Andre Tarkovsky, seemingly reverberating with ideas from Stanislavski, discusses how in life body language does not often reflect literal dialogue:

> The meaning of a scene cannot be concentrated within the words spoken by the characters. 'Words, words, words—in real life these are mostly so much water, and only rarely and for a brief while can you observe perfect accord between word and gesture, word and deed, word and meaning. For usually a person's words, inner state and physical action develop on different planes. They may complement, or sometimes, up to a point, echo one another; more often they are in contradiction; occasionally, in sharp conflict, they unmask one another. (Tarkovsky, 1987: 75)

Before such insights from a master filmmaker were written, Stanislavski created blocking outside of Chekhov's text, visualizing their movements and actions as motivated by the inner psychology of the characters—these drives made visible in the blocking. We see Konstantin torturing himself over the anticipation of the play and for Nina, who is worried that her parents won't approve of her performing on the stage.

The behavior of these characters—their body language as mapped out by Stanislavski—reflects his desire that actors embody characters who reflect the contradictory nature of inner and outer behavior as observed in the subtext of real life.

This blocking physicalizes what is on Konstantin's mind and it is this foundation I want beginning filmmakers to utilize when analyzing and planning the blocking in their films. Let's look at another example, a few moments later in the same scene:

Chekhov's script:	**Stanislavski's notes:**
NINA: My father and his wife have forbidden me to come here. They say you're bohemians … They're afraid I might go on the stage … But I feel drawn here, to the lake, like a seagull. Oh, my heart is so full of you (*Looks round*).	
KONSTANTIN: We're quite alone.	Nina pulls her hand away quickly and listens, as though she could hear someone coming. Glances behind a bush up-stage where the hot-houses are. Konstantin gets up, walks across, goes over behind the bush, and comes back, saying "There's no one there." He then sits down on the other side of Nina. A pause during which Konstantin tries to draw Nina towards himself. A long kiss (*five seconds*), after which Nina tears herself away from him and runs to the tree in the foreground—on the left of the audience. During the pause Konstantin walks over to her and kneels, leaning against the rocking bench with one hand and searching Nina's eyes.
NINA: I thought there was someone there …	
KONSTANTIN: There's no one there (*A kiss*).	
NINA: What tree is this?	
KONSTANTIN: An elm.	
NINA: Why is it so dark?	
KONSTANTIN: Well—it's evening. Everything's getting dark. Don't dash away after the play, please don't.	As he says this, he kneels.
NINA: I must.	
KONSTANTIN: And what if I went to your place, Nina? I'd like to spend the whole night in your garden, looking at your window.	
NINA: You'd better not. The watchman is sure to see you. Besides, our dog isn't used to you yet, and he'll start barking.	Konstantin siezes her hand and kisses it. Nina is sitting with her back to him.
KONSTANTIN: I love you.	
NINA: Sh-h …	Nina snatches her hand away and runs off rapidly to the seat near the hot-house where she hides from Yakov behind a bush.
KONSTANTIN (*hearing footsteps*): Who's there. Is that you, Yakov?	
YAKOV: Yes, sir.	(Stanislavski, 1952: 149-151)

In this chapter I simply want to drive home the point that these types of actions are not only more important than the dialogue, but they are rooted in the psychology and the feelings bubbling beneath the surface of the dialogue and it is the job of the director to make visible these feelings through the blocking and body language of the actors, while it is the job of the cinematographer to capture and further visualize and heighten these moments through composition and lighting.

As Tarkovsky notes, when directors build a:

> *mise-en-scène*, [they] must work from the psychological state of the characters, through the inner dynamic of the mood of the situation, and bring it all back to the truth of the one, directly observed fact, and its unique texture. Only then will the *mise-en-scène* achieve the specific, many-faceted significance of actual truth. (1987: 74)

This is what I feel Stanislavski developed at the end of the 19th century for the stage, and good filmmakers would adopt this approach, in some way, decades later. Bad narrative films (and documentaries) usually stem from scripts full of surface dialogue (or narration in documentary) lacking subtext, and with nothing left to the imagination—leaving no work for the audience—it results in spoon-fed narratives with little to hold an audience's interest. If it's a good script and the film doesn't work, it usually means filmmakers failed to tell the story visually, relying on surface dialogue rather than embodying the *mise-en-scène* with subtext, as shaped through blocking.

Now that we've established a solid foundation for visual storytelling through blocking and the body language of actors, let's look at Hitchcock and Truffaut for a few moments and discuss the importance of "pure cinema" and what it means for the contemporary filmmaker, and how the concept of pure cinema has its roots in Stanislavski's work.

Section review
1. Give an example of how Stanislavski's directing notes on blocking helped visualize his stage story.
2. Why is this approach important for filmmakers?

SECTION 3: HITCHCOCK'S KEY RULES OF FILMMAKING[6]

The director of *The 400 Blows* (1959) and *Jules and Jim* (1962), François Truffaut, sat down with Hitchcock in 1962 and picked his brain for a few days (Figure 1.3). In the introduction to the book that came out of that conversation, *Hitchcock* (1984), Truffaut, explains Hitchcock's core rules of "pure cinema" filmmaking:

1. "Whatever is said instead of being shown is lost upon the viewer"
2. "Film the thoughts of [...] characters and make them perceptible without resorting to dialogue" (Truffaut, 1984: 17).

> If the scene is dead onscreen—and a scene is nearly always dead if there is only literal dialogue occurring—the magic that we enjoy as a cinematic experience will rarely, if ever, happen.

FIGURE 1.3
Alfred Hitchcock and François Truffaut engage in a 26 hour filmmaking discussion over a period of a few days in August 1962. Present, but not in the picture, is Truffaut's translator, Helen G. Scott. The book, *Hitchcock* by Truffaut, was written from these interviews. It inspired the documentary, *Hitchcock/Truffaut* (2015) by Kent Jones.
(Image from *Hitchcock*. Simon and Schuster, 1984.)

---

[6] Some of the research in this section and in Section 7 was drawn from the author's essay, "What Video-Journalists Can Learn from Alfred Hitchcock's Cardinal Rule of Filmmaking" published in the *Journal of Film and Video*. The material for this book has been rewritten with a different focus.

Hitchcock and Truffaut discuss subtext, and Stanislavski's pioneering work with the Moscow Art Theater would foreshadow, in some ways, their discussion. I'm not aware of Hitchcock's familiarity with Stanislavski's work, but Hitchcock, like Stanislavski in his work on *The Seagull*, planned his productions out in detail, and his films are full of blocking and subtext. Hitchcock knew that audiences see and hear films. They don't read scripts or have them read to them.

If the scene is dead onscreen—and a scene is nearly always dead if there is only literal dialogue occurring—the magic that we enjoy as a cinematic experience will rarely, if ever, happen. Dialogue, as playwright and director David Mamet says, is like frosting on a cake. We need it to make the cake complete but, without applying Hitchcock's two foundational concepts, filmmakers fall into the danger of making *boring* scenes, films that are uncinematic, a cake without frosting.

But once the filmmaker understands how to make, in the words of Truffaut, "the thoughts of [...] characters" (the subtext) visible, then the job of the cinematographer (and the director) is done. By making the thoughts of characters visible we see the story unfold through the performers' bodies. It is the material Stanislavski developed in his *mise-en-scène* analysis of *The Seagull* covered in the previous section and it is his legacy in the theater. This approach would eventually work its way into film. Filmmaker and former CalArts professor Alexander Mackendrick, echoing Stanislavski, offers a clear definition of subtext in film:

> The best lines of film dialogue are sometimes those in which the real meanings lie between the words, where the spoken lines mask the true and unadulterated feelings of the speaker.
>
> Such emotions are often visible to the camera, just as they are to an observant human being, because the spoken words frame those revealing and fleeting moments that take place just before a character speaks or as an impulsive non-verbal reaction to what has just been said, [...] in shots containing perhaps a barely visible shift of focus in the eyes, an unconscious flexing of jaw muscles, or a gesticulation during a speech. (Mackendrick, 2004: 5–6)

When filmmakers follow his process, the two rules of Hitchcock and Stanislavkski will become clear and their films will begin to pulse with visual strength and audiences will take notice. Theatrical staging, of course, is different than staging in cinema, since in most instances in theater, performers play towards the audience

in one direction and from a fairly fixed distance, while in cinema the camera—becoming the eyes of the audience—can be staged in any direction and distance.

Let's move away from the stage analysis we examined with Stanislavski and see how these ideas play out in a dialogue scene from Hitchcock's *Strangers on a Train* (1951). In a video essay, Kristian Ramsden notes how Hitchcock engaged in visual storytelling by emphasizing the use of eyes (the eye-lines), the duration of shots, as well as the size of shots—all of which determine who holds the power in a scene. Again, the elements of the body language reveals the subtext. (See Figure 1.4.)

> The process of making the thoughts of characters visible is the process by which we see the story unfold through the performers' bodies.

The eyes and the amount of time the camera spends on Bruno in the scene (14 seconds) reveals that Bruno holds the power, Ramsden explains. Despite what's said in the dialogue, the visual elements, not the dialogue, tells the real story as seen in the visual cues of the actors' body language.

Note, for example, in frame 3 of Figure 1.4, Bruno's demeanor. Ramsden describes how Bruno provides intense focus, his body language showing how he holds power. Guy, on the other hand, reveals anger, fear, and relief during the conversation, Ramsden says, as shown through the use of the actor's eyes (frame 2). Bruno holds his gaze steady, while Guy's reactions shift moment to moment in a subservient way. When Hitchcock cuts to a close-up of Bruno (as shown in the same cut in frames 5 and 6), the dramatic tension increases.

FIGURE 1.4
Kristian Ramsden examines how Hitchcock shapes the power relationship between the two characters, Guy and Bruno, through the blocking of this scene. But rather than focus on dialogue, Hitchcock wants us to focus on the subtext, the body language of the performers.
(Images courtesy of Kristian Ramsden ©1951 Warner Bros.)

As Truffaut said about Hitchcock's films, the dialogue is only a small part (the most inconsequential part) of the cinematic experience. The dialogue can certainly be important, but the life of a narrative film extends from the facial reactions, eyes, gestures—the body language of the performers—all designed to capture "the most complex and subtle relationships between human beings" (Truffaut, 1984: 18). Hitchcock trained his actors to perform for cameras, especially during a close-up: "how to use their face to convey thought, to convey sex, everything, in an unstated subtle way" (Gottlieb, "Hitchcock on Truffaut", 2013: 11).

Mackendrick describes the power of the close-up and the futility of simply focusing on the filming of surface dialogue:

> Study, frame by frame, the performance of an expressive actor in a close-up and you may be able to find the precise images where the spark of thought or feeling ignites, those impulsive moments that then find expression in the delivery of a line. In the hands of competent filmmakers, even the most seemingly inconsiderable dialogue can provide a significance that would be lost if there were more talking. If a scene is genuinely interesting because it is cinematic (*in the sense that without speech we can comprehend most, if not all, of what is happening*), then the added component of the spoken word will probably contribute something. If the scene is uninteresting in cinematic terms, then layer upon layer of dialogue will only make it more so. (2004: 6; emphasis added)

If the eyes hold one of the most important elements in shaping the subtext of a character, then the close-up must be a key tool in shaping subtext, especially during intimate moments. Scholar Sydney Gottlieb feels that more work needs to be done in studying "the full range of 'looks' embodied in [Hitchcock's] films—some of which are *not* exercises of power, control, abuse, or voyeuristic pleasure—and the ways in which they are presented and interrelated" (Gottlieb, 2013: 14).

If this work is important in understanding the visual language found in fiction films, then what needs to be done in documentary films to make them more visual in relationship to the body language of subjects? If documentary filmmakers prioritize glances, gestures, and other elements of body language like a Hitchcock film, then they, too, engage in the creation of "pure cinema." Instead of crafting the actors' bodies through blocking, the documentary cinematographer must take note of real life as it happens.

I explore documentary work towards the end of the chapter. Let's examine how a scene from Truffaut's *The 400 Blows* illustrates subtext through body language in film. The scene begins as we see Antoine crossing a street with a friend. As he crosses, he sees his mother kissing a man that's not his father. (See Figure 1.5.)

Although it's a short scene, the blocking reveals the subtext, as Gottlieb notes, through a "complex choreography of several kinds of looks in this scene: direct, returned or reciprocated, and averted" (Gottlieb, 2013: 14). The dialogue does not propel the story forward. Rather, the most interesting aspect of this scene stems from the body language of the performers, because it is here that we begin to see the inner life of the characters come alive while emotions shift moment to moment, as the mother and son comprehend the enormity of the situation in this brief encounter.

In commenting on this scene, Hitchcock tells Truffaut:

> [Antoine] looks and he sees [his] mother going along there. [See Shots 4–6]. The mother turns her head and sees [her son] looking in her direction. The boy turns his head, embarrassed, and the mother turns her head, embarrassed. [See Shots 7–8.] Now when they meet, with [...] that in the background, they don't like to look at each other, they don't look at each other, they avoid each other's looks when they first meet again. (Gottlieb, 2013: 20.)

What are these emotions made visual as they flow out from the body language? The mother looks away in embarrassment that she's been caught by her son (7a–b). Antoine glances away in shame as he sees his mother kissing a strange man (8a–b). He doesn't want his friend to see and further his shame, so he quickly pulls his friend across the street (11–12), the thoughts of the characters manifested in the blocking and body language delivering a visual story in less than thirty seconds (twelve cuts in six setups). (See Figure 1.5; sequence order goes from top to bottom; letters are in the same cut.)

These are the internal moments made physical that Hitchcock, Tarkovsky, and Mackendrick talk about as the key element in making strong visual films, and for which Stanislavski experimented onstage. A less skillful director would focus on dialogue, spoon-feeding the audience with information about how they should think about what they are seeing. But filmmakers who focus on the visual story, as manifested in blocking, allow the audience to discover these storytelling moments through visual cues, making the connection betweene exterior and interior reality through their own imagination. Make visual the subtext and film that. Otherwise, surface dialogue leads to weak and boring films.

VISUAL STORYTELLING THROUGH BLOCKING   CHAPTER 1   19

FIGURE 1.5
A scene from Truffaut's *The 400 Blows* (1959). Hitchcock, in a discussion with Truffaut, notes how the mother looks away from her son, Antoine (7), and he looks away from his mother (8)—body language conveying the emotional beats of shock and shame, giving the scene power, because it makes the inner thoughts of the characters physical, one of the magical elements of cinema. (Images ©1959 Les Films du Carrosse and Sédif Productions.)

Section review
1. According to Truffaut, what are two strong rules Hitchcock used that filmmakers should follow?
2. What are some ways we can make the thoughts of characters visible?
3. What, according to Mackendrick, makes a scene cinematic?
4. Why is dialogue not really important in film?

> Make visual the subtext and film that.

SECTION 4: BODY LANGUAGE AND BLOCKING IN *GIRL WITH A PEARL EARRING*

Smart movies begin with smart scripts, and a good cinematographer and a good director start with script analysis in order to discover clues about how to make visible the underlying emotions that create magical moments of pure cinema. In a short scene from *Girl with a Pearl Earring* (2003), screenplay written by Olivia Hetreed (based on the novel of the same name by Tracy Chevalier), we will examine how the scene was changed by the director, Peter Webber, by taking into account the process of favoring visual storytelling over dialogue.

In this case, we do not have the director's notes, but, unlike the example from Stanislavski, we do have the actual production we can look at, just as we did with the scenes we looked at from Hitchcock and Truffaut. We also have the script to compare the scene. The director of photography, Eduardo Serra, is a Portuguese cinematographer, who also shot *Unbreakable* (2000), *Blood Diamond* (2006), *Harry Potter and the Deathly Hallows: Part 1* (2010), and *Part 2* (2011), holds to a strong visual storytelling method. I consider *Girl with a Pearl Earring* a perfect example of "pure cinema," where the cinematography, the blocking, and body language of the performers show the story visually, the dialogue being an adjunct to the visual (rather than the other way around, which leads to weak filmmaking).

Griet, a young woman hired in the artist Johannes Vermeer's household as a servant, becomes enamored of Vermeer's paintings and, bit by bit as Vermeer sees promise in her, he begins to mentor her about his art. At the same time, sexual tension builds between them, although this attraction is never stated once in the film's dialogue. Rather, it is made visual through the subtext, the body language of the actors. The scene is less than one page and, as edited, runs about ninety seconds. Here's the scene as written (Figure 1.6):

```
INT. ATTIC DAY

Griet and Vermeer are at work preparing colours; Griet
grinding bone black, Vermeer kneading a paste of precious
blue lapis lazuli. Vermeer clears his throat.

                    VERMEER
          Why did you move the chair?

Griet pauses, not uncertain, but wanting to say rightly what
she means.

                    GRIET
          When you took the map from the
          painting of Mistress Van Ruijven -
          it was better.

She puts down the muller, thinking it through carefully.

                    GRIET (CONT'D)
          The clear space below her arm, it
          balances the wall above now. She is
          not trapped.

She has finished and looks up at him for his reaction but he
stands still and silent for a long time. At last he starts
working again, Griet picks up her muller too. Almost at once
he stops.

                    VERMEER
          so. I never thought to learn from a
          maid.

They are both very still, their hands next to each other by
the bright pigments. His beautiful long, white fingers, so
close to hers they can feel each other's warmth. Then
suddenly a clatter of footsteps and voices below; MARIA
THIN'S voice, a warning tone.

                    MARIA THINS
          Griet, are you up there?
```

FIGURE 1.6
Scene from the screenplay, *Girl with a Pearl Earring* by Olivia Hetreed (2003); based on the novel of the same name by Tracy Chevalier.

As we watch the scene, the dialogue is not nearly as important as the emotional beats and facial reactions flowing shot-to-shot, capturing "the most complex and subtle relationships between human beings," as Truffaut noted about Hitchcock's films (Truffaut, 1984: 18).

We can see how Vermeer tests Griet. In an earlier scene, she had moved a chair in Vermeer's studio that impacted the composition of one of his paintings. The description, "She puts the down the muller, thinking it through carefully," emphasizes the intelligence and creativity that impresses Vermeer and reveals a level of attraction that's more than he should be feeling. The writer indicates this with two lines in the description of Vermeer's reaction to Griet's thoughtful response:

1. "She has finished and looks up at him for his reaction but he stands still and silent for a long time. At last he starts working again, Griet picks up her muller too. Almost at once he stops."

This blocking note reveals the intent of the screenwriter to visualize the inner psychological conflict within Vermeer, a process that helps bring similar psychological truth to the scene that Stanislavski must have wrestled with in interpreting moments from Chekhov's *The Seagull*.

Vermeer processes Griet's response and realizes that she's right and this stops him in his tracks, because she has no artistic training and falls below his station. Thus he dismisses her initially, refusing to give her the satisfaction of an answer, and he goes back to work. He concedes her point: "Almost at once he stops." At the same time, this makes her more attractive to him. This interpretation comes from this next description: "So. I never thought to learn from a maid," a line not used in the film.

2. "They are both very still, their hands next to each other by the bright pigments. His beautiful long, white fingers, so close to hers they can feel each other's warmth. Then suddenly a clatter of footsteps and voices below; Maria Thins' voice, a warning tone."

This is Griet's scene, her point of view ("His beautiful long, white fingers") and the mutual attraction stems from this description: "... so close to hers they can feel each other's warmth." The plural, *they can feel*, indicates this mutual attraction, rather than the singular feminine, *she can feel*. But it is forbidden as indicated by Maria yelling up as she looks for her and offers "a warning tone." There's no visualization of this attraction and warning in the script, other than these notes. The director (along with the cinematographer) would interpret these moments visually and heighten this tension through the actors' bodies and behavior.

Let's look at the shots of this scene from the film and discuss them. (See Figure 1.7.)

VISUAL STORYTELLING THROUGH BLOCKING CHAPTER 1 23

FIGURE 1.7
In this scene from *A Girl with a Pearl Earring*, subtext is shown through the body language of the performers and reveals mutual attraction and a heightening of sexual tension with the lingering glance and hands that touch (cuts 8–11). Frames 11a and 11b are the same shot showing the before and after action.
(Images ©2003 Lions Gate Films.)

There are twelve cuts in this scene and six setups (different angles of shooting). It begins with an extreme close-up on Griet's hands mixing the blue pigment, a cut that's about 14 seconds long, followed by a shot of the master painter, Vermeer, mixing his color that lasts about 17 seconds. Both shots utilize a shallow depth of field and engages a key light motivated by sunlight coming through a diffused window.

While Griet's actions are matter of fact and shows a certain assurance in mixing the color—as if she's done this before—Vermeer's movements, in contrast, reveal a certain hesitancy to his actions. He takes about 5–6 seconds to set aside his spatula he uses to mix the paint and reaches for the oil. This hesitation indicates that he has something on his mind. These two cuts (1 and 2) comprise a third of the scene and, remarkably, it tells the story through the hands of the performers. This foreshadows the strong implication later in the scene, when their hands touch.

At 32 seconds into the scene, Shot 3 goes wide, establishing the geometric space and the spatial relationship between the two. We can see the tools, paints, oils, and the window in the far wall. Griet's face, hooded, hides a lot of her expressions, which is more outwardly shown through her hands. Vermeer's face looks down as he works. At 39 seconds, still in the wide shot, she glances over at his work, but not at him, signifying her station as a servant and her shyness towards him.

We hear the sounds of scrapes of the tools, but no music. The ambient sound—along with the absence of dialogue—builds a certain amount of tension. The shot ends at 43 seconds and cuts to 4 (from the second shot setup), held only for five seconds this time. It reveals the repetitive action of Vermeer setting down the spatula as he reaches over for the oil. We see Griet's hands as she mixes the paint in the background, out of focus.

The scene then cuts to 5, a close-up oblique profile of Griet and Vermeer, with him in focus in the foreground, dominating the scene. The shot lasts about six seconds, and occurs as he asks the question: "Why did you move the chair?" The 48 seconds leading up to the first line of dialogue is filled with pregnant pauses as the two go through their actions. We know there's something on Vermeer's mind, a question he wants to ask due to moments of hesitancy shown in his body language earlier in the scene. This is strong visual storytelling.

In 6, we get a reverse angle close-up, matching the previous oblique profile shot, the focus now on Griet for six seconds. She responds, "She looked trapped."

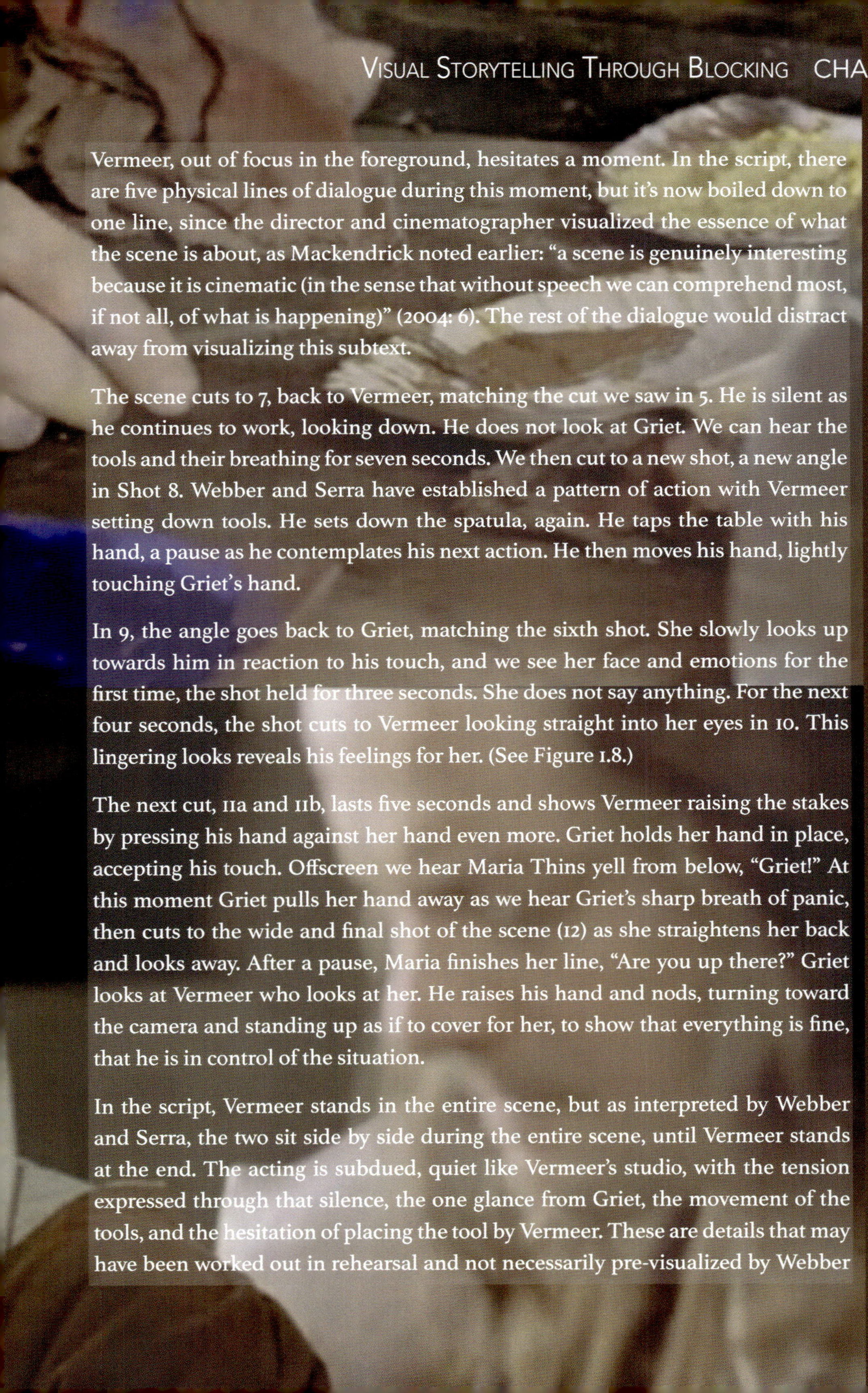

Vermeer, out of focus in the foreground, hesitates a moment. In the script, there are five physical lines of dialogue during this moment, but it's now boiled down to one line, since the director and cinematographer visualized the essence of what the scene is about, as Mackendrick noted earlier: "a scene is genuinely interesting because it is cinematic (in the sense that without speech we can comprehend most, if not all, of what is happening)" (2004: 6). The rest of the dialogue would distract away from visualizing this subtext.

The scene cuts to 7, back to Vermeer, matching the cut we saw in 5. He is silent as he continues to work, looking down. He does not look at Griet. We can hear the tools and their breathing for seven seconds. We then cut to a new shot, a new angle in Shot 8. Webber and Serra have established a pattern of action with Vermeer setting down tools. He sets down the spatula, again. He taps the table with his hand, a pause as he contemplates his next action. He then moves his hand, lightly touching Griet's hand.

In 9, the angle goes back to Griet, matching the sixth shot. She slowly looks up towards him in reaction to his touch, and we see her face and emotions for the first time, the shot held for three seconds. She does not say anything. For the next four seconds, the shot cuts to Vermeer looking straight into her eyes in 10. This lingering looks reveals his feelings for her. (See Figure 1.8.)

The next cut, 11a and 11b, lasts five seconds and shows Vermeer raising the stakes by pressing his hand against her hand even more. Griet holds her hand in place, accepting his touch. Offscreen we hear Maria Thins yell from below, "Griet!" At this moment Griet pulls her hand away as we hear Griet's sharp breath of panic, then cuts to the wide and final shot of the scene (12) as she straightens her back and looks away. After a pause, Maria finishes her line, "Are you up there?" Griet looks at Vermeer who looks at her. He raises his hand and nods, turning toward the camera and standing up as if to cover for her, to show that everything is fine, that he is in control of the situation.

In the script, Vermeer stands in the entire scene, but as interpreted by Webber and Serra, the two sit side by side during the entire scene, until Vermeer stands at the end. The acting is subdued, quiet like Vermeer's studio, with the tension expressed through that silence, the one glance from Griet, the movement of the tools, and the hesitation of placing the tool by Vermeer. These are details that may have been worked out in rehearsal and not necessarily pre-visualized by Webber

FIGURE 1.8
A scene from *A Girl with a Pearl Earring*. We get a reaction shot from Griet after Vermeer touches her hand in cuts 8. The romantic attraction is clear from the body language of the performers.
(Images ©2003 Lions Gate Films.)

or Serra. In either case, we can see how the interpretation of the scene focuses on visual storytelling, minimizing the dialogue, showing the sexual tension build as they look at each other and as their hands touch, as well as the forbidden nature of that touch when Griet pulls her hand away.

This level of visual storytelling is something that needs to be worked out ahead of time on paper. It can be changed as much as needed in production as the actors and director work on the scene, but the actions and subtext giving rise to those actions found in the blocking and body language should be made clear in preproduction so when changes are made on set they stay true to the director's interpretation of the underlying story as indicated in the script, even if the script itself isn't fully adhered to.

In this next section, we will take a script and interpret it in two different ways, guiding the reader through the process of visualizing subtext.

Section review
1. What elements of blocking did the director use in *Girl with a Pearl Earring* to help reveal the visual story?
2. In one sentence, what is the story in this scene?
3. Justify this answer with a visual analysis of the scene.

SECTION 5: DISCOVERING DRAMATIC ACTION THROUGH SCRIPT ANALYSIS IN OZU'S *TOKYO TWILIGHT*

To reinforce the concept of how basic dramatic principles involve conveying actions characters take—and in the process visualizing the story—let's look at Aristotle's *Poetics* (his lecture notes examining story structure found in ancient Greek plays). In this work, he lays out the foundation of drama in Western culture and we find similar patterns in most contemporary films. Filmmakers owe much of their understanding of dramatic tension and characters from this text. A couple of key points on character, plot, and action in Part VI stand out:

> Tragedy [the drama] is the imitation of an action; and an action implies personal agents [people], who necessarily possess certain distinctive qualities both of character and thought; for it is by these that we qualify actions themselves, and these—thought and character—are the two natural causes from which actions spring, and on actions again all success

or failure depends. Hence, the Plot is the imitation of the action—for by plot I here mean the arrangement of the incidents.

[…] Now character determines men's qualities, but it is by their actions that they are happy or the reverse. Dramatic action, therefore, is not with a view to the representation of character: character comes in as subsidiary to the actions. (S. H. Butcher translation, 1961)

It is interesting to note that Aristotle describes "thought and character" as the "two natural causes from which action spring," grounding the discussions about visualizing subtext by Stanislavski, Hitchcock, Truffaut, and Mackendrick in drama. Characters are defined by the actions they take. These actions spring from their needs and desires (thoughts or the inner emotional life of characters), and the sequence of actions they take and react to determine how the story unfolds, creating what we call plot ("the arrangement of incidents").

Thus, the first step in analyzing a script or a scene involve answering four questions of dramatic action, which takes as back to the analysis we saw in Stanislavski's work, as well as in the films we looked at for Hitchcock, Truffaut, and Webber:

1. *What does each character want?* The inner desires, needs, wants of the characters define who they are.

2. *What do they do to get what they want?* Their desires drive the action and creates the plot.

3. *What prevents them from getting what they want?* If characters get what they want with no resistance, then there would be no conflict, and not much of a story, since conflict feeds the plot. And sometimes characters don't get what they want, but what they need.

4. *Whose point of view is it?* The character going through an emotional change in a film (or scene). Knowing who "owns" the scene—usually the one with the most at stake, the most to lose—helps to determine the shots needed to reveal that point of view.

Once we've answered these questions, we have, in essence, discovered and defined the core emotions in a scene and the relationships among the characters.

As those emotions become clearly defined, we can visualize them through blocking and body language (good actors will do this work naturally and they will come up with creative ideas that may be better than ours), but we must begin with this before any other work on the film can be done since the emotions, the subtext, is what drives all of the other choices filmmakers must make.

Let's examine a scene from Yasujiro Ozu's *Tokyo Twilight* (1957), screenplay by Kogo Noda and Ozu (I have transcribed the scene from the film; I have also replaced the character names with Boy and Girl). (See Figure 1.9.)

```
EXT. PARK--CLOUDY AFTERNOON

Overlooking a busy port of a harbor. Ambient outdoor sounds.
Two people sitting close, a young man and woman (late teens
early 20s). They sit quietly, not looking at each
other--like they've shared bad news too difficult to
contemplate--as the sounds of the city and harbor
reverberate around them.


                    BOY
          This is terrible. How can this be?

                    GIRL
          What's terrible?

                    BOY
          You're absolutely sure?

                    GIRL
          You think I'm lying to you? You
          think I could lie about this?

                    BOY
          No, I don't ... but what a mess.

                    GIRL
          I'm the one in trouble. Much more
          than you. Please be serious. Stop
          looking so indifferent.

                    BOY
          Indifferent? It's all I've been
          thinking about since you told me.
```

```
                    GIRL
          But you've been avoiding me.

                    BOY
          That's not true.

                    GIRL
          You've been running away from me!
          [Beat.] What are we going to do?

                    BOY
          I wonder if it's even mine.

                    GIRL
          Who else's could it be? Whose do
          you think it is? Are you that
          suspicious?

                    BOY
          It isn't that.

                    GIRL
          Then what do you intend to do? What
          am I to do?
```

The girl cries. The sounds of the city get louder. The boy sits quietly.

```
                    BOY
          Hey. ... Hey. Stop crying like
          that. Let's think it over.
```

She continues to cry.

```
                    BOY
          What a mess.
```

He looks at his watch.

```
                    BOY
          I have to go now. I've got to meet
          Professor Otsuka at 6:30. Wait for
          me at Etoile, will you? I'll be
          there by 9:30, ok?
```

He gets up.

```
                    BOY
          I'm going. Be sure to wait for me.
```

He walks away as we see her sitting alone.

FIGURE 1.9
A scene from Yasujiro Ozu's *Tokyo Twilight* (1957), transcribed by the author.

Let's answer the four dramatic questions, but there is no one set of right or wrong answers. This is a subjective process of interpretation by the filmmaker, but the questions must be answered and choices made in order to discover ways to block and shoot the scene. *Everything in this chapter leads to answering these questions.*

1. **What does each character want? This is the scene objective.**
   - The Boy wants his freedom. He's in college and wants to avoid the responsibility of being a father.
   - The Girl wants the Boy's support in deciding what to do about her pregnancy.

2. **What do they do to get what they want? These are the actions, the different tactics or sub-objectives, they take in an attempt to get what they want.**
   - The Boy questions the legitimacy of her claim, falls into denial, and makes an excuse to get out of there.
   - The Girl asks the Boy to share blame for the pregnancy and cries to appeal to his conscience.

3. **What prevents them from getting what they want? This creates conflict, which helps an audience connect with characters.**
   - The Girl attempts to block the Boy's desire to delay the decision about what to do about the pregnancy, asking him to share in the blame by making him feel guilty through crying.
   - The Boy overcomes the girl's guilt and tears, by asserting an excuse about a late appointment.

4. **Whose point of view is it? This is the side the filmmaker takes, the person who owns the scene and the one the audience wants to succeed.**
   - The Girl—she has the most to lose and she wants the Boy to help her. By the end of the scene, she realizes that he is not going to help her.

In this interpretation (which is fairly clear in the script and Ozu's film), the Boy gets what he wants, but she does not. With the inner life—the desires and needs—of the characters discovered through this dramatic analysis, we can now translate these dramatic needs physically through a variety of steps or actions the character takes (the blocking and body language), and the composition, camera movement, and lighting will reinforce all of this. (But we're only looking at the blocking in this chapter.)

Section review

Take one scene from a film script—either your own or from a professional film and answer the four dramatic analysis questions for this scene.

1. What does each character want?
2. What do they do to get what they want?
3. What prevents them from getting what they want?
4. Whose point of view is it?

SECTION 6. VISUALIZING SUBTEXT THROUGH BLOCKING AND BODY LANGUAGE IN OZU'S *TOKYO TWILIGHT*

To reiterate, the blocking is where, when, and how subjects are placed and move in the composition. How they are placed, when they move, where they move from, where they go, and any body language conveyed are dependent on the interpretation of the story. These movements (the blocking of the performers) need to be motivated (rather than random); otherwise, random movements not grounded in the story will appear unmotivated, therefore weak, on screen. The job of the director is to shape the blocking of the performers in each shot, while the cinematographer, often working with the director, needs to choreograph the camera with these movements. The cameraperson must be hyperaware of body language and movement in an unrehearsed environment.

In short, blocking depicts the story by and through actors' bodies—their body language, eye lines, gestures, and movement through space—and this blocking must be tied to every shot, whether the camera is locked down or moves. Whatever decision you make as a cinematographer when shooting, be aware that blocking and camera movement are intrinsically tied together.

Begin by conducting the dramatic analysis, then visualize the script through your own blocking notes.

1. *How do you visualize the actors' movements and body language based on their dramatic needs, the subtext, as the scene unfolds?*
2. *What is the starting point and the end point?*
3. *Where does the scene shift?*

Use the dramatic needs and wants of your characters and build it visually from these answers and make sure there is a progression of action in the scene. It should not be static—the characters should change emotionally over the course of a scene (as well as over the course of the film). By defining their dramatic needs—and the actions they take to meet those needs step by step—we can then begin to visualize the story.

In the scene from *Tokyo Twilight* I developed as an exercise in a cinematography and directing class (in the Creative Media & Film program at Northern Arizona University), the first thing you'll note is how I've deleted the original actions as described through the transcription of the scene. By removing the original blocking notes, I'm freed from simply recreating the scene as envisioned by Ozu and this is a technique I learned from Stanislavski. This gives me a clean slate and it provides room for an open interpretation of the scene shaped by my own sensibilities and vision. (See Figure 1.10.)

> **Use the dramatic needs and wants of your characters and build it visually from these answers and make sure there is a progression of action in the scene.**

```
EXT. PARK  CLOUDY AFTERNOON

Overlooking a busy port of a harbor. Ambient outdoor
sounds. Two people sitting close, a young man and woman
(late teens early 20s). They sit quietly, not looking at
each other  like they've shared bad news too difficult to
contemplate  as the sounds of the city and harbor
reverberate around them.

[SHOOT in LIBRARY. Hushed whispers. People walk by. Gets
loud as the tension escalates.]

                    BOY
          This is terrible. How can this be?

                    GIRL
          What's terrible?

                    BOY
          You're absolutely sure?

                    GIRL
          You think I'm lying to you? You
          think I could lie about this?

                    BOY
          No, I don't ... but what a mess.
```

Boy paces back and fourth, eyeing others outside the frame. She is sitting, her back leaning against the stacks.

She stands and grabs his hands, forcing him to sit on the ground with her.

He pulls away, gently, but gets up and

                    GIRL
        I'm the one in trouble. Much more
        than you. Please be serious. Stop
        looking so indifferent.

                    BOY
        Indifferent? It's all I've been
        thinking about since you told me.

                    GIRL
        But you've been avoiding me.

                    BOY
        That's not true.

                    GIRL
        You've been running away from me!
        [Beat.] What are we going to do?

                    BOY
        I wonder if it's even mine.

                    GIRL
        Who else's could it be? Whose do
        you think it is? Are you that
        suspicious?

                    BOY
        It isn't that.

                    GIRL
        Then what do you intend to do? What
        am I to do?

~~The girl cries. The sounds of the city get louder. The boy sits quietly.~~

                    BOY
        Hey. ... Hey. Stop crying like
        that. Let's think it over.

~~She continues to cry.~~

                    BOY
        What a mess.

He looks at his watch.

                    BOY
        I have to go now. I've got to meet
        Professor Otsuka at 6:30. Wait for
        me at Etoile, will you? I'll be
        there by 9:30, ok?

~~He gets up.~~

                    BOY
        I'm going. Be sure to wait for me.

He walks away as we see her sitting alone.

Blocking notes (in red):
- grabs a book, thumbing through it absent-mindlessly, trying to come up with a plan that can get him out of there. She stands and grabs the book from him.
- She steps up close to him, confronting him, face to face. He steps back.
- She pushes him to the bookshelves, somewhat seductively, kissing him on the cheek. She pulls away and turns her back to him, slowly stepping away from him.
- Dead silence. Several beats. A tear roles down her cheek.
- Boy puts his hands on her shoulders from behind, then tries to hug her, but she pulls away.
- The girl slowly sits back down in despair, staring into space (does not look at him).

FIGURE 1.10

A scene from Yasujiro Ozu's *Tokyo Twilight* (1957). I've removed most of the blocking developed by Ozu and reset the location and the style of the scene in order to express my own sensibilities. My blocking notes are in red and they represent the actions (or tactic) each character takes to attempt to get what they want.

Why not just have the actors perform the emotions called for in a script? Because acting does not work that way, unless you want bad acting, reverting to the 19th-century overacting style Stanislavski fought against. In his acting text, *An Actor's Work*, he demonstrates this. He emphases the point that acting is not a process by which to convey emotion: "Acting is action. *The basis of theatre is doing, dynamism. The word 'drama' itself in Ancient Greek means 'an action being performed'*" (Stanislavski, 2008: 40)—as we noted above in Aristotle's *Poetics*.

Therefore, if we map the dramatic need of characters, actors can take the actions they need in an attempt to attain their desire. This is much easier and more natural for actors to do than attempting to have them *will* emotion into being, which is not acting, but emoting. This is the reason why a director should never tell a performer to act an emotion. Stanislavski, writing as the teacher Tortsov, responds to his students after they attempted to perform an emotion:

> "How, in your opinion," asked Tortsov, "can you sit on a chair and will yourself to be jealous, furious, or sad without a why or wherefore? Can you summon up 'creative action?' You've just tried to do it and nothing happened, no feelings sprang to life and so you had to start playacting, using your face to demonstrate non-existent experiences. You can't squeeze feelings out of yourself, you can't be jealous, love, suffer for the sake of being jealous, loving, or suffering. You can't force feelings. That only leads to the most repulsive kind of ham acting. So, when choosing an action, leave your feelings alone. […] perform actions in a genuine human fashion. You must not play passions and characters but react under the influence of passion, in character." (Stanislavski, 2008: 43)

As noted in his later work, *An Actor's Work on a Role*, Stanislavski stresses how actors "start with physical actions that are stable and manageable" in order to tap into the psychological—"we can use physical actions to arouse emotions" (Stanislavski, 2010: 78). This is the reason I map out the physical actions of characters. The physical actions grow from the underlying psychological needs and wants of characters, and good actors will feel those emotions bubble up from the physicalization of the subtext.

My blocking notes are provisional. It helps me to envision the scene, but I'm not necessarily held by it, because I know my performers will come up with other interpretations of their characters, which is fine, and they may create even better ideas. However this foundation gives me a strong starting point, because it visualizes the subtext in a physical way, which is where I want to be when engaging in visual storytelling. At the very least, if there are changes, I now know where I need to go emotionally with the scene—and as long as changes make the visualization of the emotions clearer and stronger during rehearsals, the time spent envisioning the scene through blocking notes makes that decision-making process much easier.

This visual blocking utilizes Hitchcock's rule (and reiterated by Truffaut, Tarkovsky, and Mackendrick) as the foundation of visual cinema: If you strip away the dialogue and are still able to follow the story visually through the blocking (and composition), you've done your job as a director and cinematographer.

> **If you strip away the dialogue and are still able to follow the story visually through the blocking (and composition), you've done your job as a director and cinematographer.**

I've set the scene at NAU's Cline Library in order to control the environment for my classroom experience. But it also gave me tools to help depict visually both characters feeling trapped by their circumstance. The first blocking note reveals the emotions of the two characters, physically:

> *Boy paces back and forth, eyeing others outside the frame. She is sitting, her back leaning against the stacks.*

The Boy pacing back and forth visualizes his emotion as hinted in his line: "This is terrible. How can this be?" It also reveals his state of mind in trying to find a way to escape the situation (his scene objective, and the pacing reveals the first step or sub-objective in meeting this goal). He panics. He wants out of there and is trying to find the best, most polite excuse to get out. The Girl sitting and leaning back embodies the idea of someone who just gave bad news and now awaits a response.

It would be easy to keep her sitting down when the boy says, "You're absolutely sure?" but I want to energize her. In Ozu's film, she stays sitting during the entire scene—and it certainly worked for Ozu in the 1950s—but in 2017 (when this scene was shot as an exercise) I want her active, fighting for what she wants. So when she states—"You think I'm lying to you? You think I could lie about this?"—I want her to stand up, grab his hand, and pull him down next to her in order to force him to stop pacing and make him listen to her, for that is her dramatic need (her objective), to get him to share in the responsibility and to help her with the decision as to what to do about her pregnancy. This physical action embodies the sub-objective of getting his attention.

But he still has his dramatic need—to remain free, to delay the decision, to escape from it. So his getting up, turning away, and thumbing through a book are ways to make physical—visualize—that need. He's not yet ready to leave (since he's not *that* rude), but he's trying to find a moment to collect his thoughts, to come up with an excuse, his next sub-objective. She escalates the dramatic action by grabbing the book from him, tossing it aside, stepping closer, confronting him face-to-face, and pushing him against the bookshelves. In this note, I envisioned her being somewhat seductive, kissing him on the cheek as another tactic in order to try and get him to help her, to remember the good times they've had together.

However, it comes all crashing down when he says, "I wonder if it's even mine." With that there's no seduction—only anger. And to translate that anger into something physical, she steps away and turns her back to him and she hits the climactic moment of the scene: "Then what do you intend to do? What am I to do?" Her back to him visualizes her loneliness and disconnection from him, foreshadowing her giving up on him. There's a moment of stillness as she realizes that he probably isn't going to help her and she begins to cry and it is her last tactic to try and get what she wants from him, by making him feel guilty.

He tries to cover it by hugging or touching her, but this is displacement, his attempt to ease her pain in this moment so he can buy more time. He really wants to get out now and he makes his escape with an excuse about a late appointment, leaving her in despair, visualized as she slowly falls to the floor, leans against the book stacks, and stares off into space—making physical her despair.

Another director and another cinematographer would likely interpret this scene differently. There is no one "right" interpretation. Each person will approach their work and analysis differently. At the moment of my analysis, this visualization of the scene gave me a strong interpretive stance, visualizing the emotional beats rising and falling throughout the scene. This is a core feature of the director's job and by extension the cinematographer's job—especially if the director is not as visually inclined as the cinematographer.

> At the moment of my analysis, this visualization of the scene gave me a strong interpretive stance, visualizing the emotional beats rising and falling throughout the scene. This is a core feature of the director's job and by extension the cinematographer's job—especially if the director is not as visually inclined as the cinematographer.

Changing point of view

So what might this scene look like if it's decided that the Boy is in love with the Girl? It will change the entire tone and intent of the scene and it would *demand entirely different blocking* in order to make physical these different emotions. It would also shift to the Boy's point of view, and ultimately lead to different choices in composition and lenses.

The fundamentals of the dramatic action changes with this new interpretation:

1. **What does each character want?**
   - The Boy wants to be with the Girl, but he still has responsibilities and wants his life to stay on track.
   - The Girl wants a full commitment from him, but she is unsure of his level of responsibility.

2. **What do they do to get what they want?**
   - The Boy tries to comfort her, playfully, and kisses her to prove to her that he loves her.
   - The Girl pulls away, realizing that love is more than romance. It's a grown-up responsibility.

3. **What prevents them from getting what they want?**
   - The Boy certainly tries to prove his love, but in the end, his appointment is more important, but he thinks he has earned a delay. He can talk to her about it later, his conscience at ease, his college career still on track.
   - The Girl realizes that the Boy will not give up *everything* for her, even his goal to graduate college. She needs him here, now, as a potential father.

4. **Whose point of view is it?**
   - The Boy's. He will lose his chance to stay in college and lose his life plan if he becomes a father now. In this case he does not change in the scene. He attempts to maintain the status quo.

Here's what the scene might look like with the new blocking based on this interpretation. (See Figure 1.11, next page.)

> **As the emotions become clearly defined we can visualize them through blocking and body language.**

~~EXT. PARK--CLOUDY AFTERNOON~~
~~Overlooking a busy port of a harbor. Ambient outdoor~~
~~sounds. Two people sitting close, a young man and woman~~
~~(late teens early 20s). They sit quietly, not looking at~~
~~each other--like they've shared bad news too difficult to~~
~~contemplate as the sounds of the city and harbor~~
~~reverberate around them.~~

                    BOY
          This is terrible. How can this be?

> The boy kneels in front of her, his hands touching her knees.

                    GIRL
          What's terrible?

                    BOY
          You're absolutely sure?

                    GIRL
          You think I'm lying to you? You
          think I could lie about this?

> The girl stands up and she pulls away from his clinging.
>
> He looks up at her.
>
> He pats the ground next to him, but she turns away.

                    BOY
          No, I don't ... but what a mess.

                    GIRL
          I'm the one in trouble. Much more
          than you. Please be serious. Stop
          looking so indifferent.

                    BOY
          Indifferent? It's all I've been
          thinking about since you told me.

                    GIRL
          But you've been avoiding me.

> He jumps up and tries to kiss her.
>
> But she turns her face to the side.
>
> He kisses her. She relents for a moment and receives the kiss, then pushes him away.

                    BOY
          That's not true.

                    GIRL
          You've been running away from me!
          [Beat.] What are we going to do?

                    BOY
          I wonder if it's even mine.

                    GIRL
          Who else's could it be? Whose do
          you think it is? Are you that
          suspicious?

> He takes her hand and looks into her eyes and smiles, laughing.
>
> She laughs back, taking his sarcasm.

                    BOY
          It isn't that.

> He kisses her again, playfully.
>
> She pulls away, afraid of their future. She sits down.

                    GIRL
          Then what do you intend to do? What
          am I to do?

The girl cries. The sounds of the city get louder. The boy sits quietly.

```
                    BOY
        Hey. ... Hey. Stop crying like     │ The boy sits down next to
        that. Let's think it over.         │ her and hugs her.

She continues to cry.                      │
                                           │ She does not look at him.
                    BOY                    │
        What a mess.                       │ He takes her hand. She
                                           │ still does not look at him.
He looks at his watch.                     │
                                           │ He reaches up to her face
                    BOY                    │ and turns her towards him.
        I have to go now. I've got to meet │
        Professor Otsuka at 6:30. Wait for │ He touches her stomach,
        me at Etoile, will you? I'll be    │ gently.
        there by 9:30, ok?                 │

He gets up.

                    BOY
        I'm going. Be sure to wait for me.

He walks away as we see her sitting alone.
```

FIGURE 1.11
A scene from Yasujiro Ozu's *Tokyo Twilight* (1957) with the new blocking notes in red. This time, the point of view is from the Boy's perspective and he is in love with her.

The actions now convey the new intentions of these characters. Again, she loses, but from this point of view, there's still hope that she will get what she wants. He does not come across as irresponsible. This approach to blocking—making physical the underlying intentions and emotions of the characters—is actually the foundation of good acting. By making these emotions physical (rather than trying to make actors emotional), then you can work with actors to direct them to do actions that the cinematographer can physically see. When you *see* it, then you should begin to feel it, and the truth of the scene will come out. At this point—and really only at this point—will you be ready to shoot the scene. A good cinematographer will plan the right composition and lenses that best capture these emotions, which we'll cover in the next chapter.

Section review

1. Take the scene you've chosen from the previous section and interpret it. Block it out on paper. (Or you may use this same Ozu scene and interpret it differently.)

2. Work with two actors and develop the scene in a real space. Let the actors bring new interpretations to the blocking—as long as it stays true

> to the intent you're trying to bring across. Try this with different points of view. Don't worry about shooting this, yet. Focus on the actions and performances. Can you follow the story after stripping away the dialogue?

After determining the initial blocking, the next step, covered in Chapter 2, involves visualizing the composition of the blocking and body language through the camera and by lens choices—the key component to composition, as well as with camera movement.

SECTION 7: BODY LANGUAGE AND SUBTEXT IN DOCUMENTARY

Documentary filming requires the utmost concentration and focus from cinematographers—those operating the cameras, capturing moments of life as it unfolds in front of them. Blocking is not typically planned out ahead of time—blocking occurs in real time, unrehearsed, and is simply where the subjects stand and move in relationship to each other as they express behavior in their daily lives. Therefore, the cinematographer must concentrate on emotional beats flowing through their subjects moment to moment, taking visual notice of all the elements of body language found in fiction films. They must know when to hold focus on a hand gesture, the glance of an eye, the nuance of facial expressions. If they're not in tune with their subjects and building such trust that this behavior occurs naturally, then it's nearly impossible to capture powerful footage.

Kirsten Johnson, cinematographer for such documentaries as *Cameraperson* (2016), among others, discusses the process of building trust with subjects:

> You made some sort of an [unspoken] pact with the person, that they're going to reveal the most terrible things of their life. You're here and they're talking and suddenly you realize, if you move, it is a breaking of this bond. Yet, you're trying desperately to think of, "how am I going to cut this into a sequence?"

For example, she says:

> Suddenly, you see someone pressing their fingernails against their arm and you can see they're hurting themselves. You then have to decide

if you either want to potentially change their behavior by shifting your placement or capture it from across the room with the long lens. By merely making your subjects aware that you have noticed something, you can change a whole scene. (Nord, 2016)

This balance of keeping the camera rolling and getting footage needed without breaking the bond between cinematographer and subject is key in capturing emotional moments that become the subtext of the film. While Stanislavski—and later, filmmakers—shaped these moments in their *mise-en-scène*, relying on actors to portray a certain interpretation of what directors, perhaps, imagined, the cinematographer in documentaries relies on their own sensibilities to find and record these moments as they happen. The director may provide guidance, but there's usually no retakes in documentary work. This required the cinematographer to be especially alert to the nuances of human behavior.

David MacDougall, one of the most important visual anthropologists working in the field of observational cinema, provides a keen understanding of how human behavior is expressed through body language:

Within the face, the eyes are the apotheosis of the quick, the most alive and sensitive parts of the body, seemingly afloat in liquid and protected by the dry outer covering of the lid. The lid is the eye's instrument of revelation. […] The eyes are therefore the part of the body most carefully watched for disjunctions between social performance and inner feeling. Next the hands are most often studied for such clues (as in poker games). It is appropriate that the fingerprint, the other unique mark of individuality, should be found at the most sensitive extremities of touch, and that we should call the flesh beneath the fingernail "the quick." The human voice, another imprint of identity (now recognized in the "voice print"), is a further site of the quick. In listening to voices, our differentiation of the senses begins to blur. Voices have textures, as though perceived tactilely and visually. Produced by our bodies, they are distinctive physical manifestations of ourselves. Like our eyes, they can be "covered" by closing our lips—but also by language, which is how civilization imposes its laws on the animal sounds we make. (MacDougall, 1998: 52)

For MacDougall, "the quick" is a form of filmic "uncovering, or revelation"—"that which is tender, alive, or sensitive beneath an outer protective covering"

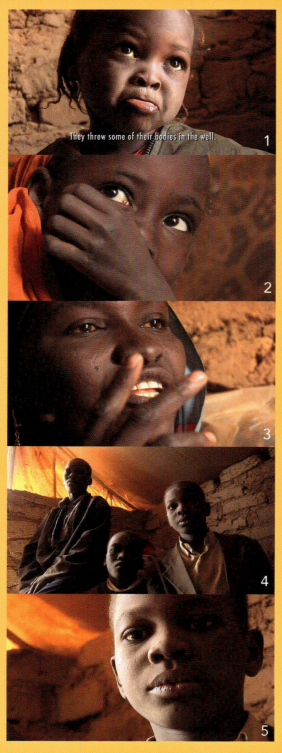

and "[w]e experience it as a sudden exposure, a contrast between dull and sensitive surfaces" (MacDougall, 1998: 50). It is that which reveals subtext, the underling emotions of the documentary subject.

In photojournalist Travis Fox's short documentary, "Crisis in Darfur Expands: Testimonials" (6:04), published by *The Washington Post* (March 7, 2007), we can see moments of the power of facial expression and the eyes of his subjects as he films in a refugee camp. (See Figure 1.12.) Fox's video can be found at www.vimeo.com/1293941.

Anima Abakr (3), a survivor along with some of her children of a Janjaweed attack (1, 2, 4, 5), explains to Fox what happened. We hear the story she tells, a witness testimonial recorded on video, but the most intriguing aspect of Fox's story involves the use of facial expressions and body language of Abakr and her surviving children (1, 2, 4, 5). These elements express a pathos through Fox's lens—a form of cinematic writing—as we are told that not all of her children made it out, Fox expressing, as Truffaut says about Hitchcock, a "unique ability to film the thoughts of [...] characters and make them perceptible without resorting to dialogue" (1084: 17).

The body language found in Fox's short piece echo with human sincerity or authenticity similar to the blocking Stanislavski conceived for his actors in Chekhov's *The Seagull*. Instead of giving his subjects blocking notes, Fox "writes" his "notes" in the moment with his camera, capturing the emotions of facial expressions, gestures, and the movement of his subjects as it unfolds in front of his lens, the process of attaining moments of what MacDougall calls the quick. Later in the edit, he shapes the sequence, the pauses, the

FIGURE 1.12
Travis Fox focuses on the body language of his subjects in order to reveal the underlying feelings.
(Images ©2006 *The Washington Post*.)

sound design, and so on, in the end creating a "dramatic effect by purely visual [and aural] means," as Truffaut would say about the films of Hitchcock (1984: 17).

The techniques utilized by Fox, here, stem from what visual anthropologists Grimshaw and Ravetz describe as not necessarily being "about creating an accurate transcription of the world" (2009: 17). That would be simply documenting, recording literally what's in front of the camera. Filmmakers do much more than this, as Grimshaw and Ravetz note: "Instead it hinges upon connection, expressed in an almost intangible, empathic moment. How to render this moment concrete is the problem that confronts the observational filmmaker" (2009: 36). As Stanislavski attempted to inscribe psychological truth in his notes on *The Seagull*, and by extension onto his actors' bodies in production, the documentary cinematographer confronts this psychological truth through the lens of her camera in an attempt to create empathy in the audience. And that empathy is shown visually through body language.

> Documentary filmmakers record expressions, gestures, and looks (the intimate emotional beats) of their subjects, capturing more than dialogue.

At one point Abakr pauses (3). Fox takes advantage of this silence to fill it with ambient sound of wind hitting the tent as we see close-ups of Abakr and her children (4 and 5). Utilizing a cinematic technique, Fox takes this moment to visualize (and auralize) the emotion of her story, where a less sure hand would have filled that apparent emptiness with more dialogue or narration, which would have strangled the story, cinematically. But it is in such spaces that we often discover the subtext of a scene, the dramatic tension that reveals much more than what is said on the surface, allowing us to, perhaps, find that "intangible, empathic moment" Grimshaw and Ravetz write about, moments that I feel Stanislavski was attempting to render onstage in his own way with Chekhov's play.

If such visual moments can help reveal a deeper truth, to clarify human relationships within the conditions they live, then it's imperative that documentary filmmakers discover and record them by paying attention to the gestures, the looks, the full expression of their subjects, because, as Truffaut says, "the essential is elsewhere" (not in the dialogue), but "it is by studying their eyes that we can find out what is truly on their minds" (Truffaut, 1984: 17).

MacDougall's thoughts reinforce this notion: "Much of the film experience has little to do with what one sees: it is what is constructed in the mind and body of the viewer. Films create a new reality in which the viewer plays a central role, or at least is invited to do so" (70–71). It is within the *seeing* of the facial expressions and the eyes that we, as the audience, can construct—*perceive*—the inner life of the characters, in which this new reality or story is created.

Utilizing observational filmmaking techniques, documentary filmmakers must train their eyes to perceive "discerning resonances" found in the "sounds, gestures, movement, rhythm" in a scene, a process by which, "paradoxically, allows their subjects to breathe" (Grimshaw and Ravetz, 2009: 118 and 63).

Let's look at a sequence from Netflix's original series, *Chef's Table* (season 1, episode 3: "Francis Mallmann"). (See Figure 1.13.)

Detail shots hone in on Mallmann's coooking with his son helping (1–9), which connects us to his family life in a positive way. The warm colors from the fire and candlelight (10–12) bring out the romantic feel. The composition in this footage reveals activity, but also emotion (see 5, 8, and 12), revaling warm, familial subtext.

FIGURE 1.13

Will Basanta's cinematography from an episode of *Chef's Table*, reveals a sequence over two and a half minutes, where we can see the emotional expression from Francis Mallmann and his family as he cooks a simple meal. What is the subtext? What does this visual sequence tell us about Mallmann? What does the filmmaker want us to feel about him? The camera records an intimate portrait of family life. (Sequence read top to bottom, first column, then second column onto the next page, cuts 1–13.) (Images ©2015 Netflix.)

VISUAL STORYTELLING THROUGH BLOCKING CHAPTER 1   45

> If documentary filmmakers avoid utilizing narration as a primary storytelling tool (what Hitchcock might refer to as "explanatory dialogue" in fiction films), and instead engage in the visual techniques of noticing the body language of their subjects, then they, like Hitchcock, can end up "filming the most complex and subtle relationships between human beings" (Truffaut, 1984: 18).

In fiction or narrative filmmaking, the director can shape her vision through the actors' bodies and capture it through cinematography, shape the set in the production design, decide what actors wear through the costume design, but in documentaries these elements—other than cinematography—is rarely crafted.

The inner subjective lives of documentary subjects must be "found" through externalized visual evidence (the subject's body language, facial expressions, the eyes, and tone of voice), resulting in the revealing of "such intimate emotions as suspicion, jealousy, desire, and envy" (as Truffaut said about Hitchcock's scenes, 1984: 18). Of course, Basanta writes a different kind of story than Hitchcock would with his lens. As seen in this sequence, Basanta captures an intimate and safe portrait of a family life that's full of love, authenticity, and tenderness, these moments revealed in the visual evidence of his cinematography.

If documentary filmmakers avoid utilizing narration as a primary storytelling tool (what Hitchcock might refer to as "explanatory dialogue" in fiction films), and instead engage in the visual techniques of noticing the body language of their subjects, then they, like Hitchcock, can end up "filming the most complex and subtle relationships between human beings" (Truffaut, 1984: 18).

Section review
1. What does it mean to film "the most complex and subtle relationships between human beings"?
2. As a documentary filmmaker, what does it mean to write with a camera?
3. What are some of the techniques Travis Fox and Will Basanta use to tell their story visually?
4. How do they express pathos through their respective cameras?

WORKS CITED

Allen, David. *Performing Chekhov*. Taylor and Francis, 1998.

Aristotle. *Poetics*. Trans. by S. H. Butcher. Hill and Wang, 1961.

Baron, Cynthia. "Stage Actors and Modern Acting Methods Move to Hollywood in the 1930s. *Cinémas* 25.1 (2014): 109–129. www.erudit.org/fr/revues/cine/2014-v25-n1-cine01837/1030232ar

Dill, Bill, ASC. "Elements of Composition" in *Learning Cinematography: 1 Narrative Fundamentals*. Lynda.com. 2016. www.lynda.com/Filmmaking-tutorials/Cinematography-01-Narrative-Fundamentals/423992-2.html

Fox, Travis. "Crisis in Darfur Expands: Testimonials." 7 March 2007. *Washington Post*, 2006. www.vimeo.com/1293941

Gottlieb, Sidney. "Hitchcock on Truffaut." *Film Quarterly*. Summer 2013: 10–22.

Grimshaw, Anna and Amanda Ravetz. *Observational Cinema: Anthropology, Film, and the Exploration of Social Life*. Indiana University Press, 2009.

Hetreed, Olivia. *Girl with a Pearl Earring*. Screenplay. 2003. www.awesomefilm.com/script/girlwithapearlearring.pdf

Hitchcock, Alfred, dir. *Strangers on a Train*. Cinematography: Robert Burks. Warner Bros., 1951.

Hurlbut, Shane, ASC. "Blocking and Matching Coverage." *Shane's Inner Circle*. Blog. August 2017. www.hurlbutvisuals.com/blog/2017/08/blocking-and-matching-coverage-2

Jones, David Richard. *Great Directors at Work*. University of California Press, 1986.

Lang, Fritz, dir. *Metropolis*. Cinematography: Karl Freund, Günther Rittau, Walter Ruttmann. Universum Film, 1927.

MacDougall, David. *Transcultural Cinema*. Princeton University Press, 1998.

Mackendrick, Alexander. *On Film-making: An Introduction to the Craft of the Director*. Edited by Paul Cronin. Faber and Faber, 2004.

McTeague, James H. *Before Stanislavsky: American Professional Acting Schools and Acting Theory 1875–1925*. The Scarecrow Press, Inc., 1993.

Still from *Chef's Table* "Francis Mallmann." DP: Will Basanta. (Image ©2015 Netflix.)

Mitter, Shomit. *Systems of Rehearsal: Stanislavski, Brecht, Grotowski,* and *Brook.* Routledge, 1992.

Netflix. "Francis Mallmann." *Chef's Table.* 1.3. 2015. www.netflix.com/title/80007945

Nord, Liz. "'Search for Revelations': Invaluable Cinematography Advice from DP Kirsten Johnson." Nofilmschool.com. 27 September 2016: www.nofilmschool.com/2016/09/kirsten-johnson-cinematography-documentary-masterclass-ciff

Ozu, Yasujiro, dir. *Tokyo Twilight.* Shochiku Eiga, 1957.

Ramsden, Kristian. "Alfred Hitchcock: Dialogue versus Pure Cinema." YouTube.com. Take Me To Your Cinema channel. 25 April 2016. www.youtube.com/watch?v=nQQgI9jNCuw

Stanislavski, Konstantin. *An Actor's Work: A Student's Diary.* Translated by Jean Benedetti. Routledge, 2008.

— *An Actor's Work on a Role.* Translated by Jean Benedetti. Routledge, 2010.

— *The Seagull Produced by Stanislavski.* Edited by S. D. Balukhaty. Translated by David Magarshack. Dennis Dobson, Ltd., 1952.

Stockwell, John, dir. *Crazy/Beautiful.* DP: Shane Hurlbut, ASC. Touchstone Pictures, 2001.

Tarkovsky, Andrew. *Sculpting in Time.* Translated by Kitty Hunter-Blair. University of Texas Press, 1987.

Truffaut, François, dir. *The 400 Blows.* DP: Henri Decaë. Les Films du Carrosse and Sédif Productions, 1959.

— *Hitchcock.* Simon and Schuster, 1984.

Webber, Peter. *Girl with a Pearl Earring.* DP: Eduardo Serra. Archer Street Productions, Delux Productions, Pathé Pictures International, 2003.

From Netflix's *Jessica Jones*. A lesson in how lens reveals character. (Image ©2015 Marvel Studios and Netflix.)

CHAPTER 2

VISUAL STORYTELLING THROUGH LENSES AND COMPOSITION

OVERVIEW

The director tends to hold the full visual flow of each scene in her head. The cinematographer must execute that vision, translating each scene into a number of shots in physically visual ways that can be captured on camera. As cinematographer Bill Dill, ASC says:

> We photograph physical things to stand in for the things we can't photograph. We can't photograph love, redemption, happiness, peace, war, or chaos. So we photograph physical things and actions. And give them meaning so the audience understands what those things represent. (Dill, 2016)

The composition—the physical visual elements framing the foreground, middle ground, and background bordered by a certain focal length of a lens—is the most important tool a cinematographer can use. It is designed to capture, in the most compelling way possible, the blocking and body language of performers, as explored in Chapter 1. It also frames the arrangement of all the other elements of the visual story, such as the setting, props, costumes, and lighting. This chapter covers elements of composition, lenses, and camera movement (composition in motion) in order to create engaging cinematic stories. My focus is not technical. The key knowledge of this chapter includes the psychological exploration of lenses and composition, providing filmmakers the tools to help make choices based on how the director *directs* the eye of the viewer in order to shape the story and the correlative emotional content of each shot. Choices in composition should fundamentally allow the audience to receive all of the necessary information for them to follow the story, visually. That comprises the director's job. A cinematographer should utilize the tools outlined in this chapter to envision the director's plan.

I break this chapter into five sections, providing definitions and case studies from the Netflix series *Godless*, *Jessica Jones*, and *The Crown*, as well adding composition and lens choices to the scene in Ozu's *Tokyo Twilight*, which I analyzed in Chapter 1.

1. Ten tools of composition
    - Shot size and lenses
    - Camera height and angle
    - Camera motion
    - Focal depth of field
    - Light and dark
    - Line and linear perspective
    - Layers
    - Weight
    - Color
    - Texture
2. Shooting for the edit
    - Coverage
    - Eye lines
    - Point of view and cutaways
    - 180 degree rule
    - Jump cuts
    - Kuleshov effect
3. Case study in lenses and composition from *Jessica Jones* with DP Manuel Billeter
4. Case study in lenses and composition from *Chef's Table* with DP Adam Bricker
5. Case study in lenses and composition from Ozu's *Tokyo Twilight* class project reinterpretation

Cinematographers must understand blocking in order to discover and execute the subtext through their camera and lighting work.

SECTION 1: TEN TOOLS OF COMPOSITION

Composition involves how all the elements in a shot look, where they are placed, and what they look like through a particular lens. There are at least ten elements cinematographers can use as tools in shaping the look and feel of a film.[1] I'll provide a short description of each, then give examples as a visual guide. Other than the first, these are not in any particular order of importance, since many of them may be used simultaneously in shots. The first five are basic and should be practiced in introductory courses. The other five tend to be more advanced and should be applied to the filmmaker's practice after mastering the first five.

1. *Shot size and lenses:* the shot size determines what an audience sees in a composition, whether it is wide, medium, or close (in combination with camera placement), and this size determines levels of intimacy in a shot. At the same time, the focal length of a lens shapes how we perceive the shot size, reinforcing the psychology of a scene. This section goes deep into the psychological impact of lenses.

2. *Camera height and angle:* the placement of the camera—low, level, or high—impacts how we perceive subjects and objects from a psychological/power point of view. Camera placement also determines the size of a shot.

3. *Camera motion:* the way to change composition in a shot. When not static (locked off), shots may be handheld, shaky, slow, or fast in motion, but in all cases it should reinforce the story, and changes in motion in a scene should revolve around emotional shifts in the story, what's called motivated camera movement.

4. *Focal depth of field:* deep focus or shallow depth of field.

5. *Light and dark:* the placement of light and shadow.

6. *Lines and linear perspective:* the placement of perceived lines on the screen denoting depth or flatness of an image, as well as the energy of horizontals, verticals, and diagonals.

---

[1] Others may argue for more or less, but these ten comprise the basics for determining key elements of composition in a practical, usable way.

7. *Layers:* the placement of foreground, middle ground, and background objects and subjects.
8. *Weight:* the size or visual "weight" of objects and subjects placed in the composition, either balancing or unbalancing it within the frame.
9. *Color:* the colors in a shot, from lighting to costumes, sets, and props.
10. *Texture:* how smooth or rough a scene physically seems, from the surface texture of furniture, floors, and walls to costumes, props, and even the skin of performers. Light placement (and resulting shadows) shape the texture, as well as the use of fog or smoke for atmospheric texture, which also determines the relative softness or sharpness of an image.

Below, I apply each tool to a scene from the opening sequence in the first episode of Netflix's limited series, *Godless* (2017), a tour de force of cinematic visual storytelling written and directed by Scott Frank, with cinematography by Steven Meizler. This sample reveals the visual power of cinematic storytelling and illustrates how all of the elements of the tools of composition were used by Frank and Meizler in a way that reveals the story beats step by step.[2]

The scene opens in dust and wind leading to low visibility for about the first third of the scene, the obscuration enhancing the story visually with mystery, we're wondering where we are and what is happening. The smoke and dust begin to lift as we see details of a massacre—both animals and people—ruined by a heart-breaking rampage, Marshal Cook scanning the remains of a small town, the only survivor singing a gospel song in front of a train wreck. The series of screen grabs reveal the 30 cuts and/or reframing of composition through camera movement. (See Figure 2.1.)

FIGURE 2.1
The opening scene to the first episode of Netflix's *Godless*, "An Incident at Creede." The shots are numbered in sequence, with letters referring to selected composition moments from camera movement within a shot.
(Images ©2017 Netflix.)

---

[2] I also want to note how the sound design (by Harry Cohen) and sound editing (by Hector Gika) shapes the entire atmosphere of this sequence. Without it, the power of the film loses its efficacy as strong visual storytelling. Take note of this when creating your film. Strong images become more compelling when accompanied by a strong sound design.

VISUAL STORYTELLING THROUGH LENSES AND COMPOSITION   CHAPTER 2   55

Aspect ratio

Although I don't place aspect ratio in the tools of composition, choosing the right aspect ratio for the story is important since the shape of the screen sets the boundaries of the "canvas" for the shoot, so it is the first technical choice a cinematographer must make.

- 1.33:1 (4:3)—The ratio for standard definition format. Rarely used, today. If used, it's designed to help provide a retro look to a film.
- 1.78:1 (16:9)—The ratio used in high definition video.
- 1.85:1—A standard widescreen format in filmmaking. Both 1.78:1 and 1.85:1 are nearly the same and provide an expansive view for the audience, helping to create a breadth of scale.
- 2:1—A widescreen format used by a variety of cinematographers who have shot such Netflix shows as *Ozark*, *Mindhunter*, and *House of Cards*, among others.
- 2.39:1—Anamorphic widescreen ratio. Significant increase of breadth and scale, typically used in "epic" films expressing an expansive scale.

The aspect ratio may not seem like it matters—especially when dealing with widescreen formats (it's rare that films are shot in standard definition formats and the broadcast standard has shifted to 16:9 in widespread adoption of widescreen televisions). However, aspect ratio determines the height and width of a frame and when you consider the blocking or staging of actors, it matters in how the audience sees the action unfold.

Godless utilizes a 2.39:1 widescreen anamorphic aspect ratio, providing an epic scale for this series. Here's what a shot would look liked from *Godless* if cropped to 1.33, 1.78, 1.85, and 2.1 with the original 2.39 ratio. (See Figure 2.2.)

The smaller ratios would not have provided the scope needed to reveal the expanse of the story for this series' western landscapes.

1. Shot size and lenses

The lens you choose determines your field of view (tied to camera distance). That's obvious. But lenses also determine how an audience feels about the story at particular moments, so examining how different types of lenses influence how we perceive a story (even if unconsciously), sets the discerning cinematographer on the path to thinking about how shots sizes and focal lengths of lenses comprise one of the most important elements of visual storytelling in cinema.

FIGURE 2.2
Different aspect ratios from the end of the scene of "An Incident at Creede" show how the expansive scale would have lost some of its impact if shot in a smaller aspect ratio. (Images ©2017 Netflix.)

We spend some extra time and space on this first tool of composition in order to explore the psychology of lenses. It seems that this is an advanced technique, but it is fundamental to visual storytelling and it should be the most important tool in the cinematographer's toolkit. Beginners who master the psychological aspects of lenses, camera height and angle, camera motion, and focal depth of field (covered in sections 1-4 of composition) will stand out.

Psychological point of view
Normal: The point of view of a person's eyesight, but this is really the perspective from a single eye (not two), and it does not include peripheral vision. *Use to establish normal behavior.*

In this scene from *Godless*, we see a normal point of view in this moving shot in 1a–1b (see Figure 2.1, p. 55). Reinforcing what appears to be a normal point of view of Marshal Cook checking out a mystery as he heads into a burning town.

Objective: Omniscient voice viewpoint. The perspective is not from a character's point of view, but the voice of the storyteller, the director. *It is outside looking in, providing information a character might not see.*

We see several occurrences of this type of shot in cuts 7, 9–11, and 20 of *Godless*. (See Figure 2.1.) These shots reinforce the story from an omniscient point of view, the eye of the storyteller providing shifting perspectives on the story.

Subjective: Subjective point of view. In an extreme example, we're seeing the scene through the eyes of a character (like a GoPro strapped to someone jumping from a plane or in a first person shooter game). *For storytelling purposes, the closer the camera is placed behind a character, such as an over the shoulder shot (OTS), the more*

> **The proper lens (at the proper distance) will reinforce the emotion found in the story as performed by the actors.**

subjective it becomes. The farther away the camera is and/or when the camera is placed more on the side looking in, the more objective the shot becomes.

In this opening scene from *Godless* (Figure 2.1) we see the story from Marshal Cook's point of view and the following shots are subjective: 1–6, 8, 12–19. Some are from his perspective, especially 12–19, while some are from a subjective view to his story (1–6). In 11a and 11b, we see an objective shot from inside the building wrap around to his perspective (in 11c).

Emotional distance and intimacy in shot sizes

Wide: Captures and sets the characters' locations in a scene. *Psychologically, it offers the least intimacy between characters.* It's similar to having a conversation between two people standing against opposite walls in a room. Provides scale in reinforcing the geometrical space of the location as a storytelling element.

The widest shot in this scene from *Godless* (Figure 2.1), is the last, when the camera cranes up on Marshal Cook's face, while pulling away at the same time, setting him as a small figure in a wide space showing the face of evil. In 2, 3, 5, 6, 7 there are wide full shots of Cook and his team that place them geometrically in the space, but not an extreme wide shot until 20.

Medium: Provides a normal conversational distance between people. *Psychologically equivalent to people having a conversation at a comfortable distance without invading personal space.*

There are many medium shots in this scene from *Godless* (Figure 2.1), notably 11 and 15, and the idea of what is medium must be put into perspective with the rest of the other shots—some are wider and closer than others when placed in comparison to other shots.

Close: Distance of intimacy. *Psychologically, we're now in someone's personal and emotional space.* This usually occurs in real life when people are in love or in a fight.

> Psychologically, the wide shot offers the least intimacy between characters.

In Figure 2.1 (p. 55), we see several close-up shots from *Godless*: 1b, 12, 14, 16, 19a. A few of these are tighter than others—they define emotions and reaction shots to what the Marshal sees and establish him as the point of view character (we see no other close-up of another living character).

The **Psychological impact of lenses chart** (pp. 60–61), summarizes some of the psychological impact of lenses, but there's no formula or hard and fast rule that a specific focal length correlates with a particular emotion. Use this as a guideline, rather than as a rule.

Psychological Impact of Lenses

Shot type and lens size	Depth of field	Uses and psychological impact
Super wide fisheye or convex lens 6–12mm	Deep focus	The image curves along the edge of the shot and causes the image to become distorted. • Provides a sense of expansiveness in wide shots. • May add comedic effect; or where distortion and confusion is needed when brought close to a subject. • Could be used to show a security camera's view, bug eyes, or even an alien.
Wide 12–18mm	Deep focus	Provides expansive clarity, a view showing details from foreground to background. Places character(s) within a heightened sense of space. A tight close-up on subjects may lead to visual distortion. (You can place the lens close to a subject in the foreground and have the background focus fall off.) • Use to ground a character in geometric space and location in wide shots. • Use to provide an expansive view of a scene. • Use to express instability or zaniness in tight shots. • Use to show discomfort between characters, since the world becomes distorted.
Normal wide 18–34mm	Deep focus Open aperture to get shallow depth of field	A step below a "normal" field of view, the standard wide angle view provides a sense of geometric space, because it not only picks up details from foreground to background through deep focus (under normal aperture), but it also covers the area around the edge of the subject when setting wide shots. A tight close-up on subjects may lead to visual distortion in lower focal lengths. (You can place the lens close to a subject in the foreground and have the background focus fall off.) • Places characters within a heightened sense of space. • Use to provide a sense of grounding in space and location in wider shots. • Offers a bit of instability or zaniness in tight shots when brought close to the subject, especially in the lower focal lengths. • Makes you feel like you're participating in the action. • May also allow for a sense of discomfort between characters, since the world becomes a bit distorted compared to the normal view of the world.
Normal view 35–55mm	Deep focus at high aperture Shallow focus at low aperture	Psychologically for viewers, this is the normal field of view for the human eye (one eye)—normal lenses do not capture peripheral vision. There's no distortion on the edge of the frame. • Use when offering a sense of "normality" to a scene and equal balance of power. • Normal lenses offer intimacy when the camera is level, because the balance of power is equal.
Fairly tight 60–100mm	Image becomes magnified and may start feeling compressed at the proper camera-subject distance. Provides shallow depth of field.	Depending on the tightness of a shot, it can provide a decent reach to get a character in a tight close-up with a shallow depth of field. The image starts getting compressed and shallow in narrow fields of view as the lenses get longer, magnifying the shot. • Use to provide focus on a single character or cutaway shot. • Use to provide a sense of distance in an intimate scene. • Brings beauty to a character (a good "portrait" lens would fall in the 85–135mm range).

Tight 100–400mm (or longer)	Magnified shot with shallow depth of field at normal aperture. Compression occurs with the lens far enough away from the subject (with proper camera–subject distance).	For reaching close when the camera is farther away from a subject—magnifies the background and foreground providing a sense of compression when the camera is properly placed at the right distance. • Use when you need to get close to a subject when the camera is farther away. • May enhance an objective view due to a distancing of intimacy in a scene. • Brings a heightened sense of beauty to a character.
Tilt shift lens (variety of focal lengths)	Shallow to deep depending on the focal length and aperture of the lens.	Allows you to adjust focus within a specific field of view within the shot, providing a highly stylized shot. • Can provide a sense of miniaturization to a scene. • Use to stylize the subject or scene, such as in a dream state or drug-induced altered viewpoint, or even an alien landscape.

Furthermore, these impacts change with camera distance, so keep in mind the emotional distance and intimacy in shot sizes in combination with the focal length of the lens. The proper lens (at the correct distance) will reinforce the emotion found in the story as performed by the actors. In many ways, the impact of how a particular lens is used or how a camera moves depends on the style of the story. The filmmaker sets the rules of consistency in how certain focal lengths, composition, camera movement, and camera angles reinforce different psychological situations.

In the example from *Godless* (Figure 2.1), we see a variety of normal and long lenses used throughout most of the shots, with a wide lens used in the final shot.

2. Camera height and angle

The height of the camera and camera angle in relationship to the subject also determines the psychological nature of a scene:

High angle shot: The camera's point of view is from on high looking down onto the subject, causing the subject to look up towards the camera. This height can be just slightly higher than the eyeline or higher. *It tends to result in a sense of subservience and weakness. There is no intimacy in this type of shot, due to the balance of power being uneven.*

As can be seen in the final shot of the scene from *Godless* (Figure 2.1, p. 55 and more detail in 2.17, p. 81), the Marshal stumbles as the camera reaches high, looking down at him as he faces a horror holding dominance over him; the high angle shot looking down onto him takes away all of his power, revealing his sense of subservience and weakness to the devastation around him, and obviously there is no intimacy, here.

> **High angle shots tend to result in a sense of subservience and weakness. There is no intimacy in this type of shot, due to the balance of power being uneven.**

Low angle shot: The camera's point of view is low, looking up at the subject, so the subject must look down towards the camera. The height can by just slightly below the eyeline or lower. *It typically gives the character dominance, authority, superiority, and strength. There is no intimacy in this type of shot, due to the balance of power being uneven.*

In Figure 2.1, cut 18 (p. 55), we see the girl appears weak—and as a victim she is—in the shot, with the perceived power in the Marshal's hands.

> **Low angle shots typically give the character dominance, authority, superiority, and strength. There is no intimacy in this type of shot, due to the balance of power being uneven.**

Level shot: Camera's lens is at eye level to the subject. *It often provides a sense of evenness of power since no one is looking down or up at someone, and allows for intimacy.* Use a level shot with a normal lens to provide intimacy in a close-up, due to the perceived equal power relationship.

In cut 1 of Figure 2.1, the Marshal and his men come out of the smoke and dust in a level shot. They're all equal as they enter an unknown situation.

Dutch angle shot: Camera tilted unevenly from the horizon line. *Tends to induce a sense of disarrangement or confusion on the part of the subject.*

In Figure 2.1, cut 20 the angle is slightly skewed, reinforcing his disorienting nature of the final shot of this scene. The lens is also wide, supporting the uncomfortable nature of this shot.

Front shot: When on axis and level, *provides the strongest intimacy since the full face is exposed*.

Again, in cut 18 of Figure 2.1, we see the woman front on, as the Marshal faces her. Even though the shot is wide, we feel an vulnerability between the Marshal and her as she sings, because she's fully open to the camera.

Side or profile shot: Sees action from the side, objectively. *It pulls us away from intimacy since we're not seeing the full face where emotion is most fully expressed.*

Visual Storytelling through Lenses and Composition CHAPTER 2

In Figure 2.1, cut 9; the victim is in a profile shot, helping to offset the character's death, lost in the lack of intimacy in that moment.

Rear shot: The furthest emotional distance from a character, since we do not see their face. *Because of this, we also feel tension because we don't know what the character is feeling, doing, or looking at.* For example, in Figure 2.1 (p. 55), cut 11c, Marshal Cook's back is to the camera, building tension as he looks down the train tracks and sees the ruin in the distance. It holds mystery since there's no clear visual of the train wreck and the victims beyond in the distance.

	Emotional Impact of Camera Height and Angle
High angle	The camera's point of view from on high looking down onto the subject, causing the subject to look up towards the camera. This height can be just slightly higher than the eye line or higher. • It tends to result in a sense of subservience and weakness. There is no intimacy in this type of shot, due to the balance of power being uneven.
Low angle	The camera's point of view is low, looking up at the subject, so the subject must look down towards the camera. The height can be just slightly below the eye line or lower. • It typically gives the character dominance, authority, superiority, and strength. There is no intimacy in this type of shot, due to the balance of power being uneven.
Level	Camera's lens is at eye level to the subject. Use a level shot with a normal lens to provide intimacy in a close-up, due to the perceived equal power relationship. • It often provides a sense of evenness of power since no one is looking down or up at someone, and allows for intimacy.
Dutch angle	Camera tilted unevenly from the horizon line. • Tends to induce a sense of disarrangement or confusion on the part of the subject.
Front	When on axis and level, *provides the strongest intimacy since the full face is exposed.*
Side	Sees action from the side. • It pulls us away from intimacy since we're not seeing the full face where emotion is most fully expressed.
Rear	The furthest emotional distance from a character, since we do not see their face. • We feel tension because we don't know what the character is feeling, doing, or looking at.

Level shots often provide a sense of evenness of power since no one is looking down or up at someone, and allows for intimacy.

3. Camera motion

Camera movement changes the composition in a shot and it should convey a clear beginning, middle, and end. It influences the emotions of a scene and what it reveals. Some filmmakers add motion for the sake of visual stimulation, and in certain cases that technique works as eye candy, failing to deliver any story substance. But when used consciously—with psychological motivation rooted in the story—camera movement reveals information and emotion, and even the passage of time, cinematically.

Motivated camera movement: Reveals emotional story intent from point A to point B. (See Figure 2.17, p. 81.) The crane up shot would typically be used as a moment of release in an edit, revealing sweeping panoramic views at the end (or beginning) of a scene. In *Godless*, it reveals, moment by moment, increasing tension as the gradual panoramic crane shot reveals even more story information.

Shaky cam shot: The handheld look. Use a wide lens to minimize extreme motion. The longer the lens, the more obvious and extreme the shake. *The camera calls attention to itself, providing a sense of disorientation, giving a newsreel or raw documentary feeling as if the action is occurring unstaged in the moment.*

Absolute motion: When the camera moves, yet stays in one place on its axis (such as on a tripod), the foreground and background move at the same rate of speed onscreen. Found in pan, tilt, and zoom shots. This does not naturally occur with our eyes in the real world, so it may reinforce unnatural feelings.

Relative motion: When the camera moves *through* space, the foreground moves more quickly relative to the background. Naturally occurring when we move through space. Found in push-in, pull-out, jib, and tracking shots.

The Psychological impact of camera movement table defines different types of camera motion, the tools required for that motion, the type of motion, as well as the uses and general psychological impact of that motion.

Psychological Impact of Camera Movement			
Type of camera motion	Tool	Motion type	Uses of motion and psychological impact
Pan	Tripod	Absolute	Covers space from left of screen to right and vice versa on a static axis (tripod). • Use to cover subject movement, moving from one subject to another to show the relationship between them in space. • Use to cover the reaction of someone. Following the eyes, the energy of one person looking at another—we pan to see what the character looking sees. • Use to cover a person drawing attention to an object and following it, used in some ways as the continuation of a physical action. • Psychologically, an audience wants to see what another character is looking at, so the pan releases this tension as we want to follow the gaze.

Tilt	Tripod	Absolute	Covers space from bottom to top of screen and vice versa on a static axis. Similar to the pan, but pointing vertically up and down rather than horizontally left and right. • Use to cover the reaction of someone. Following the eyes, the energy of one person looking up or down at another, we tilt to see what the character looking sees. • Use to cover a person drawing attention to an object and following it up or down, used in some ways as the continuation of a physical action. • Potential to reveal importance of grandeur or majesty of an object or subject, by tilting up to reveal a towering figure or object. May be menacing to the subject if shot from a low angle. • Changes the power relationship in a scene when height of the angle is changed from low to high and high to low.
Zoom	Lens	Absolute	Change focal length within a shot (quick zooms are referred to as snap zooms). • We're conscious that a camera is being used (to create the effect of newsreel footage, like a live event—someone with a camera covering an event, providing a subjective look). • Use to move close or farther away from the subject while maintaining absolute motion, so only use if the subjective view is needed. • Effective as a snap zoom to push the audience quickly and abruptly into an emotional moment, causing them to feel off balance (such as in battle scenes or some other intense physical activity), providing a subjective sense that the action is unfolding by the moment and the camera is there to cover it as it happens.
Push in (dolly)	Track, slider, steadicam, gimbal, jib	Relative	Camera physically moves closer to the subject or object. • Use to intensify or heighten emotion in a scene as the audience enters the intimate space of a subject. • Move slowly to make the shift in emotion subtle. • Move quickly for obvious impact and/or rushed feeling.
Pull out (dolly)	Track, slider, steadicam, gimbal, jib	Relative	Camera physically moves away from the subject or object. • Use to diminish emotion in a scene as the audience moves out of the intimate space of a subject, making them feel isolated or lonely. • Move slowly to make the shift in emotion subtle. • Move quickly for obvious impact and/or rushed feeling.
Parallel (or lateral) tracking	Track, slider, steadicam, gimbal	Relative	Camera physically follows the action of a character in parallel to the subject's movement. Or it reveals different action in a shot, even passing time. • Tracking away from a character creates distance from the subject and may reveal loneliness or disconnectedness from the world. • Tracking towards a character allows us to enter the emotion of a character from a distance. • Tracking with the character in a profile shot is far less intimate, but puts the audience into the scene as if they are with the character.

Jib (crane)	Jib, gimbal	Relative	Camera can physically move up and down in space, as well as allowing it to push in and/or pull out of space within the same shot. (The up or down and push or pull may be done simultaneously.) • Use to reach deep into space (of the location or set) where it may be difficult to get a shot otherwise (such as when trying to set tracks in a tight space). • Use to pull back and leave a scene, departing from a character and leaving them in a landscape—good way to exit a specific type of scene, causing a de-establishing shot. • Use to swoop into a scene and look around a space that could not be shot with another type of move. • When starting low and moving up, reveals an expanse of scenery and distances us from the emotional point of view of characters. • Looking down from above provides an omniscient view of landscape and action. • When starting high and moving low, provides a shift from omniscient POV to a personal intimacy as we enter the emotional space of the characters.
Hand-held	Hands, gimbal, steadicam	Relative	The handheld look, when done smoothly, offers a way for the visual movement to float through space. • Use to provide a sense of floating and peace. • When using choppy quick movement, then use to convey a sense of frenetic, out-of-control behavior.

As you translate the blocking and body language in your script analysis done in Chapter 1, use these charts from sections 1-3 to think closely about how to take the blocking notes and apply lens choices, composition, camera height, and camera movement effectively as one of the most powerful tools you can use when telling a story visually. Your work will stand apart form others when you master them.

4. Focal depth of field

Reveals what is in focus. Use focus to frame a shot (foreground and background). Depth of field changes with aperture and with types of lenses—a wide angle will tend to provide deep focus, while a telephoto or long lens will provide a shallow depth of field, where you can choose whether the background, middle ground, or foreground is in focus, allowing you to compose different types of framing. You can place wide and normal lenses close to a subject and decrease the focal distance, while a greater distance will increase the depth of focus. A *rack* focus occurs when changing focus within the same shot (going from foreground in focus to background in focus with the foreground falling out of focus, for example). You can also adjust depth of field by changing the aperture. Closing it up deepens the focal field of view, while opening it up makes the focus shallow. Knowing how all of these work is fundamental in using focal depth of field. (This site offers a depth of field calculator: www.dofmaster.com/dofjs.html.)

> **Deep focus shots tend to provide breadth, little mystery, or a revealing of a mystery, as well as an expansion of the mind.**

Deep focus: Foreground to background are all in focus. It reveals the importance of everything in the shot, the details, as well as the breadth and depth of the shot. *Deep focus shots tend to provide breadth, a little mystery, or a revealing of a mystery, as well as an expansion of the mind.* (See Figure 2.3.)

FIGURE 2.3
A deep focus shot reveals the train wreckage, the destruction of those killed, and the one lone survivor singing a Gospel song. Even though the background goes a bit soft, this deep focus shot helps reveal the scale of the scene, the amount of death that has occurred in the story. The fact that the train runs off the tracks disrupts our eye at the apex of where the girl is on the ground, singing, forcing our eye to go there (along with placing light on her white dress). (Image ©2017 Netflix.)

Shallow focus: Only a part of the frame is in focus, either the foreground, middle ground, or background. It focuses the eye to an important part of the frame. Usually, it's on someone's face in order to heighten the emotion. *It forces us to focus on one moment, a character's emotion; offers an ambiguous sense of depth—a lack of expansion, but a focus of intent or feelings.* (See Figures 2.4 and 2.5, p. 68.)

Rack focus: The focus changes in the shot. This is called pulling focus. *A rack focus shifts our attention along with shifting points of story through balance of power or a revealing of mystery around the edge of what's in focus; it clarifies relationships.* (See Figure 2.6, p. 69.)

> A shallow focus forces us to focus on one moment, a character's emotion; offers an ambiguous sense of depth—a lack of expansion, but a focus of intent or feelings.

FIGURE 2.4
A shallow depth of field close-up on the Marshal, reveals his pain and disbelief. A deep focus shot would scatter the energy of this emotion into the background. By keeping it shallow our entire focus is on him. By extension, it reflects the pain that we as the audience feels.

(Image ©2017 Netflix.)

FIGURE 2.5
This is a shallow depth of field shot, but it is not as shallow as the close-up in Figure 2.4. Here, the focus drops off slowly, and we can see the Marshal riding his horse with bodies in the background. But our full attention is on the church bell, perhaps a symbol of hope lost or an ironic juxtaposition of the church bell echoing in the midst of destruction, a warning that is too late.

(Image ©2017 Netflix.)

FIGURE 2.6
One of the Marshal's men calls to him. It is the first line of dialogue spoken in the scene. The shot is shallow, with the Marshal in the foreground, left, in focus, then the camera tilts down and pans right, with a rack focus on one of his deputies, as he gets his attention. This sets up the moment that there is something even worse coming.

(Images ©2017 Netflix.)

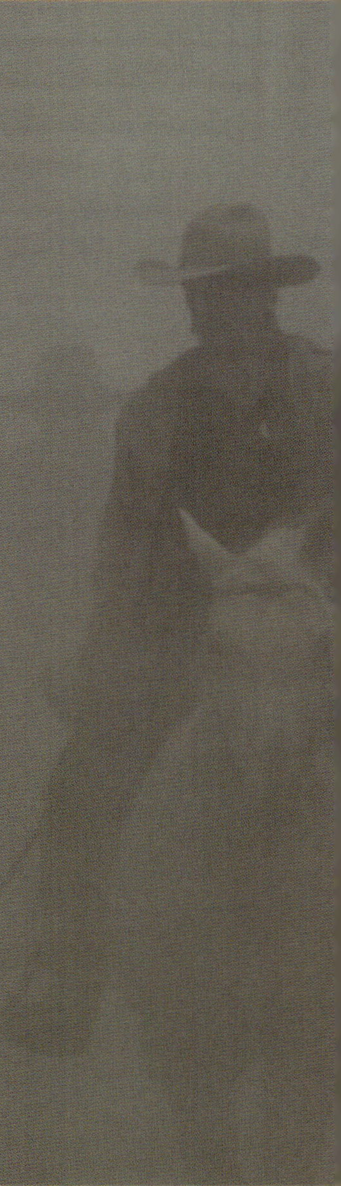

5. Light and dark

Cinematographers use light and shadow (*chiaroscuro*) to shape the details of tonality in a scene, utilizing elements of light and shadow to draw our eyes to various elements of composition. It also tends to reflect the emotional intent of a scene.

- *Darkness holds mystery and provides high energy when used in contrast with light.*
- *Light provides clarity of focus, but if "flat" (with no negative fill or shadow placement), it makes everything even, little to no contrast, and reinforces low energy.*

In Figure 2.10 (p. 73), we can see how the shadowed background stands in contrast to the side light spilling onto the woman, making her stand out. There are moments throughout the scene where the contrast is low (such as cuts 1a, 2, 3, and 5 in Figure 2.1, p. 55), while others (such as cuts 1b, 4, 6, 7, 8, 9, 10) provide high contrast so the figures stand out. Our eyes are drawn to the brightest area of the screen, so placing light and shadow is crucial in visual storytelling. Lighting is covered in more detail in the next chapter.

6. Lines and linear perspective

Filmmakers set and move their cameras in real space—full-on three dimensions—but the image that is recorded and projected is on a two-dimensional surface, so finding ways to make those two dimensions into three on a flat surface using linear perspective has been pioneered by artists since the Renaissance.

Flat shot: A shot that contains no receding lines (linear perspective). Scenes shot against a flat wall, for example, are flat. *There are some points of the story where you*

FIGURE 2.7 (background image)
The Marshal and his men are obscured in the second shot from *Godless*. Even through the building behind them—along with the Marshal taking point—reveals some sense of depth, there's no receding linear perspective. They're shot against the flat wall of the building. We begin to see detail on the Marshal and his horse, but his men behind him are more obscured, showing that he is the leader. The obscuration and flatness of the scene (shaped by smoke and dust) builds the mystery—they're heading into an unknown situation and we, as the audience,

want to shoot flat as a way to provide contrast to deep shots, but more importantly it tends to convey a sense of entrapment or "flatness" to someone's life. The energy of a flat surface is low, placid, contained, unexciting—there's no forward movement or a sense of going anywhere.

The opening shots from "An Incident at Creed" are flat—not fully due to a flat background, but reinforced by smoke and dust obscuring the background. (Figure 2.7, background image.)

The next few shots in the scene (see p. 55) show the characters riding through the smoke and dust with details revealed shot by shot.

Deep shot: A shot that contains linear perspective, lines that recede in the distance, shaping depth to a shot, creating a sense of going forward (or receding), as well as showing unconstrained or unreserved energy. It conveys high energy.

The first shot that shows cinematic depth occurs in Figure 2.8 (p. 72).Later in the scene, the Marshal looks at a train wreck, the tracks providing linear perspective drawing his (our) eyes down the length of the tracks. (See Figure 2.9, p. 72.)

Linear perspective is one of the most powerful tools a filmmaker can utilize to help tell a story visually. It draws our eyes to a point of focus or action. Diagonals provide energy to shots, as well. The reverse close-up on the Marshal reveals his despair as he scans death and destruction over the next few shots. (See cuts 12–19 in Figure 2.1, p. 55.)

are with them, trying to figure out what is going on. If the shot had started wide—the so called "establishing shot," then all mystery would have been gone and we would not be nearly as interested. That would be a form of "telling" that spoon feeds the audience. These particular shots lead us along the Marshal's point of view as he tries to figure out what happened. This is visual storytelling. It forces the audience to pay attention and figure out what is going on, as well. (Image ©2017 Netflix.)

FIGURE 2.8
Take note of the linear perspective. Even through the riders are still in smoke and dust, the receding lines drive the action forward, providing high energy as the team begins to discover the scope of the massacre.

(Image ©2017 Netflix.)

FIGURE 2.9
The Marshal in the foreground is framed in a deep focus shot, along the rule of thirds, as the receding line (linear perspective) of the train tracks draw his (and our) gaze to screen-left, the wreckage of the train in the distance.

(Image ©2017 Netflix.)

Most of these cutaway shots (p. 55, cuts 8-10, 13, 15, 17, 18) reveal detail, providing for some of the most unobscured shots in the scene, revealing how the horrific details are ingrained in his mind.

Psychological impact of lines
- Horizontal lines provide balance and evenness.
- Vertical lines emanate a sense of strength and power.
- Diagonals exude energy and potential change or imbalance.

Psychological impact of shapes
- Circles express feminine power, softness, reserved, inner, and radiant power.
- Squares and rectangles provide masculine edginess and external power; brashness.
- Triangles provide dynamic shifts in power or imbalance.

7. Layers

Shoot in layers, utilizing foreground, middle ground, and background elements in the composition in order to not only provide a sense of depth, but it also makes the environment realistic. Shallow depth of field shots will heighten one layer, while deep focus shots will allow all layers to be seen. Nearly every shot includes multiple layers in this scene from *Godless*. (See Figure 2.10.)

> - *The foreground, when in focus, provides the most power and the strongest story intent.* If the foreground is out of focus, then the shot conveys a sense of depth, foreground obstacles to be overcome between us and the subject in the middle ground. The woman in the middle ground of Figure 2.10 reveals a sense of hopelessness, despite the fact that's she's balanced in the frame. And, as being in the middle ground, there's balance to that position within the frame.

FIGURE 2.10
A boulder, out of focus, lies in the foreground, while the woman sings in the middle ground. The wreckage of the train and another body comprise the background. Even though this is a tighter shot, cutting in from the previous shot 17b in Figure 2.1, the use of layers reinforces her anguish as no life exists in front of her or behind her.
(Image ©2017 Netflix.)

The foreground reveals an ambiguous obstacle between the Marshal and the woman. The background remains in focus, but dark, highlighting her presence as a sense of balance and perhaps a sense of hope.

- *Composition favoring the middle ground helps shape balance to a scene.*
- *Composition favoring the background helps engage a sense of depth and distance.*

8. Weight

Balance: The geometrical visual size of elements in a shot. When following the rule of thirds, there's balance (which can also be configured through light, shadows, and color). This weight might balance figures in horizontal space as well as through depth, such as the one found in Figure 2.11. *Balance determines how stable a scene and/or character might be.*

In the scene from *Godless*, most of the shots are balanced—which at first glance seems an anomaly, since the characters are facing a horrific massacre that should make them all feel unbalanced, and by extension, the audience should feel that way, as well. But the Marshal remains unflappable throughout the scene, until the end, the law providing hope and stability.

Unbalanced: Occurs when graphic elements, light, dark, and/or colors are uneven in the composition within the foreground, middle ground, and background. *An unbalanced shot reinforces what is unbalanced in the character's world.* (See Figures 2.12 and 2.13, p. 75.)

FIGURE 2.11 The wagon in the foreground pulls the weight of the image to the right, while the horse and rider in the mid-ground draws our eye to the left. Note the layers in this shot, with blurred buildings in the background, filling out the balance of the image. (Image ©2017 Netflix.)

VISUAL STORYTELLING THROUGH LENSES AND COMPOSITION   CHAPTER 2   75

FIGURE 2.12
Marshal Cook rides up center of the screen, then turns screen-left. Although his face is composed along the rule of thirds, this shot is unbalanced, because he predominantly looks screen-left, crowding the left side of the screen, forcing the audience to begin to feel the character become unbalanced as he looks at the horrors around him. If he looked predominantly screen-right, then the shot would be balanced.

(Image ©2017 Netflix.)

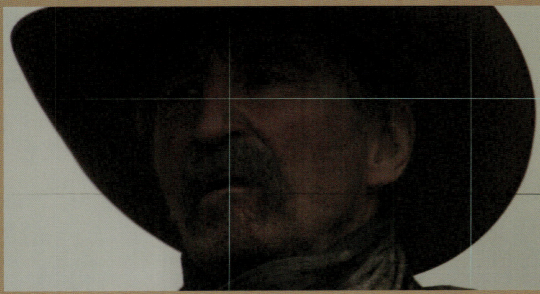

FIGURE 2.13
The rule of thirds places Marshal Cook on the lines, as it were, but as he predominantly faces screen-left in the shot, it feels a bit unbalanced because his look crowds the left frame, causing a bit of unease or anxiety in the audience.

(Image ©2017 Netflix.)

9. Color

The color is the palette of the film, determining its "look." It not only includes colors of costumes and props, but also the setting, as well as the color grade in the postproduction process. Color is one of the key components of cinematography. After researching articles in the cinematography trade magazine, *American Cinematographer*, Richard Misek dials in on the American Society of Cinematographer's (ASC) view that color falls within the cinematographer's purview. Writing in the journal, *Screen*, Misek notes:

> The ASC's view of film production can be summarized as follows: a film's director has a mental image (a "vision") of how the script will appear on screen; the DoP realizes this "vision" by registering moving images with a 'look' that corresponds to, or improves on, what the director imagined; by setting the "look" of images registered by the camera, the cinematographer is thus by implication responsible for the overall "look" of a film; colour constitutes a key aspect of a film's "look," and so falls within the cinematographer's creative territory. (2010: 405)

Color shapes how we feel about characters and the film, subconsciously. Umberto Eco argues how cultures tend to condition the colors we see, therefore "content" does not comprise the "external world. Expressions do not *signify* things or states of the world. At most, they are *used* to communicate with somebody about states of the world," a form of categorization (Eco, 1985: 162).

Colors should help shape and reinforce emotions found in a screenplay. In fiction, the director—along with her team—can consciously design (signify) how an audience feels about the world of the film, just as advertisers use certain psychology of colors to manipulate how we feel about a product in a commercial, for example, as explored by Ashton Hauff in her blog, "The Know it All Guide to Color Psychology in Marketing," where she examines some of the ways color induces or reinforces the psychology of viewers. (See Figure 2.14, p. 77.)

Throughout the scene from *Godless*, we see muted color tones, predominantly utilizing greens, browns, grays, and blacks. The negative psychological impact of green (envy, jealousy, and guilt), brown (dogmatic, conservative), gray (gloomy, sad, conservative), and black (death, evil, and mystery) all reinforce the death and destruction of the scene caused by a man betrayed by an adopted son—all information we discover later in the series. By using Adobe Color CC

VISUAL STORYTELLING THROUGH LENSES AND COMPOSITION   CHAPTER 2   77

COLORS CONVEY Emotions

BLUE	TURQUOISE	GREEN	YELLOW
(+) TRANQUILITY, SECURITY, INTEGRITY, PEACE, LOYALTY, TRUST, INTELLIGENCE	SPIRITUAL, HEALING, PROTECTION, SOPHISTICATED	FRESHNESS, ENVIRONMENT, NEW, MONEY, FERTILITY, HEALING, EARTH	BRIGHT, SUNNY, ENERGETIC, WARM, HAPPY, PERKY, JOY, INTELLECT
(−) COLDNESS, FEAR, MASCULINITY	ENVY, FEMININITY	ENVY, JEALOUSY, GUILT	IRRESPONSIBLE, UNSTABLE

PURPLE	PINK	RED	ORANGE
(+) ROYALTY, NOBILITY, SPIRITUALITY, LUXURY, AMBITION, WEALTH	HEALTHY, HAPPY, FEMININE, SWEET, COMPASSION, PLAYFUL	LOVE, PASSION, ENERGY, POWER, STRENGTH, HEAT, DESIRE	COURAGE, CONFIDENCE, FRIENDLINESS, SUCCESS
(−) MYSTERY, MOODINESS	WEAK, FEMININITY, IMMATURITY	ANGER, DANGER, WARNING	IGNORANCE, SLUGGISHNESS

BROWN	TAN	GOLD	SILVER
(+) FRIENDLY, EARTH, OUTDOORS, LONGEVITY, CONSERVATIVE	DEPENDABLE, FLEXIBLE, CRISP, CONSERVATIVE	WEALTH, WISDOM, PROSPERITY, VALUABLE, TRADITIONAL	GLAMOROUS, HIGH TECH, GRACEFUL, SLEEK
(−) DOGMATIC, CONSERVATIVE	DULL, BORING, CONSERVATIVE	EGOTISTICAL, SELF-RIGHTEOUS	INDECISIVE, DULL, NON-COMMITTAL

WHITE	GRAY	BLACK
(+) GOODNESS, INNOCENCE, PURITY, FRESH, EASY, CLEAN	SECURITY, RELIABILITY, INTELLIGENCE, SOLID	PROTECTION, ELEGANCE, DRAMATIC, CLASSY, FORMALITY
(−) ISOLATION, PRISTINE, EMPTINESS	GLOOMY, SAD, CONSERVATIVE	DEATH, EVIL, MYSTERY

FIGURE 2.14
Hauff's "Colors Convey Emotion" chart summarizing some of the key positive and negative emotions associated with certain colors. Filmmakers will find this chart useful in learning about how to utilize color in their films for subtle psychological impact. This chart does not suggest the impact of saturation versus desaturated colors. However, the intensity of color could be used to reflect the intensity of the emotion, as opposed to desaturated scenes that may lessen intensity. (Image ©2016 Ashton Hauff. Used with permission.)

(color.adobe.com), you can map the spectrum of colors in a scene by importing a screen grab to this online app. The color, of course, isn't just lighting, but the costumes, set design/location, and props. (See Figure 2.15.)

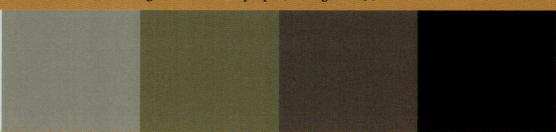

FIGURE 2.15
Using Adobe's Color, we can graph the color spectrum of a scene by importing a screen grab. Here we see the greens, grays, browns, and blacks from the opening sequence of *Godless*.
(Image courtesy of the author using Adobe CC Color.)

One of the few variances of color we see include the woman in cut 18 (Figure 2.10, p. 73) who is wearing a white dress (with tan patterns), which indicates her goodness, innocence, and purity in the stark contrast of death around her. At the same time the negative elements of white (isolation, pristine, emptiness) also reflect her predicament. This also tends to reflect, to some extent, the Marshal's white horse.

The use of color—and the intensity of colors (or lack of intensity)—reveals and reinforces emotions or subdues them based on the levels of saturation.

> **The use of color—and the intensity of colors (or lack of intensity)—reveals and reinforces emotions or subdues them based on the levels of saturation.**

10. Texture

Many people talk about how sharp an image is in filmmaking, especially as it relates to lenses—but not all films are sharp, nor should they be. Sharp images do not define cinematography from a visual storytelling perspective. This is not to say you do not need to be in focus! Although in some moments of a story soft focus may be appropriate.

We're really talking about the texture of a shot, which involves the grain or feel of surfaces and subjects in a shot, as well as the texture of light and shadow, which impacts how we perceive the texture of surfaces, such as costumes, props, the set,

VISUAL STORYTELLING THROUGH LENSES AND COMPOSITION   CHAPTER 2   79

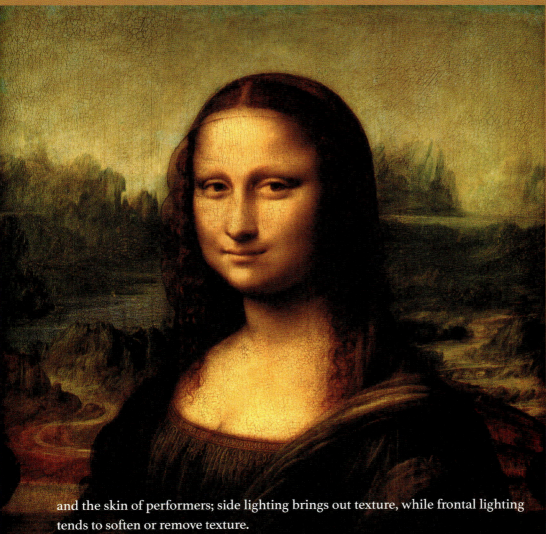

FIGURE 2.16
In Leonardo da Vinci's *Mona Lisa* (1503-1519), the artist not only creates a softness to the image in the background through diffusion ("objects penetrate mists with difficulty"), but he also shapes softness in her face through soft shadows and gradual gradation of tonality in those shadows.
(Image courtesy of Wikimedia Commons.)

and the skin of performers; side lighting brings out texture, while frontal lighting tends to soften or remove texture.

It also refers to *sfumato*, Leonardo da Vinci's utilization of diffusion in the air, such as haze on the horizon of distant objects. This technique in painting include the process by which the colors and the shading of colors (tones) gradually blend into each other, softening the image.

"The painter will demonstrate various distances by the variation of color of the air interposed between objects and the eye," Leonardo writes. "He will demonstrate how the species of objects penetrate mists with difficulty. He will demonstrate how mountains and valleys are seen through clouds in the rain" (quoted in Isaacson, 2017: 375). (See Figure 2.16.)

Sharp

To attain a sharpness of image, choose a deep depth of field. *This will bring across sense of clarity with little to no ambiguity intended, visually.* (See Figure 2.17.)

FIGURE 2.17
Despite the dark shadow areas, this segment from this shot from *Godless* reveals a sharp shot, where there is little to no diffusion. We can see sharp edges around the desk and the murdered telegraph men.
(Image ©2017 Netflix.)

Also note, in Figure 2.18 (p. 81), the clarity, here. The crane shot is the clearest in the entire sequence. Why at this point? There's no longer any ambiguity in what has occurred in Creede, a sense of hopelessness and disbelief seizes Marshal Cook as he stumbles to his knees. With everything in sharp or near-sharp focus, the filmmakers drive home the point through visual storytelling that the horrific deeds have been revealed and that at some point justice must be sought.

FIGURE 2.18 (facing page)
There's no longer any ambiguity to the horrors Marshal Cook faces in Creede in the final shot from the opening sequence of "An Incident at Creede," episode 1 of *Godless*. The focus is sharp, reinforcing the unambiguous nature of Cook's realization that the evil actions done are horrific as he looks up at a boy who has been hung, and realizes that the perpetrators must be brought to justice.
(Image ©2017 Netflix.)

Visual Storytelling through Lenses and Composition   CHAPTER 2

Soft (sfumato)

Any time you utilize a shallow depth of field shot, you're engaging, to some extent, a process of *sfumato*.

However, it is more typical that you're engaging a deep focus with haze, fog, smoke, or other type of aerial diffusion in the distance. Although there is clarity in the foreground, and to some extent, clarity in the middle ground, when the background is soft, we will sense an element of ambiguity, a bit of mystery of what is ahead. (See Figure 2.19.)

FIGURE 2.19
In this shot from *Godless*, we can see mist and smoke in the distance, softening the background, with the softness of the hills similar to background mountains in Leonardo's *Mona Lisa*. (See Figure 2.16, p. 79.)
(Image ©2017 Netflix.)

Although the heavy smoke and dust have dispersed, compared to the opening shots of this sequence, the obscuration of detail in Figure 2.19 helps to continue the mystery or ambiguity. We clearly see a train wreck, but we don't know if there are survivors.

Section review
1. What are ten tools of composition? Define each.
2. What are the psychological uses for each tool of composition?
3. Take a scene from one of your favorite films or television dramas and identify several tools of composition used in each shot.
4. How are the different tools of composition being used to support the story, psychologically?

SECTION 2: SHOOTING FOR THE EDIT

Without an understanding of how shots fit within an edit, then you may end up wasting people's time. You should know what shots you need and why each scene is crucial when setting up each shot and delivering usable shots to the editor. This section describes some of the basic rules for orientation of the viewer geometrically in space, and the importance of delivering such shots to the editor.

1. *Coverage* Some filmmakers—especially those who are not sure how each shot will be cut—fall back on this safety feature, which involves running the scene multiple times in order to shoot a master (wide), medium, and a close-up on each actor. In this way, the editor is assured a variety of shot sizes when cutting the scene together.
2. *Eye lines* What or who a character looks at draws the eyes of the audience and they will want to see what they're looking at or the reaction of the person they're looking at. There is a lot of potential energy stored in a glance or a look of a performer and this information must be shot in order to release this potential energy. (See Figure 2.20.)

FIGURE 2.20
In this shot from *Jessica Jones* (episode 2.2 "AKA Freak Accident"), we see Jessica look down, her eyes draw us towards what she's looking at, which requires a cutaway shot.
(Image ©2018 Marvel Studios and Netflix.)

3. *Point of view and cutaways* Shooting inserts (cutaways) or details of objects or views of what a character sees, such as flowers on a table or a key being inserted into a door. It forwards the story in some way, visually, so the audience doesn't miss important story detail. (See Figure 2.21.)

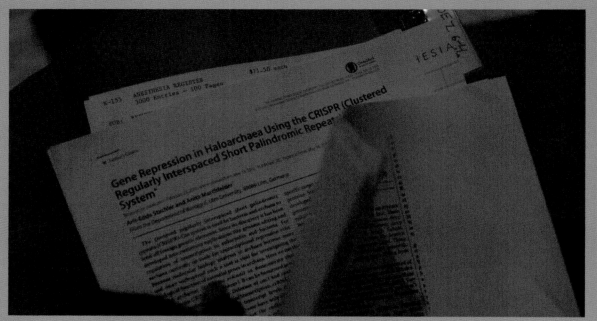

FIGURE 2.21
Now we see a cutaway of what Jessica sees, in a scene from *Jessica Jones* (episode 2.2 "AKA Freak Accident").
(Image ©2018 Marvel Studios and Netflix.)

It could also entail a detail shot cut into a shot that is not motivated by a character's glance, such as the interstitials of nature, trains, signs, and other objects found in between many sequences in most of Yasujiro Ozu's films, the shots providing a poetic transition from one scene to another. (See Figure 2.22, p. 85.)

4. *180 degree rule* The camera faces objects or performers from one direction along 180 degrees. As long as the camera stays facing that direction and doesn't switch to the opposite side of that imaginary line, the actors and objects will face the proper screen direction. If you cross the line, then the characters and objects will face the wrong screen direction. By maintaining this rule, you maintain continuity in the edit and maintain consistent screen direction in the geometrical layout of the scene. (See Figure 2.23, p. 85.)

Visual Storytelling through Lenses and Composition   CHAPTER 2   85

FIGURE 2.22
A different type of cutaway used by filmmaker Ozu in *Late Spring* (1949), the shots of the vase and the rock garden do not forward the plot or action, but are used as visual rest notes. They transition us from one scene to another.
(Image ©1949 Shôchiku Eiga.)

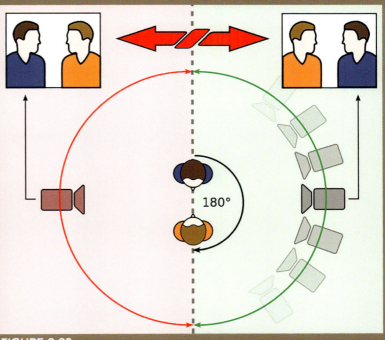

FIGURE 2.23
If the camera stays on one side of the line—anywhere facing that line—the screen direction of the performers will stay oriented in the proper direction, such as seen here where the character in blue faces screen-left, for example. If the camera crosses the line into the red zone, then the character in blue now faces screen-right, the opposite direction from where they were first filmed, leaving the audience disoriented in their geometric layout of the screen direction.
(Image courtesy Grm wnr. Creative Commons.)

5. *Jump cuts*

When there is a lack of continuity in a shot—whether it's from shooting the wrong screen direction, or not providing a cut on action—the edits can lead to jump cuts, and sometimes the filmmaker delivers this in order to provide a cut that disorients and fulfills the emotional intent of the story. (See Figure 2.24.)

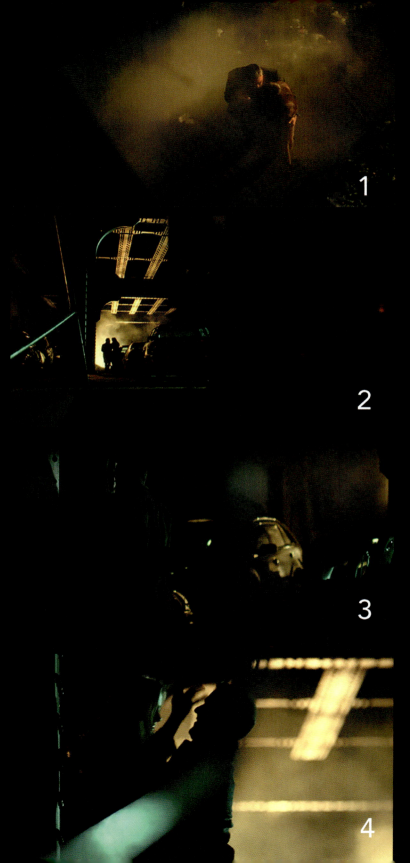

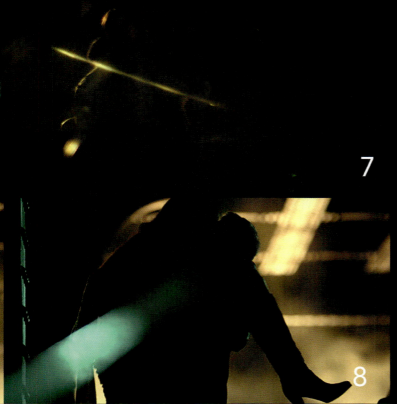

FIGURE 2.24
In this scene from *Jessica Jones* "AKA Ladies Night," we see jump cuts between cuts 1–2 and 7–8, with continuity between 3–6. Also note that the cut between 6 and 7 crosses the line, with 8 cutting back to the original position, crossing back to the original line. This reinforces the emotion of the scene as Jessica watches the couple become intimate as she takes pictures with her camera, providing evidence of infidelity for her client. The discontinuity through jump cuts jumps time in certain moments, allowing the audience to fill in the gaps, and because the scene depicts an intimate encounter, there are a certain amount of emotions running amok, justifying the jump cuts, as well.
DP Manuel Billeter.

(Image ©2015 Marvel Studios and Netflix.)

6. Kuleshov effect

Early Russian filmmaker Lev Kuleshov conducted an experiment where he used existing footage of a bowl of soup cut against a close-up of an actor; then a shot of a young girl in a coffin followed by a cut of the same shot of the actor; and then a shot of a young woman lounging on a sofa cut against the same image of the actor, again. In each case—although the shot of the actor holds the same expression in every shot—the audience perceived a different emotion, proving that the juxtaposition of different content reverberates with different emotions based on the context of the preceding shots and the shots following.

Bill Dill, ASC, applies this concept to cinematic storytelling in this way:

> Much of what we do with visual storytelling in film derives from the effect that one image has on another. Keep in mind that we will give the audience a limited amount of time to view the image. In some cases, maybe only half a second. So it's not only the sequence of images that creates the effect the filmmaker wants, it's also the timing of those images that will affect the audience's perception. (Dill, 2016)

The juxtaposition of shots—and scenes—impact how the audience perceives and feels the story. The length of the shots creates part of the rhythm and pacing of a scene (along with the sound design). So it is important to control and visualize the shots when thinking about the shots that precede and follow each other, because that's where the heart of the story lies.

In this low key sequence from the second season of Netflix's *The Crown* (2017) in the episode "Beryl," we see Prime Minister Macmillan driving with his wife, who states she will end her affair with another man, since he is now the PM. The sequence shows the simple shots of their back and forth discussion with the camera and editing delivering medium shots of the two, intercut with shots of the car driving (1–9). (See Figure 2.25.)

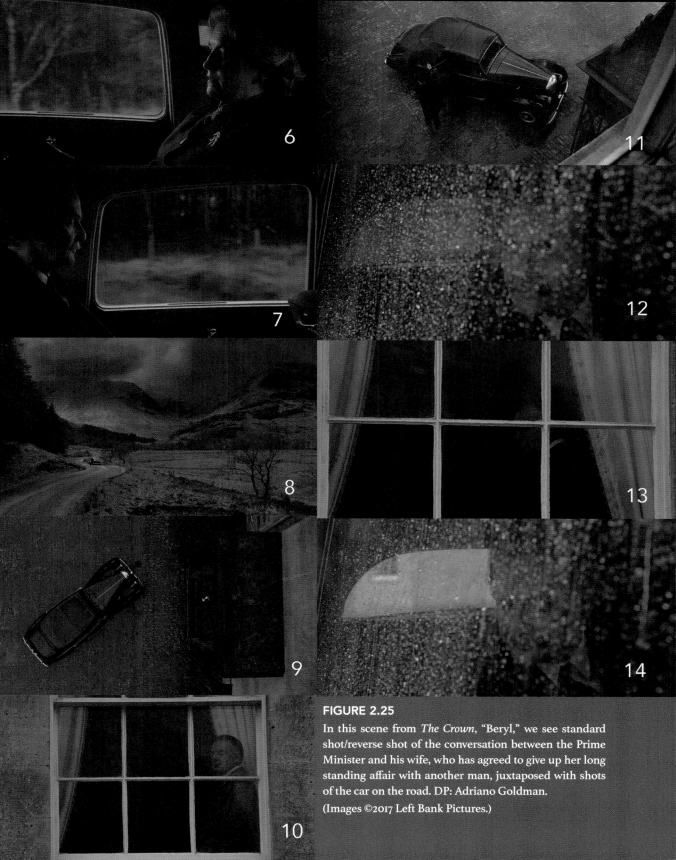

FIGURE 2.25

In this scene from *The Crown*, "Beryl," we see standard shot/reverse shot of the conversation between the Prime Minister and his wife, who has agreed to give up her long standing affair with another man, juxtaposed with shots of the car on the road. DP: Adriano Goldman.
(Images ©2017 Left Bank Pictures.)

Note how the blocking makes clear their separation as they sit far apart from each other and they never look at each other (2–7). After the car arrives at the man's house, we see the shot of the him looking out of the window (10), followed by the PM looking up at him from the car (12). After the man in the window walks away (13) the PM looks down (14).

The juxtaposition of the shots of the man and Prime Minister Macmillian reveals the strength of the Kuleshov effect as a visual storytelling tool. The man looking out of the window conveys a fairly neutral expression (10 and 13) and the shot of the PM looking up at him is also neutral (12), but when placed within the context of the discussion previously about the PM's wife wanting to end the affair with this man, the shots at the end of this scene take on added emotional weight.

We don't need to be told that the man is lording over the PM, since he knows that the PM's wife loves him and we don't need to be told through dialogue that the PM is saddened by the fact that his wife loves this other man since the visual story shows us this with his glance down in the last cut (14). The emotional arc is made physical in these shots and they convey the story of the PM defeated.

Take note, also, of the camera height. The man in the window is shot from a lower angle—which is justified by the PM sitting in the car below the window—but it gives that man power over the Macmillan's personal life. If the filmmakers were to interpret this scene differently, then the PM would have gotten out of the car. Furthermore, the rain also reinforces the PM's defeat. Again, if the PM was to be depicted as a stronger character, perhaps this would have been a sunny day and he would have stepped out of the car and confronted the man, which would have required the cinematographer to use a different camera height in order to empower him.

In many ways, the Kuleshov effect requires the filmmaker to engage in the creation and building of visual evidence for the unfolding story and emotions embedded in each shot, the evidence resonates with new meanings based on what shots are chosen before, during, and after each shot in a scene. In this way, filmmakers rely on visual evidence rather than on dialogue to forward stories.

Applying this concept to documentary, visual anthropologist David MacDougall explains the importance of visual storytelling in nonfiction filmmaking:

> If social experience cannot finally be translated, except by first being conceived linguistically, it can be made perceptible in images and sounds. But how well we perceive the experience of others depends upon fields of consciousness we share with them. This involves a transcultural process (now in the process of crossing cultural boundaries) and a willingness to enter into a sympathetic contract with others, including the filmmaker or writer as intermediary. Consciousness includes the domain of tacit knowledge, evoked only in the interstices and disjunctions of what can be physically shown. Gaining access to this requires an awareness of what is absent. (MacDougall, 1998: 272–273).

What's absent? Language as exposition, a crutch of interview-based documentary filmmaking, and filmmakers like MacDougall prefer the effervescent moments of subtext captured visually by the composition of the lens—and through the juxtaposition of certain shots—the Kuleshov effect becomes the very means by which the story visually unfolds in the edit. The visual elements become the means by which the story is told, rather than through the exposition of language. "In asking his viewers to engage with an argument made through the medium of film, MacDougall raised the possibility that observational techniques might serve as a basis for intellectual inquiry pursued by means of non-textual forms," Grimshaw and Ravetz note in their book, *Observational Cinema* (2009: 84).

The visual (and aural) elements become the means by which the story is told, rather than through the exposition of language.

In this way, MacDougall engages in a type of cinematography (and editing) that cinematic storytellers have been doing in fiction when utilizing the Kuleshov effect as the means to tell a story through visual evidence. By doing so, filmmakers like MacDougall challenged the expository storytelling methods of conventional documentaries.

"In breaking the norms of expository film that reported on or reconstructed experience, [filmmakers like MacDougall] were attempting to render people's lives more fully—not in the sense of more accurately or completely but existentially," write Grimshaw and Ravetz (2009: 82).

By focusing on the existence of characters in moments of a "specific human encounter," Grimshaw and Ravetz argue, "MacDougall works cinematically to persuade, [...]. Through careful, patient camera work mirrored by the fine-grain detail of the sound track, the filmmaker assembles a case based upon the meticulous amassing of small observations that comprised a series of propositions about the nature of reality perceived" (2009: 82–83). They reference MacDougall's masterwork, *To Live with Herds* (1972), a film documenting the Jie tribe's fading pastoral life in the face of encroaching industrialization and modernization.

In one sequence in the film, the Jie must sell some of their cattle and oxen to raise money to pay government taxes—directly challenging their pastoral livelihood, since they don't live to make or use money. MacDougall edits a series of shots that reveal this tension without relying on an omniscient voice of narration to explain what is going on. Through visuals, he lays out the evidence, moments of emotional tension, argument, a giving up, and self-reflection. (See Figure 2.26.)

Cuts 1–7 builds up and places us into the action where the Jie must sell their cattle, and they take what they can get as reluctant sellers (6-10). Cuts 11–13 reveal the aftermath of the sale, followed by a quiet moment as one of the Jie looks off in into the distance (14). A fade to black breaks the sequence, but this is followed by a relentless sandstorm (15)—a visual and aural force metaphorically revealing their way of life slowly being lost. The power of the edit, using the Kuleshev effect across entire sequences, allow fiilmakers to create visual arguments within the film itself without relying on narration.

Section review

1. What does it mean to shoot for the edit?
2. Identify five rules of editing and explain why these rules exist and when you might want to break them.
3. What is the importance of the Kuleshov effect in relationship to visual storytelling and visual discourse?
4. Take one of your favorite scenes from a film, television drama, or documentary and identify how the Kuleshov effect helps forward the story, visually.

FIGURE 2.26 (facing page)
In this sequence from *To Live with Herds* (1972), we can see how David MacDougall utilizes visual and audio elements to build an argument without relying on the words of a narrator. DP: David MacDougall.
(Images ©1974 Berkeley Media.)

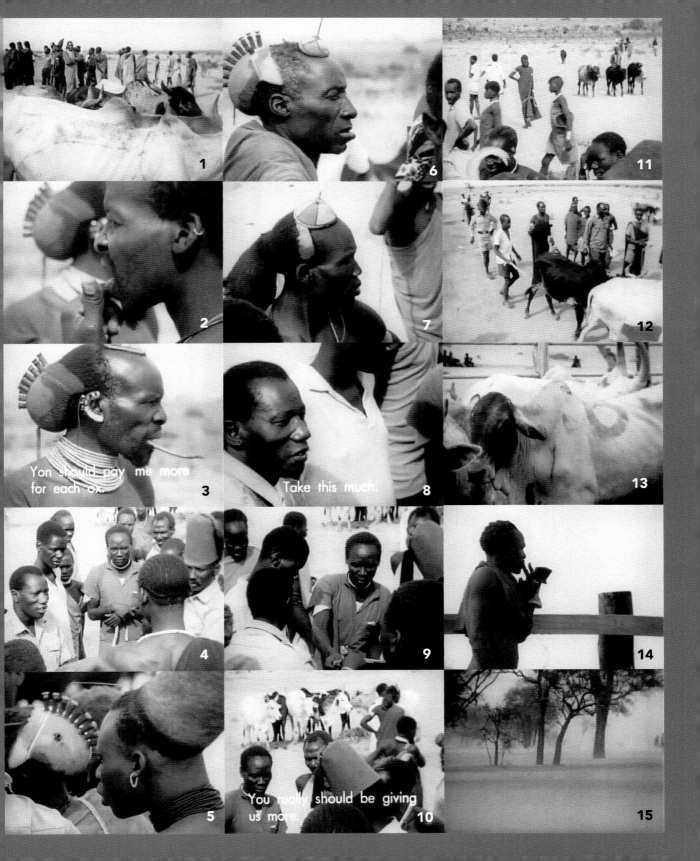

SECTION 3: CASE STUDY IN LENSES AND COMPOSITION FROM *JESSICA JONES* WITH DP MANUEL BILLETER

The following scene from *Jessica Jones* ("AKA Ladies Night") provides an example of how different types of shots are used to help shift perspective in a story. (See Figure 2.27.)

Let's analyze this scene shot by shot.

1. a-b: The filmmakers chose a slow push-in dolly down the hall towards Jessica's private-eye office, Alias Investigations. This approach accomplishes two things, cinematographer Manuel Billeter says in an interview with me: "It helps in keeping the theme of putting obstructions between the camera and the character of Jessica Jones, forcing the audience to peel away the layers which were set up by us in order for the audience to get to the core of her character." It also was used as an establishing shot for Jessica's world, of where she lives, he adds. "Just looking at the detail, such as chipped paint, the two-tone color on the walls, as a way to focus the audience on those narrative elements. The slow moving shot extends the time, allowing the audience to take in the scenery, the situation, and the landscape, if you will, that Jones is in."

FIGURE 2.27
A variety of shots and angles uses objective and subjective viewpoints in this sequence from *Jessica Jones* (AKA "Ladies Night"). Jessica has to defend herself as she breaks the bad news to her client about his wife's infidelity and he attacks her.
DP Manuel Billeter.
(Image ©2015 Marvel Studios and Netflix.)

Billeter notes how the scene also references both the source material of the comic book and Jack Nicholson's detective character in the opening of *China Town* (1974), an homage to both the detective genre and the original comic book. It was important that there would be a long hallway in a pre-war building as it is archetypically New York, Billeter exlains. A shallow depth of field heightens the uncertain nature of the action, the focus sharpening as we get closer to the door.

The shot is objective, because we're looking from the outside, the director and cinematographer easing us into the story, forcing us to ask what is going on—setting up a certain mystery so that we're forced to watch and listen in order to discover the unfolding action of Jessica's world. The wide/medium shot also prevents any kind of intimacy to occur in the shot, but it also—especially through the camera movement—provides a sense of us participating in the scene, eavesdropping on the argument. The camera angle is low, putting the man, silhouetted against the window, in a position of power. This helps make the audience feel that this man is a threat, reinforcing the yelling we hear in the scene.

2. An objective point of view from above as the man is thrown through the window by Jessica. It sets up the cutaway in 3 as we see photos drop from his hand. The shot is medium-wide as we enter the man's world, shot on a normal wide lens (probably a 24mm) with deep focus. This choice heightens the discomfort we feel in the violent situation, perhaps feeling for the man being thrown through the window. The lens choice reinforces the zaniness of the violence occurring in the shot, giving us a sense of instability, as well as a bit of surprise as we're not expecting this violence.

> **The lens choice reinforces the zaniness of the violence occurring in the shot, giving us a sense of instability, as well as a bit of surprise as we're not expecting the man to be thrown through the window.**

3. The camera switches to the man's point of view (subjective) as we see the photographs providing the visual evidence we saw Jessica take in the previous scene. (See Figure 2.24, pp. 86–87.) The previous shot (2)

utilizes a creative way to reveal that this person being thrown through the window was the person who hired Jessica to find evidence about his girl's infidelity. The camera is closer revealing a bit of intimacy as we bear witness to what the man sees—the details of the photographs—which looks like it was shot on a normal lens, the only moment of stability found in the scene.

4. The camera cuts back to an objective view as Jessica surveys the damage in a wide shot from down the hall (from the same point of view found in the first shot). We are not allowed to enter the feelings Jessica expresses. In many ways, this shot provides a geometric perspective on the scene as a way to get our bearings after seeing the violence. The lens is normal, providing a sense of stability or balance in the scene as Jessica begins to take control of the situation.

5. We cut back to a low angle perspective as Jessica looks down through her broken window at the man (who presumably looks back up at her in a subjective point of view) as she says his bill is due. "We cut to this high angle looking down," Billeter explains, "to the low angle shot looking up at her, but she's upside down, which gives us the perspective that the man she has thrown through the window is looking back up at her and sees her upside down. That's actually," he adds, "a very compelling way, and a very interesting way, and a strong way to introduce her character when in the first shot you really see her, she's upside down!" This angle reveals who holds the power in the scene, reinforcing the understanding—visually through the composition—that Jessica is in control. The shot is closer, a frame within a frame, showing Jessica as a no nonsense person who uses force to solve her problems. Through the normal lens choice the cinematographer visually restores a sense of balance of power back into Jessica's hands.

The wide lenses Billeter uses in shooting *Jessica Jones* helps make the character "inclusive of the environment she's in," he explains.

The wide lenses Billeter uses in shooting *Jessica Jones* helps make the character "inclusive of the environment she's in," he explains.

> It also gives us the opportunity to play with frames within frames. It is absolutely a story element, a narrative element—a configuration of not presenting her entire character. It adds a visual tension that will hopefully trigger something in the audience when they see it. With wide lenses we wanted to take advantage of the visual nature of the story.

A normal lens, for example, would have told that story differently.

Billeter describes how the opening scenes set up the character of Jessica Jones for the entire series. "You never get a second chance to make a first impression. We set the tone from these very first sequences of the show," he says. "The way you meet someone, it's fundamental in the way you see them for the first time."

Section review
1. How does Billeter use the tools of composition to introduce and tell the story of the character, Jessica Jones?
2. How might you use ideas from Billeter in some of your own work?

SECTION 4: CASE STUDY IN LENSES AND COMPOSITION FROM *CHEF'S TABLE* WITH DP ADAM BRICKER

Let's analyze the following sequence from "Dominique Crenn." (See Figure 2.28, p. 100.)

> 1–13: The first thirteen cuts (or change of frame from camera movement) sets up the visual story of how Crenn goes into the field to taste the ingredients she'll use for her creations. Peter Jacobsen, the owner of Jacobsen Orchards in Yountville, California, shows her several crops, including figs, as she smells and tastes them. The cut from 4 to 5 is a jump cut as the editor chooses to jump time between an herb and a fig. Frames 5-9 focus on a fig that bleeds milk, revealing that it isn't ripe. Cuts 9 and 10 utilizes another jump, as Jacobsen picks a ripe fig and hands it to Crenn (11), carrying the frame to 12 as she taste it on a close-up.

13–23: A cutaway is then used to carry a line of one of her poems she uses in her restaurant: "Nature rejoice, chasing childhood memories" (13) used as a transition to an interview shot (14) where she talks about how she first tasted a fresh tomato from her family's garden when she was three or four. Music is also used to take us into the interview and the memory: "You can eat something and remember that forever," Crenn says. The handheld fluid camera movements reinforce the style of this story. Cutaway shots (15, 17, and 21) guide us poetically along her story (without it being literal), the shots of nature filling in for her memories of eating a tomato (18 and 19) as soft electronic tones play in the background. A shot of the clouds (23) end the sequence, transitioning us to the next section of the story.

This entire sequence moves us through her interactions with Jacobsen, revealing the care she takes in choosing the right ingredients for her food. DP Adam Bricker uses a handheld camera to capture the unfolding story visually, reframing as he searches for strong compositional moments, holding mainly to medium and close shots, along with a few tight detail shots. The first half (1–11) uses a lot of deep focus shots (with elements of some focal fall off), but the second half of this sequences utilizes a lot of shallow depth of field work (cuts 12–21) as the editor chooses these shots to reflect the story of her childhood memory, our attention focused on the story, the shallow depth of field work reinforcing that focus and the dreamy feeling being expressed through those memories. The sequence ends in sharp focus with a shot of the clouds in the sky, pulling us out of this story and into the next one.

The shallow depth of field shots evoke a dreamlike moment of memory. The smooth handheld operation offers a sense of floating and peace, which reflects the poetic story being told visually through that movement. At the same time, this *vérité* style footage intercuts with a formal interview as Crenn tells the story of tasting tomatoes when she was three or four years old. The elements of memory add poetic depth to the visual story of her tasting a fig, which extends to the story about the care she takes in choosing fresh ingredients for her creations.

> The smooth handheld operation offers a sense of floating and peace, which reflects the poetic story being told visually through that movement.

FIGURE 2.28
Vérité style footage intercuts with formal interview footage of Dominique Crenn, memories intermingling with the present. DP: Adam Bricker. (Images ©2016 Netflix.)

Unlike a narrative film, Bricker, who operates the camera, says that he "cannot control where the subject is going to go, but you can control where the camera is in relationship to the subject. You're looking for depth in the background," visual elements that support the story. These compositional choices are designed to support editorial, to make sure the editor and director have the shots needed to tell the story.

They're not trying to find "journalistic truth," Bricker explains to me, by waiting for any one moment, but, instead, are "trying to shape emotion visually." By going handheld, Bricker finds not only the best compositional angle (and light), but he's free to push in to "grab a slow-motion close-up of someone's face, for example, something that you inherently know is cinematic and emotive. Later, in the edit, that shot might tell the emotional story and support that narrative journey," he adds.

Section review
1. How does Bricker use the tools of composition to visually tell a nonfiction story?
2. Why do you think he says that he's not looking for "journalistic truth" when filming *Chef's Table*?

Adam Bricker uses a handheld camera to capture the unfolding story visually, reframing as he searches for strong compositional moments, holding mainly to medium and close shots, along with a few tight detail shots.

SECTION 5: CASE STUDY IN LENSES AND COMPOSITION FROM OZU'S *TOKYO TWILIGHT* CLASS INTERPRETATION

The following is an examination of lens choices based on the script analysis in a scene from a recreation and reinterpretation of Ozu's *Tokyo Twilight*. This section includes notes of how this scene was blocked (described in Chapter 1), but now with planned camera angles, shots sizes, and lenses in order to guide the reader through the process of choosing lenses and composition based on psychological reasons that reinforce the blocking and the emotional elements of the story. Note that the final choices in blocking and lenses evolved during the rehearsal process. The camera notes on the script, below, were provisional and helped plan for the day's shoot. During the shoot, the initial ideas tend to shift naturally during the rehearsal process. (See Figure 2.29.)

Dirty OTS on boy.
Normal 35mm. Handheld. MS
Back and forth OTS MS
Shallow DoF to highlight the isolation.

CU, moving from her to him. 16mm

EXT. STREET--CLOUDY AFTERNOON

Ambient outdoor sounds. Two people sitting close, a young man and woman (late teens early 20s). They sit quietly, not looking at each other--like they've shared bad news too difficult to contemplate--as the sounds of the city reverberate around them.

[SHOOT in LIBRARY. Hushed whispers. People walk by. Gets loud as the tension escalates.]

          BOY
This is terrible. How can this be?

          GIRL
What's terrible?

          BOY
You're absolutely sure?

          GIRL
You think I'm lying to you? You think I could lie about this?

          BOY
No, I don't ... but what a mess.

          GIRL
I'm the one in trouble. Much more than you. Please be serious. Stop looking so indifferent.

          BOY
Indifferent? It's all I've been thinking about since you told me.

          GIRL
But you've been avoiding me.

          BOY
That's not true.

Boy paces back and fourth, eyeing others outside the frame. She is sitting, her back leaning against the stacks.

She stands and grabs his hands, forcing him to sit on the ground with her.

He pulls away, gently, but gets up and grabs a book, thumbing through it absent-mindlessly, trying to come up with a plan that can get him out of there. She stands and grabs the book from him.

She steps up close to him, confronting him, face to face.
He steps back.

Visual Storytelling through Lenses and Composition   Chapter 2

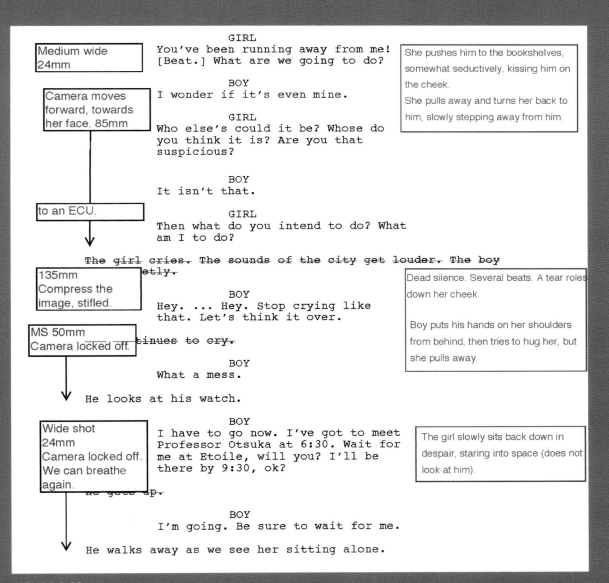

FIGURE 2.29
The script with the notes on lenses, composition, and camera movement, along with the original blocking notes in the right column as discussed in Chapter 1. The lens choices and shot sizes, as well as camera movement, all reinforce the emotional needs and shifts occurring in the scene.

Note: In this class exercise, we did not deal with lighting, so all lighting is from the practical fluorescents in the library with no alteration—so the lighting does not look good! (Lighting will be examined in the next chapter.) This exercise simply covers elements of lens choices and composition based on blocking ideas and emotions developed from the script analysis provided in Chapter 1.

Below, I provide several representational stills from my beginning cinematography class exercise, which again, focused on blocking, composition, and lens choices. The scene also was shot by different students on a Canon C100 Mark II with Rokinon primes, so if you look at the video you can clearly see differences in style as different students practiced with the camera. The student performers are Mikayla Khramov and Sean Lang. This scene is not perfect, but it does strongly show how lens choices complements, or rather, reinforces the emotional intent of the blocking and body language of the performers, revealing the emotional story visually. Remember, no lighting or lighting modifiers were used in this scene. The full sequence can be seen in Figure 2.30 (p. 105). Individual shots are found in Figures 2.31–2.35 (p. 106-115). The full scene is at: www.vimeo.com/201876721.

Note that I did not start wide with the so-called establishing shot—because there's no such rule in using such a shot when opening a scene. Rather, the 35mm provides me with the Girl's perspective, because I've made the choice that it is her scene—she's the one with most at stake. Note also how the original notes discussed the over the shoulder (OTS) as going back and forth between the Boy and Girl. During the shoot, I scrapped this initial idea in order to focus on the blocking in this particular moment, her demeanor becoming more agitated as he paces, forcing her to get up grab him and pull him down next to her in cuts 2–4 of Figure 2.30.

Lens choice and composition size, as well as depth of field, should stem from the visual blocking/body language analysis, which grows from the script analysis of characters' needs and wants.

VISUAL STORYTELLING THROUGH LENSES AND COMPOSITION   CHAPTER 2   105

FIGURE 2.30
In this full sequence we can see how the blocking flows, shot by shot, along with a reference to the focal length of each lens. Reinterpretation of a scene from Ozu's *Tokyo Twilight*. No lighting or modifiers were added. (Images courtesy of the author.)

FIGURE 2.31
Cut 1: We start with a normal 35mm lens of the Boy, over the shoulder, "dirty" (meaning we see the Girl's shoulder in the foreground) medium handheld shot from the Girl's perspective; the normal lens situates us in the scene from her point of view. The camera placement and the medium shot provide information of the Girl's nervous tension as we see the Boy pacing in the background, in soft focus, which helps reinforce how his expectations of her has not yet been made clear to her.
(Image courtesy of the author.)

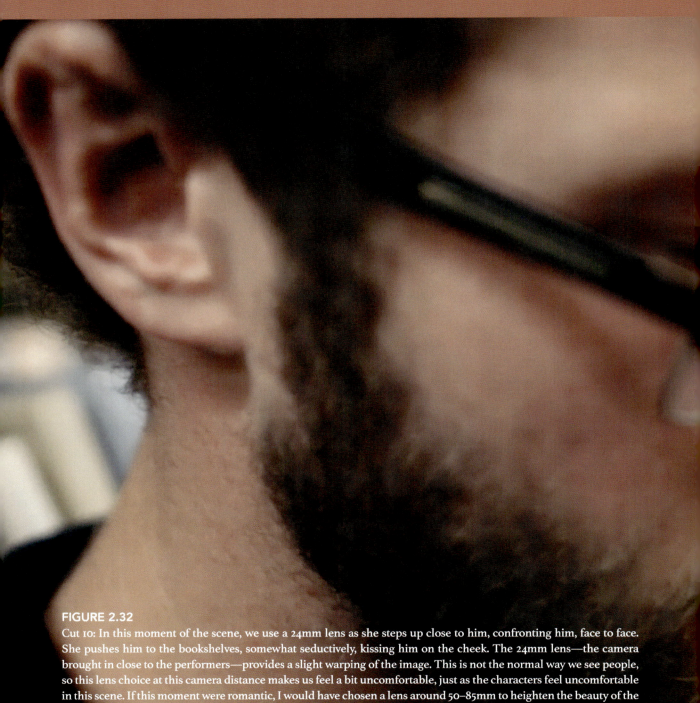

FIGURE 2.32
Cut 10: In this moment of the scene, we use a 24mm lens as she steps up close to him, confronting him, face to face. She pushes him to the bookshelves, somewhat seductively, kissing him on the cheek. The 24mm lens—the camera brought in close to the performers—provides a slight warping of the image. This is not the normal way we see people, so this lens choice at this camera distance makes us feel a bit uncomfortable, just as the characters feel uncomfortable in this scene. If this moment were romantic, I would have chosen a lens around 50–85mm to heighten the beauty of the moment, but that would have been the wrong interpretation for this shot.
(Image courtesy of the author.)

VISUAL STORYTELLING THROUGH LENSES AND COMPOSITION   CHAPTER 2   109

FIGURE 2.33
Cut 17: I want to jump to the end of the scene of a wide shot using the 24mm lens, showing how it feels differently in relationship to camera distance. Here, the lens is perfect for isolating her in an empty space, trapped by bookshelves thrusting back into the distance with linear perspective. The camera height is high, looking down, further disempowering her. A normal height or a low angle looking up would be at odds with the story intent. She's lost him and we feel it and see it through the composition, the lens choice, and the blocking. Also note that this is the only wide shot in the scene. By holding it to the end, the shot expresses contrast to all of the other tighter shots seen previously, providing dynamic contrast to what preceded it, giving this moment more power to the story.
(Image courtesy of the author.)

FIGURE 2.34
Cut 16: With this shot we see the power of 85mm portrait beauty lens of the Girl, as we see the Boy out of focus in a shallow depth of field walking out of the shot, leaving her alone. This lens reinforces two things here. One, the longer lens with the shallow depth of field isolates her in the shot. Our attention pulls away from the Boy as he exits, reinforcing her reaction—her feelings—about him, heightening her disappointment. A wider lens with deep focus would express her feelings differently. At the same time, there is a slight perspective compression through the magnification of the lens that binds the two characters together; even as he exits, we still feel her emotionally hanging on to him.
(Image courtesy of the author.)

85mm

VISUAL STORYTELLING THROUGH LENSES AND COMPOSITION   CHAPTER 2   113

Visual Storytelling through Lenses and Composition   CHAPTER 2   115

FIGURE 2.35
Cut 8: This is an unplanned shot that we discovered during the rehearsal of the scene. As part of the storytelling, the height of the camera—level to her—along with the long 135mm focal length of the lens provides a strong reaction shot as she argues with the Boy. It also gave us a comedic effect as he attempts to ignore her. The more he ignores her the angrier she gets, which motivates her to stand up and get into his face. The perspective compression of the image and the narrow field of view of the 135mm lens also allows us to save the wide shot until the end. The long lens also isolates her in the shot, allowing us to focus on her actions, which reinforces the story at this moment—she's fighting for his attention, as he continues to ignore her. Finally, the long lens heightens her beauty—why would he ignore her? (Image courtesy of the author.)

Section review
1. Analyze a scene for dramatic action (or use the one you wrote for Chapter 1) and now add notes on composition and lens choices for each shot. Justify each choice through the psychology of lenses, camera movement, and other elements of composition based on your story choices and interpretation.
2. Shoot a 1–2 page scene using these tools of composition (or draw out a storyboard, if needed; free download at: https://wonderunit.com/storyboarder/).

In this chapter, we applied an understanding of ten different tools of composition for visual storytelling in filmmaking. After asking questions of the script and each scene, be sure to translate the emotional content in each scene into visual blocking and body language (as examined in the first chapter), even if it's just provisional before the rehearsal process begins. Filter those visual emotional beats through different tools of composition covered in this chapter, including the psychological impact of shot sizes, depth of field, focal length of the lens, camera height, and camera movement, among others.

WORKS CITED

Dill, ASC, Bill. *Learning Cinematography: 1 Narrative Fundamentals.* Lynda.com, 2016. https://www.lynda.com/Filmmaking-tutorials/Cinematography-01-Narrative-Fundamentals/423992-2.html

Eco, Umberto. "How Culture Conditions the Colours We See" in *On Signs.* Edited by Marshall Blonsky. The Johns Hopkins University Press, 1985: 157–175.

Frank, Scott. *Godless*. "An Incident at Creede." Netflix, 2017. DP: Steven Meizler. https://www.netflix.com/title/80097141

Grimshaw, Anna and Amanda Ravetz. Observational Cinema: Anthropology, Film, and the Exploration of Social Life. Indiana University Press, 2009.

Isaacson, Walter. *Leonardo da Vinci*. Simon & Schuster, 2017.

Hauff, Ashton. "The Know it All Guide to Color Psychology in Marketing + the Best Hex Chart." CoSchedule Blog. 18 April 2016. https://coschedule.com/blog/color-psychology-marketing

MacDougall, David. *Transcultural Cinema*. Princeton University Press, 1998.

MacDougall, David and Judith MacDougall. *To Live with Herds* (1972). Berkeley Media, 1974.

Misek, Richard. "The 'look' and how to keep it: cinematography, post-production and digital colour." *Screen* 51.4 (2010): 404–409.

Netflix. "AKA Ladies Night." *Jessica Jones*. 1.1. Marvel and ABC Studios, 2015. DP: Manuel Billeter. https://www.netflix.com/title/80002312

Netflix. "Beryl." *The Crown*. 2.4. Left Bank Pictures, 2017. DP: Adriano Goldman. https://www.netflix.com/title/80149008

Netflix. "Dominique Crenn." *Chef's Table*. 2.3. Chef's Pictures One, 2015. DP: Adam Bricker. https://www.netflix.com/title/80007945

Netflix. "AKA Freak Accident." *Jessica Jones*. 2.2. Marvel and ABC Studios, 2015. DP: Manuel Billeter. https://www.netflix.com/title/80002311

Ozu, Yasujiro. *Late Spring*. Shochiku Eiga, 1949. DP: Yuharu Atsuta.

From Scott Frank's *Godless*.
(Image ©2017 Netflix.)

Still from *Blade Runner*. DP: Jordan Cronenweth.
(Image ©1982 Warner Bros.)

CHAPTER 3

VISUAL STORYTELLING THROUGH LIGHTING

OVERVIEW

In this chapter I will first cover the psychology of lighting, including some basic definitions, followed by six elements to consider when lighting a scene. Then I'll examine exposure, and provide examples exploring the dramatic analysis and lighting for indoor and outdoor scenes. I will not, however, cover the technical aspects of how to set up lights nor will I show the different types of lighting you can use. There are many resources—from books to online video tutorials—that dig into this. Rather, I will focus on how lighting makes visible and elucidates the story elements of blocking and subtext we covered in Chapter 1 and composition in Chapter 2. Examples will be drawn from *Blade Runner*, *Blade Runner 2049*, "Fragments" (a short fiction piece sponsored by Canon, which includes behind the scenes lighting setups), *Jessica Jones* (with material from a personal interview with the DP, Manuel Billeter), an exercise from my cinematography class, and an analysis of lighting in the Netflix series, *Chef's Table* ("Dominique Crenn"), including material used from a personal interview with Adam Bricker, one of the DPs for that series.

There are six sections in this chapter:

1. The psychology of lighting
    a. Foundation
    b. Light placement terminology
    c. Six elements of lighting
2. Some basic tools of exposure
3. Indoor day and outdoor day setup examples from "Fragments"
4. Outdoor night case study from *Jessica Jones* with DP Manuel Billeter
5. Indoor night case study from Ozu's *Tokyo Twilight* class project reinterpretation
6. Documentary lighting case study from *Chef's Table* with DP Adam Bricker

SECTION 1: THE PSYCHOLOGY OF LIGHTING

Foundation

If the composition, lenses, blocking, and camera movement shapes what audiences *look* at onscreen, lighting determines how they *feel* about what they see. Lighting is the most powerful ally in helping filmmakers sculpt the feel of their films. Vilmos Zsigmond, ASC, says that the "type of lighting we use actually creates the mood for the scene" (Fauer, 2008: 332).

Studies on the impact of lighting on the psychology of humans tend to involve the placement of light as an architectural experience in public spaces, offices, and private homes. Some of this research is useful to cinematographers—since they help shape the feeling of a scene through light. In the journal, *Psychology*, scholars Rosella Tomassoni, Giuseppe Galetta, and Eugenia Treglia from the Department of Human, Social, and Health Sciences at the University of Cassino and Southern Lazio, Cassino, Italy, examine how light is more than a "stimulus that influences most the human perception, but also the psychophysical well-being of the individual in everyday life," they write in their essay, "Psychology of Light: How Light Influences the Health and Psyche" (Tomassoni, 2015: 1216). Among other things, they examine light as "an environmental 'cognitive map' and a psychophysical *driver* of human perception" (2015: 1217). Light, as a form of physical stimulation, evokes sensations, emotionally. They continue:

> Within a home or working space, light is able to induce—according to its intensity, saturation, and modulation—specific emotional states, but also activate specific cognitive skills inside the perceiver (Flynn, 1977): dynamism, relaxation, privacy, visual clarity, excitation, productivity, efficiency, but also stress, sleepiness, sadness, agitation, restlessness, anxiety. The individual response by a subject exposed to the light is variable inside the range between the extremes of a light source, that can be bright/dim, uniform/non-uniform, central/perimeter, warm/cool: in short, it is possible to induce a change of the psychophysiological responses by the perceiver through the alteration/modulation of the nature and typology of light stimuli within a continuum of variations, allowing also the measurement of subjective impressions in lighting conditions (Flynn et al., 1979; Boyce, 2003). (Cited in Tomassoni, 2015: 1217)

These researchers do not break down exactly how different types of lighting evoke different emotional responses, but they explore how lighting in home and work environments are designed to either stimulate productivity or its opposite, including stress-inducing elements of agitation, restlessness, and anxiety. And the key takeaway for cinematographers includes knowing when and how to create lighting that engages a sense of dynamism, relaxation, privacy, visual clarity, excitation, and so forth in relationship to the story they're lighting. These qualities are highlighted or balanced between the extremes of bright or dim, uniform or not uniform, central or perimeter within the geographic space, as well as the more obvious warmth and coolness of the color temperature. In addition, researchers also recognize the power of sound and the use of color in enhancing the psychophysiological stimulation of light:

> the synesthetic possibilities of human perception, and the range of emotional responses by each individual exposed to the light, grow if—besides the impact generated by a light source—we also add a sound stream, such as a piece of music. Moreover, colored light may evoke a tactile sensation in the perceiver (according to the range of chromatic hue), manifesting itself in the form of perceived temperature, implementing modalities of synesthetic perception in the human: in this way, the individual may be able to 'feel' the light (Berry, 1961). (Cited in Tomassoni, 2015: 1217)

By exploring how to use the lighting elements described in the "Psychology of Light" article, beginning cinematographers can apply some of these findings as a way to help shape lighting that an audience of their film may "feel." Indeed, master cinematographers have trained their eyes to shape light that creates feeling through a strong interpretation of the story content—one of the key means by which a script becomes "physical."

> "[I]t is possible to induce a change of the psychophysiological responses by the perceiver through the alteration/modulation of the nature and typology of light stimuli within a continuum of variations, allowing also the measurement of subjective impressions in lighting conditions […]" (Tomassoni, 2015).

Cinemtographers notice how light needs to support the emotions of a story, whether a scene should be relaxed or anxious, dynamic or calm, express clarity or haziness, sadness or joy, and so forth. Before proceeding, here are the names of the different lighting setups. When filmmakers talk about 3-point lighting, they're talking about the first three terms below, and a 4-point setup would include background lighting.

Light placement terminology

Key: The main light source of the scene (a window, a table lamp, overhead lighting, a fireplace, and so forth). Know where the motivated light source is and add lights, if needed, to reinforce it accordingly. Can be hard or soft quality.

Fill: Lights used to fill in shadows caused by the key light. Usually a soft quality, and dimmer than the key light. This may simply be light reflecting from a bounce board or a wall, for example.

Back and rim: Lights placed behind characters to separate them from the background (sometimes called a hair light). It's usually a hard light placed high, with the light falling on a character's head, her hair and shoulders lit in such a way as to pull her from the background, usually some light spills onto the cheek, offering contrast to soft lighting. The rim light is also known as a 3/4 rear kicker.

Background: Lighting placed in the background of the set or location, designed to separate it from the foreground, giving the scene visual depth and atmosphere. These could be street lights, lights in a store, a hallway light inside, across a street, and so forth. These help to create visual depth in cinema.

Six elements of lighting

The quality of light refers to what it looks like and what it feels like. What it looks like is what you see on the surface. The feel, on the other hand, conveys the emotion shaped by light. You can shape the look and feel of a film by paying attention to these six elements of lighting:

1. **Quality:** Hardness or softness of lighting.
2. **Intensity:** Amount or brightness of light hitting a surface.
3. **Direction:** The direction and height of light sources. The direction of the light determines how we perceive surface textures.

4. **Texture:** Surface quality; the quality of the diffusion in the air; also can indicate the placement of light and how it shapes the quality of shadows.
5. **Contrast:** Ratio of light to shadow.
6. **Color temperature:** The color of the light source, measured in degree Kelvins.

Most of these elements work in a direct relationship with each other in a dynamic way.

In addition, light the set or location in layers. Lighting is *the* key tool in helping to provide depth in the two-dimensional surface of a screen. If cinematographers simply light actors in the foreground, for example, then they will appear flat in a scene. If they light the background, place actors in the midground, and light a foreground object, then cinematographers sculpt cinematic depth and help add atmosphere to a story.

Below are examples of these six elements of lighting and my attempt to describe some of the psychological aspects of lighting—it is by no means exhaustive, but it will provide ways to think about how to utilize these six different types of lighting design elements. Use them in conjunction with the psychology of color covered in the previous chapter. (See Figure 2.14, p. 77.)

1. **Quality**

Hard
Direct, producing harsh edgy shadows. This can come from a sunny day or an unblocked light pointing directly at a subject. Hard lights are especially effective as backlight and rim light sources. *May be used to express harshness, starkness, or negative emotions of a character and/or environment. When predominate with shadows, it intensifies the drama.* (See Figure 3.1, p. 124.)

Soft
Indirect, created by reflecting or diffusing the light—an overcast day or a scrim or sheet dropped between the light source and the subject, or simply bouncing light off a white art board, or even reflecting light off a wall or ceiling. *When predominate, it may be used to express the softness, warmth, or positive emotions of a character and/or environment of a scene. Romantic.* (See Figure 3.2, p. 125.)

FIGURE 3.1
Here we see the effects of a hard background and rim light source set high hitting Rory Batty (Rutger Hauer) from behind creating strong light along his hair and shoulders in *Blade Runner* (1982). There's a soft key light coming low from the 3/4 front, screen-right, hitting the front of his arms and the screen-right side of his torso, as well as the dove. In-scene lights on the right add harshness and increases the drama. It is the moment in the story when Batty let's go of the dove and decides not to kill Rick Deckard, so the lighting reinforces the dramatic element of Rory making his decision before he dies. The scene is as stark as his choices are limited. DP: Jordan Cronenweth.
(Image ©1982 Warner Bros.)

As in Figure 3.2 from *Blade Runner*, most lighting will contain a mix of hard and soft light, especially when dealing with hard back lighting, such as the use of rim (or hair) light. This does not take away the psychological intent of soft light sources.

The overall intent of lighting should reflect the story. The rim light, in this particular moment of the scene—along with the constantly moving spotlight effect—reveal the environment they're in, such as passing air traffic with "headlights" and searchlights revealing the surveillance element of the state. The key light is soft, reinforcing the romantic or tender moment of the scene as both characters let down their guard, but they're still in this harsh environment that is just outside the window.

VISUAL STORYTELLING THROUGH LIGHTING   CHAPTER 3   125

FIGURE 3.2
In this scene from *Blade Runner* (1982), Deckard (Harrison Ford) looks at Rachael (Sean Young), who has arrived at his apartment after discovering she's a replicant. Deckard is in love with Rachael and even though it's his job to "retire" replicants, he will not kill her. A roving spotlight (hard source) flashes through the window in the background, causing rim light effects on Rachael, but the key light source is soft, washing Deckard and Rachael in soft light, supporting the romantic scene. DP: Jordan Cronenweth.

(Image ©1982 Warner Bros.)

2. Intensity

How bright, or intense, do you want the light? This does not indicate hard versus soft light sources, but the brightness of the lights. There may be several light sources in a scene expressing varying degrees of light intensities. It is only in rare instances that all light sources are of the same intensity in a scene. By changing the light intensity in the space, the cinematographer creates texture and physical depth, helping to shape the three-dimensions of space. When examining the psychology of light intensity, keep in mind the overall look and feel of the scene you're trying to convey. (See Figures 3.3 and 3.4.)

Low intensity: (usually a soft light source, but not always the case):

1. *Positive:* romantic, soft, relaxing, private
2. *Negative:* dim, dark, mysterious, sleepy, sad

High intensity: (usually a hard light source, but not necessarily so):

1. *Positive:* bright, clear, exciting, dynamic
2. *Negative:* stabbing, searching, agitated, anxious, stressed, restless

FIGURE 3.3
In this scene from *Blade Runner 2049* (2017), Deckard (Harrison Ford) confronts K (Ryan Gosling), who is searching for him. With a variety of light intensities, we see bright light sources in a window in the background and also from the screen-left window, which provides the motivated key on K's right side of his face—this is where the intensity is the highest, placing Deckard in silhouette in the foreground. Where the two characters are placed, the lighting is predominately low intensity, helping to convey the mystery of the scene. Will Deckard shoot K? Is K really Deckard's son? Will he be accepted? At the same time, the warm hues and the soft lighting also reveal elements of relaxation, providing a tension between the positive and negative elements of low intensity lighting. Contrast this with Figure 3.1 (p. 124), where the hues are cool and the scene appears more deadly. DP: Roger Deakins.
(Image ©2017 Warner Bros.)

VISUAL STORYTELLING THROUGH LIGHTING   CHAPTER 3   127

FIGURE 3.4

In this scene from *Blade Runner 2049* (2017), cinematographer Roger Deakins uses soft but intense monochromatic lighting for K's (Ryan Gosling) entrance to a post-apocalyptic Las Vegas hotel. There are no harsh shadows, the lighting is diffused, providing a soft, but intensely omnipresent, light source, reinforcing K's anxiety and restlessness as he searches for Deckard, who he thinks may be his father.

Running the screen image through Adobe Color (color.adobe.com), we can see the predominately orange hues, which heighten the courage, confidence, friendliness, and success of K, all of which reflect the psychology of color being used in this scene. (See orange in Figure 2.14 "Color Convey Emotion" chart, p. 77.)

At the same time—and perhaps most importantly—this color negatively reflects K's ignorance about his origin and about being tracked, which will lead to Deckard's capture.

DP: Roger Deakins.

(Image ©2017 Warner Bros.)

3. Direction

The direction of the light will determine the placement of shadows and, consequently, the physical texture of objects and people. When lighting is "motivated," it refers to a light from a particular source, such as a fireplace, window, lamp, or the sun. Many cinematographers will use motivated lighting.

Front: Conveys little to no drama; no mystery; what is seen is obvious.
Lighting hitting the subject on-axis to the camera, offers the fewest shadows and tends to flatten the image. It fails to sculpt features. (See Figure 3.5, p. 130, for an example of front lighting.)

Side: Creates dramatic tension and texture, sculpting the scene with light and shadow; increases mystery and dramatic tension.
Shadows increase as the light shifts off-axis of the camera and to the rear of the subject. Light from the side increases texture. The dramatic mood of a scene tends to increase with more shadows. (See Figure 3.2, p. 125, where the side lighting heighten textures on Deckard's face.)

Back (including 3/4 Kicker or Rim): Provides a bold edge to characters; tends to bring out strength; adds texture; helps reinforce depth.
A bright, typically hard light source placed 3/4 rear of the performer. Separates the actor from the background of a scene. Helps provide depth to the shot, fulfilling an important component of lighting in layers. In Figure 3.2, p. 125, we can see the hard light source, separating Rachael from the background, sculpting her in a dark space. The rim light in Figure 3.1, p. 124, not only separates Batty from the background, but with the help of the wet surface of his skin from the rain, we see texture.

Background: Helps to provide depth to a scene conveying a sense of scale that allows for spatial context. Also creates a sense of mystery when used to shape silhouettes. It reinforces grandness of scale.
If no other lights are used in front of the subject, backlight will create a silhouette. (See Figure 3.3, p. 126, for an example of how a silhouette is used.) Helps separate the foreground object or subject from the midground and background, creating depth. Also, the light at the end of the hall in the background of Figure 3.3 conveys depth.

Height (low to high)
The height of the light source will determine the length of shadows. A light placed high will minimize shadows, while lights placed low will increase shadows caused by the lit subject or object. Lights placed level from windows will express a sunrise or sunset. Low level lights usually point up as security lights, or used to light a part of a building or some other object. Lights placed high pointing down usually indicate a high sun, which, if placed outside of windows, will bounce off floors and wall, scattering the light with a soft quality.

4. **Texture**

Texture reflects the placement of shadows (negative fill) in a scene and how shadow placement shapes the surface of an object. It may include both the use of gobos on a light source casting shadows or the surface of an object in the setting. A venetian blind with a light shining through would provide visual texture, for example. A polished coffee table would express a different texture than a piece of rough antique furniture. Light position shapes exture. If you want to see more texture on a subject or object, then the light needs to come more from the side than the front. The front placement of a light minimizes texture. Texture can also refer to the amount of diffusion in the atmosphere, such as fog, particles of dust, smoke, and so forth, which become pronounced when lit from behind.

Increasing shadows reveal texture, which increases the dynamic intensity or drama or mystery of a character and/or scene. Decreasing texture (by using frontal lighting) tends to decrease tension, mystery, and dynamism, while heightening elements of clarity, purity, and passivity of a character or scene. (See Figure 3.4, p. 127, for a scene with a lot of aerial texture in Blade Runner 2049. See also Figures 3.5–3.7 for additional examples of texture on the following several pages.)

> **Light quality tip**
> Set a light closer to a subject, the softer it gets, while the farther away it is, the harder it gets, since it becomes more of a point source, causing the hard light quality to stand out. Also, the inverse square law of light means when you double the light distance, the light will be four times dimmer. If you halve the distance, it'll increase in brightness by four times.

FIGURE 3.5
In this scene from *Blade Runner* (1982), Rachael (Sean Young) walks towards Deckard (from his point of view), who has arrived at Tyrell Corporation to question the head of the company. Deckard is told that Rachael is Tyrell's daughter. Take note of the front light on Rachael, minimizing any sense of texture in her costume, hair, or face. She's sculpted as a form of beauty and purity. Even though we do not know she is a replicant at this moment in the scene, the cinematography helps to foreshadow the mystery of her background by

VISUAL STORYTELLING THROUGH LIGHTING   CHAPTER 3   131

placing her purity, clarity, and no guile (as represented by front lighting), within a lot of shadows, aerial diffusion, and a black dress. Light hits the polished floor, reflecting what appears to be the surface of water. In fact, the scene includes light pointed through the surface of actual water, which contains mirrors, reflecting the light as moving texture (ripples) on the walls. (The light/water setup would be repeated by Roger Deakins in *Blade Runner 2049*.)
DP: Jordan Cronenweth.
(Image ©1982 Warner Bros.)

FIGURE 3.6

In this scene from *Blade Runner* (1982), Rachael (Sean Young) looks at Deckard during the Voigt-Kampff test to see if she is a replicant. The side light, a hard light source, placed as a 3/4-rear kicker, sculpts the edge of her cheek and hand; it not only provides high contrast (see Contrast, p. 136), but also brings out strong texture in her hair, heightens the smoothness of her skin, and reveals detailed texture in her hand, along her thumb and fingers. Also note the diffusion of the bluish smoke from her cigarette (pronounced with the back light).

The focal depth of field falls off, placing the focus on Rachael, revealing elements of dynamism and a sense of excitation. At the same time, the soft lighting on her face tends to invite a sense of relaxation, perhaps a sense of the romantic, since it's clear that Deckard falls for her in this scene.

Consulting the color chart on p. 77 (Figure 2.14), the ambient turquoise color tends to express femininity, as well as a level of sophistication and protection; the contrasting hues of yellow, red, and orange mix—tending to bring out intellect, passion, and confidence, respectively, according to the psychology of color, and Rachael does fit within this profile.

For *Blade Runner* fans, the golden light in her eyes was the means by which the director wanted to distinguish replicants from humans in a visual way.
DP: Jordan Cronenweth.

(Image ©1982 Warner Bros.)

FIGURE 3.7

In this scene from *Blade Runner* (1982), Deckard (Harrison Ford) looks at Rachael during the Voigt-Kampff test. The key light, coming from 3/4 front, textures Deckard's face and clothing. It also reveals a sense of contrast as the top half of his face falls off into shadow, while the bottom half expresses high intensity of light. (This is where the use of flags and scrims can be used to sculpt where and how light falls onto a subject.) In the psychology of lighting, certain kinds of light help increase productivity and efficiency, which certainly reinforces Deckard's demeanor in this scene.

With heightened shadows, we also feel a sense of mystery and tension in high contrast lighting, and the mystery deepens as Deckard realizes that Rachael is a replicant, not a human, as he was told by Tyrell. The colors here—browns, tans, and a little bit of blue—heighten the friendliness (brown) of Deckard, his conservatism (brown), his dependability (tan), and his masculinity and integrity (a hint of blue in his shirt), all of which stands in contrast to Rachael's setup in the reverse angle. DP: Jordan Cronenweth.
(Image ©1982 Warner Bros.)

5. Contrast

High contrast: Offers the most potential for heightening dramatic scenes. High contrast scenes usually contain high stakes, or high drama, or mystery.

There is a wide range of light levels from shadows (dark grays and blacks) to highlights (light grays and whites). It requires the use of negative fill to block light sources in order to create shadows. Think *film noir*, for example, *Casablanca* (1942). (See Figure 3.8.)

FIGURE 3.8
Shot of Sam (Dooley Wilson) and Rick (Humphrey Bogart) from *Casablanca* (1942), revealing a high-contrast, *film noir* look. Notice the lighting in the midground and background to help sculpt cinematic depth in the scene. Rick must decide to continue to wallow in self-pity or try to engage the love of his life, who has just shown up with her husband. If little shadow was used, the impact of the scene would dissipate. DP: Arthur Edeson.
(Image ©1942 Warner Bros.)

A modern version of *film noir*, Blade Runner (1982), utilizes high contrast in nearly every scene, as well as taking advantage of color. (See Figure 3.9.)

FIGURE 3.9
In this scene from *Blade Runner* (1982), Deckard meets Rachael at Tyrell Corporation. The sun, low in the sky behind angular buildings, offers a dynamic backdrop to the scene. Hard source rim lights pull both characters away from the window, as light bounces off the table behind them. The high contrast of dimly-lit faces and silhouetted torsos and chairs deepen the mystery and tension in this scene. The stakes are high, since Deckard must hunt down the escaped replicants who have been violently killing humans.

VISUAL STORYTELLING THROUGH LIGHTING   CHAPTER 3   139

In Tyrell's office, the person who is in control of the scene, Tyrell, wants to use Deckard's Voigt-Kampff test as a way to see how long it takes Deckard to discover that Rachael is a replicant. High-contrast scenes usually contain high stakes for characters. If this scene was shot in low contrast with minimal shadows or minimum changes in light intensity, the scene would lose its energy—we wouldn't be *feeling* the right lighting design. DP: Jordan Cronenweth. (Image ©1982 Warner Bros.)

Low contrast: *The dramatic stakes are usually low in scenes with low contrast lighting.*

Also called high key lighting and it offers a minimal range of light levels from shadows to highlights. When lighting the face, the contrast ratios on both sides of the face are usually even, or close to even, as typically found in comedies.

See Figure 3.4 (p. 127) for an example of a lower contrast scene from Denis Villeneuve's *Blade Runner 2049* (2017). In that scene, K (Ryan Gosling) searches for Deckard, and the landscape he enters presents the viewer with otherworldly, post-apocalyptic lighting of Las Vegas. K stands in contrast to the orange-red hues of a presumable sunset, the dust in the air scattering the light, making it soft and lowering the contrast, the light wrapping around him in similar intensity, but his dark clothing provides contrast in the scene. An extreme example of low contrast used in a high stakes scene, can be found in George Lucas' *THX 1138* (1971). (See Figure 3.10.)

FIGURE 3.10
Robert Duvall sits in a low contrast scene from *THX 1138* (1971). The image appears flat due to the lack of shadows or negative fill in the space. The skin tones stand out as a key element of contrast. THX 1138 (Robert Duvall) is imprisoned in an empty white space that seemingly continues in infinite white. Lucas' experimental film goes against the stereotype of prison scenes found in cinema. DPs: David Myers and Albert Kihn.
(©1971 American Zoetrope and Warner Bros.)

> **Lighting ratios**
> The ratio of brightness of one light compared to another is a measurement tool cinematographers use, usually with a light meter. For example, a cinematographer may want the ratio of a foreground key light on a subject to the background four times brighter. This would be a ratio of 4:1. With the same ISO set for a scene, the cinematographer may determine an f-stop setting of 5.6 to properly expose the subject's face. The background would then need to be exposed at f/11 (two stops closed up would be four times less light). Lighting ratios are commonly used to light faces with the key light on the subject's up (camera) side of their face, with the fill, the darker side, on the opposite down side, facing the camera.

6. **Color temperature**

Different chemicals burn at different wavelengths, producing different colors depending on whether the lamp is halogen, tungsten, fluorescent, sunlight, and so on. Also, the color temperature of sunlight changes over the course of the day and whether or not it's cloudy. Color temperature is measured in degrees Kelvin (K).

Ambient color temperature and the intensity of light influences human biological circadian rhythms. Color temperature of natural light changes throughout the day, so an understanding of it isn't just about setting "accurate" color temperature in-camera—creative choices can be shaped to reflect the moods associated with circadian changes. A study published in *Trends in Cognitive Science* discusses how the internal "clock is a more intimate and pervasive regulator of cognition and mood, with roles far beyond the timing of sleep" (Kyriacou and Hastings, 2010: 260). Lighting design goes well beyond filmic lighting. It includes lighting for workplace quality and performance, neonatal intensive care units, therapeutic lighting design for the elderly in nursing homes, and even lighting design for developing countermeasures for sleep and circadian disruption in space flight.

Therefore, understanding the nature of lighting and color (see Figure 2.14, p. 77) can help determine what color temperature to use in visualizing the story in strong ways, whether we're utilizing the sun or simulating it for different times of day (or using practical lights for different kinds of color temperatures)—and shaping these with color gels, as well as set, props, and costume colors. Note, in Figure 3.9 (p. 138), where we see Deckard and Rachael in *Blade Runner*, the color temperature of the scene falls between 2700–3000K, the scene full of warm hues. These warm hues are predominantly gold, a color that psychologically tends to express a sense of wealth, wisdom, and prosperity; along with gold's more negative connotations (egotism and self-righteous behavior).

We can begin to feel that the color choice in this scene is the proper choice, not only as a means of expressing the beauty and wealth that Tyrell Corporation exerts in the universe of *Blade Runner*, but Tyrell's own egotistical hubris, which will later bring him down. Furthermore, the warm color temp also "facilitates relaxation, while daylight-white light is stimulating" (Knoop, 2006: 68)

In the color temperature bar, on the facing page, we can see more examples of the color temperature of different light sources. (See Figure 3.12.)

Section review
1. What are the six elements of lighting? Define each.
2. Examine a scene from one of your favorite films or television dramas, identify the elements of lighting, and explain how the lighting supports the story.
3. Reverse engineer one of the shots from this scene and draw a floor plan of where you think the lights are placed and identify how they are utilized (key, fill, back, background) and examine how the qualities of lighting reinforce the story.

White balance tip
Do not manually white balance during a sunrise or sunset because you would be adjusting that lovely golden glow into white, and you don't want to lose the golden glow!

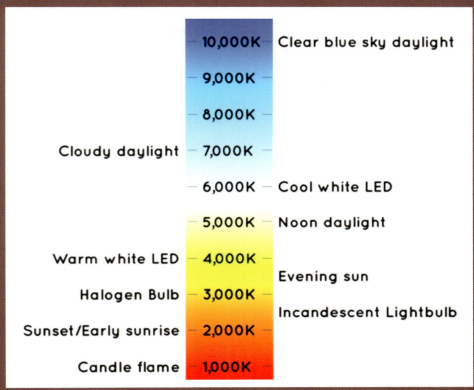

FIGURE 3.12
Color temperature bar indicating the color temperature of different types of natural and artificial light, as well as day over time.
(Image courtesy of ilumi.co ©2015 ilumi. Used with permission.)

Shadow tip
Increasing shadows reveal texture, which increases the dynamic intensity or drama or mystery of a character and/or scene. Decreasing texture (by using frontal lighting) tends to decrease tension, mystery, and dynamism, while heightening elements of clarity, purity, and passivity of a character or scene.

SECTION 2: SOME BASIC TOOLS OF EXPOSURE

This section shifts to the technical, because, to control lighting, there must be an understanding of how to control the intensity of the light.[1]

1. *Zone system:* A system that can be used to plan contrast ratios and dynamic range.
2. *Histogram:* A display tool to measure the dynamic range of light and shadow.
3. *Waveform:* Another type of display tool to measure the intensity of light in any spot in a given shot, and can help you perceive dynamic range.
4. *Aperture and ISO:* The iris that controls the amount of light hitting the sensor. Open the iris to let in more light, which results in a shallow depth of field; close up the iris to decrease the amount of light, and it also deepens the focal depth of field. The ISO adjusts the senstivity of the sensor to light.
5. *ND filters:* A modifier placed in front of the lens designed to block a certain amount of light.
6. *Shutter angle and frame rate:* A 180 degree shutter angle provides the standard cinema look; for cameras that don't use shutter angles, the shutter speed should be set to double the value of the frame rate. A camera shooting at 24 frames per second (standard cinema projection), would need a shutter speed of 1/48 per second, equivalent to a 180 degree shutter angle.
7. *Lighting modifiers:* Silks are used to soften the light quality, scrims cut light intensity, and flags block portions of light. They're designed to help the cinematographer sculpt the look and feel of the light through fill and negative fill (light and shadow).

1. The zone system

One of the tools to plan the ratio of light and shadow, the contrast ratio, and light intensity, revolves around the zone scale—an arbitrary scale indicating the tonal values from dark to light in an 11-step black–gray–white gradation, numbered 0–10 (0 = black; 10 = white; see Figure 3.12). Zones 0–3 represent black and deep shadow values (details and texture in an image can begin to be seen in zone 2, while 3 shows dark details and some texture, and 4 reveals

---

[1] Some of this material is drawn from my book, *DSLR Cinema*, 3rd edition (Focal Press, 2018), with new material and examples added for this book.

landscape shadows and dark foliage). In addition, zones 4–6 represent face tones (from dark-skinned to Caucasian facial tones).

The mid-gray of 5 represents brown skin tones and sky; this is also the reflective value of an 18% gray card used for white balance. Zones 7–9 hit lighter grays and highlights (an 8 would reveal texture in snow, whereas 9 would represent blown-out highlights, and 10, pure white). Each zone number indicates a doubling in brightness from the previous zone; the gray in 6 is twice as bright as the gray in 5; the gray in 7 is four times brighter than 5 (each step is a multiple of two). The black in 1 is half as bright as in 2. The doubling and halving of the gray scale is similar to the doubling and halving of the exposure range in f-stops. (See Figure 3.12.)

FIGURE 3.12
Zone scale from 0–10, referring to a quantification of a black-to-white gradation. One zone is twice as bright as the next when moving toward the white, while it's half as bright when moving toward the black.
(Image courtesy of the author.)

Simply put, the zone scale is a tool filmmakers can use to train their eye in controlling how much light should be in a scene—to properly shape the exposure range of cameras. You don't need to use it as a technical tool for every shot, but practice with it so you can begin to see the potential range of darks to brights and learn where your camera can handle the exposure or dynamic range.

If you want to expose for zone 5 (the "correct" exposure for an 18% gray card), set your lights and place your subject, angle the 18% gray card so that it reflects the same light as your subject, and take your reading. The 18% gray card refers to the reflection and absorption of light (18% of the light is reflected, while 82% is absorbed). If you get an exposure reading of f/4 on your light meter for your particular ISO setting, then that's your f-stop setting, and the rest of the tonal

> **The zone scale is a tool filmmakers can use to train their eye in controlling how much light should be in a scene—to properly shape the exposure range of cameras.**

Shadow side of hair is at zones 2 to 3, while the lit side of the hair comes in at 7 and rolls off to 3.

Blacks crush in at 0, while the blue daylight falls in at zone 6. The fill side of Boy's face (Sean Young) hits zone 5.

range will fall off or increase depending on the amount of intensity in other areas of the shot. If you want to see details in the shadow, for example, make sure you set the background lights three stops less (f/11) than the f/4 level on the face.

Let's look at an indoor night shot from an in-class cinematography exercise to see how we can use the zone system practically. In Figure 3.13, we see tonal values of 0 to 6—black to brightly lit skin tones.

For your reference, a typical Caucasian face has a reflectivity of 36%; a brown face, about 16%; a black face, 10%. Green leaves have a 14% reflectance, while black velvet is at 2%. Light grays reflect 70% of light, while off-whites reflect 80% (Viera, D. and Viera, M., 2005: 54).

Visual Storytelling Through Lighting   CHAPTER 3   147

The 3/4 rear kicker strikes Sean Young's face at zone 9, rolling off to zone 4 on the fill side of his face (screen-left).

The Girl's side (Mikayla Khramov), out of focus in the foreground, comes in at zone 4.

FIGURE 3.13
We could recreate this interior bar shot using the zone system by quantifying the tonal range of black-gray-white from a cinematography exercise. To accent the darkness, we let the blacks fall off, revealing little to no detail in much of the area behind the performer, Sean. We can begin to see details in the 2–3 range, while 4 and 5 allow us to clearly see the patterns and texture on the his jacket, shirt, beard. Zone 6 is typically the value of Caucasian skin tones, and we can clearly see the detail, here. The screen-right side of his face contains fill light, while the hard key blasts out at 9–10, with a roll-off to a 4 as it gets darker in the shadows. The background goes from 0–3, with some detail in the soft focus of the ceiling (the jukebox light on the back wall clips out at 10).
(Image courtesy of the author.)

2. Histogram

If you don't have a light meter, you could use the histogram graph found on most cameras to "read" the range of tonal values in the shot, and adjust the camera's exposure or ISO setting accordingly. The histogram represents the amount of your scene that's bright or dark (the tonal values). If the meter shows a high value on the left side of the screen, the image is overall dark, showing the image to be "crushed" (a lot of detail lost in the blacks); high values on the right side of the meter reveal the image to be mostly bright and could be blown out. The gray values fall in the middle, so the 18% gray card reference representing the mid-range point will be equivalent to a histogram reading in the middle of the graph.

When applied to the zone scale, the readings on the left 40% of the graph would represent 0–3 (the dark grays and blacks), 4–6 (the middle gray tones) would fall into the middle of the graph (20–30%); while brighter gray tones, highlights, and white would fall along the right 30–40% of the graph. (See Figure 3.14.)

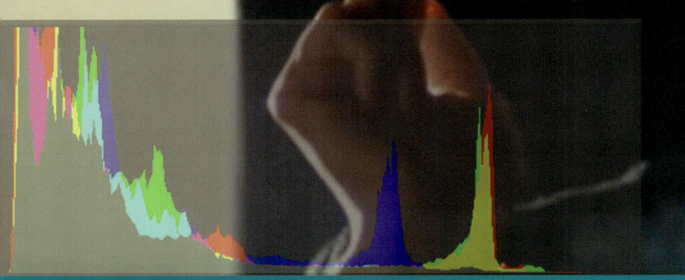

FIGURE 3.14
Histogram profile of a shot from *Blade Runner* (1982). Here we see the spread of colors and tone on a scale that shows the range of darks to brights. The scale reads high-intensity lights (the brights) on the right side, while low-intensity lights (the darks) fall on the left side. Here we see that most of the image is dark (no surprise).

VISUAL STORYTELLING THROUGH LIGHTING   CHAPTER 3   149

What's interesting is the spread of shadows on the left, as well as the colors, the teal in the shadows, the yellow in the highlights (showing the yellow light screen-left, but also some yellow and reds, as well as green, in the highlights pulling from the skin tones). (The image was created using the histogram tool in Photoshop and laying the tool onto a screen grab.)
(Image ©1982 Warner Bros.; histogram image by Kurt Lancaster.)

3. Waveform

The waveform shows the brightness of values on a vertical scale (zero being the darkest and 100 being the brightest), corresponding to a horizontal point on the image (the left side of the scale represents the left side of the image, reading left to right). This tool is found in most cinema cameras. A general rule is to keep the skin tone values of the waveform between 55–75 for a good exposure. If the image is crushed towards zero, you're underexposed. If the scale pushes to 100, then you're pushing overexposure.

You may create a high-contrast image by placing your exposure along the full range of the scale—but that's not necessary. Sometimes you want to control the exposure range in the scene to minimize contrast, for example. As we can see in the waveforms, below, from *Blade Runner* and *Blade Runner 2049*, the first image is definitely high contrast, but the values do not go much above 75, nor fall near zero; in the second, the image expresses low contrast with values ranging from 15–55. (See Figures 3.15 and 3.16.)

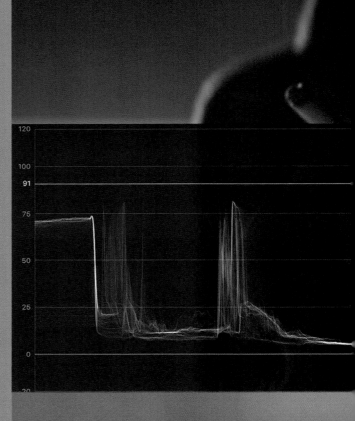

FIGURE 3.16
In *Blade Runner 2049*, we can see how the orange hues are monochromatic in the scene, and we can also see how the medium contrast range of 15–55 really reveals how an image can be shaped without using high contrast, but still remain dramatic. (The waveform images were created by sending the images to Final Cut Pro, then importing back into Photoshop for layering onto screen grabs.)
(Image ©2017 Warner Bros.; waveform images by Kurt Lancaster.)

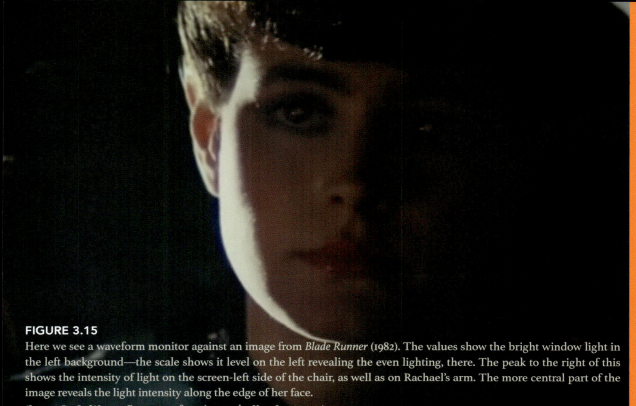

FIGURE 3.15
Here we see a waveform monitor against an image from *Blade Runner* (1982). The values show the bright window light in the left background—the scale shows it level on the left revealing the even lighting, there. The peak to the right of this shows the intensity of light on the screen-left side of the chair, as well as on Rachael's arm. The more central part of the image reveals the light intensity along the edge of her face.
(Image ©1982 Warner Bros.; waveform images by Kurt Lancaster.)

4. Aperture and ISO

ISO determines the light sensitivity of the camera's sensor. Low ISO (such as 100–200), is typically used for outdoor daylight, anything bright, while high ISO (1250, 2500, and higher) is designed for low light. Usually, the higher ISOs will increase the noise level of the sensor. Low ISOs tend to result in less noise. The adjustment of each full level of an ISO setting (100, 200, 400, 800, 1600, 3200, 6400, 12800, and so on) is equivalent to a full stop opening of the aperture (the amount of light introduced into the camera). For example, let's say your ISO is set at 800 and you're at f/2.0 aperture, but it's too bright; you could close up one full stop and go to f/2.8 or you could go to ISO 400, which is equivalent to stopping down one full stop. In the former choice your depth of field would change, while in the latter, it would stay the same.

Closing or opening the aperture determines more than just how much light enters the camera. It also influences the depth of field of the shot. The lower the f-stop, the more shallow the depth of field becomes. Higher f-stops increase the depth of field. Note how the focal depth of field increases with the distance to the subject; the depth of field decreases with the subject closer to the lens. Long lenses also decrease the focal depth of field. For example, a subject 20 feet away with a 50 mm lens at f/1.4 has a depth of field of 4.15 feet, while a subject at two feet has a depth of field of less than half an inch. A long telephoto lens will also create shallow depth of field. (See Figure 3.17.)

(T-stops are used in cimea, while f-stops are used in photography. They're similar, but T-stops take into account the degradation of light through its lens, so they're actually more accurate.)

To calculate depth of field, see www.dofmaster.com/dofjs.html and scroll down to the cinematography section, then choose the sensor size.

FIGURE 3.17 (facing page)
The f-stop setting determines the depth of field, as can be seen with the focal plane changing in the corresponding images with Preston. At f/2.8, f/4, and f/5.6, the background chairs are out of focus, while they begin to get sharper at f/5.6 and above. Depth of field calculation based on 5D Mark II, Zeiss Contax 50 mm f/1.4 at a distance of approximately 4 feet (using the depth of field calculator at: www.dofmaster.com/dofjs.html).
(Image courtesy of the author.)

VISUAL STORYTELLING THROUGH LIGHTING   CHAPTER 3   153

2.8

Distance ~4' f/2.8: DoF = 3.85" (from 3.85'-4.17')

4

Distance ~4' f/4: DoF = 5.4" (from 3.79'-4.24')

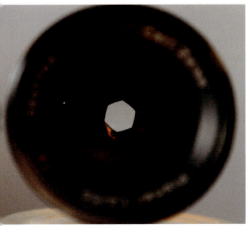

5.6

Distance ~4' f/5.6: DoF = 7.68" (from 3.71'-4.34')

5. ND filters

Filters can change the quality of a lens, diffusing an image to make it slightly soft. The most important ones are designed not only to protect your lenses from scratches, but also to filter the amount of light hitting the lens; they are called neutral density (ND) filters. This type of filter allows you to keep the aperture open under bright light conditions; the filter essentially stops down the f-stop aperture setting—without closing the iris—the amount depending on the type of filter used, allowing the filmmaker to maintain a shallow depth of field with an open iris. Filters can be screwed onto the lens or dropped in front of the lens when using a matte box, or they can be conveyed electronically if the camera has a built-in neutral density function. The Canon C200, for example, uses physical filters that are moved electronically.

Filters are assigned different numbers depending on their density, their ability to block out light. ND2 will be labeled 0.3, providing for a one f-stop equivalent reduction (see table below). Companies also make variable ND filters (called faders) so you can adjust the filter without having to switch them out.

ND Filter Type	Density	f-Stop Reduction
ND2	0.3	1
ND4	0.6	2
ND8	0.9	3
ND16	1.2	4
ND32	1.5	5
ND64	1.8	6

6. Shutter angle and frame rate

Typically, you would follow the 180-degree shutter angle rule. The shutter in a film camera would normally be half a circle (180 degrees), so if the film speed is 1/24 of a second (24 fps), you would double that to get the shutter speed (1/48). NTSC video shoots at 30 fps, while PAL (European standard) is 25fps, so with NTSC you would typically shoot at 1/60 of a second shutter speed. Shane Hurlbut, ASC, however, considers this "a recipe for delivering images that look like video, not film":

> I use a 1/40th or a 1/50th of a second shutter. You never go above that. Anytime you go above, it starts looking like video. By just going up to

1/60th of a second it instantly takes a beautiful 5D that gives filmic images and turns it into a video camera. The more you sharpen the image, the more it looks plastic. I use the motion blur to soften the crispness of HD video. Shooting at a 1/50th is like shooting with a 200 degree shutter. I shot the whole *Rat Pack* (1998) on a 200 degree shutter—I loved that look. So setting the proper shutter speed is important in helping to attain the film look. (Seymour, 2010)

In addition, film typically runs at 24 frames per second, and provides one of the benchmarks for getting the film look, which engages a judder effect when shooting (and that's part of the film look, too).

7. Lighting modifiers

Scrims are used to control the intensity of light, silks to control the light quality (from hard to soft), and flags to act as negative fill by blocking light sources. These are foundational tools for the cinematographer to control the light. (See Section 3, p. 156–161, for the use of modifiers used in the short, "Fragments.")

Section review

1. What are seven tools of exposure? Define each.
2. How would you apply the different tools of exposure?
3. Take a shot from one of your favorite films and examine the zone scale, waveform, and histogram on that shot.

> Closing or opening the iris determines more than just how much light enters the camera. It also influence the depth of field of the shot. The lower the f-stop, the more shallow the depth of field becomes. Higher f-stops increase the depth of field. Note how the focal depth of field increases with the distance to the subject; the depth of field decreases with the subject closer to the lens. Long lenses also decrease the focal depth of field. For example, a subject 20 feet away with a 50 mm lens at f/1.4 has a depth of field of 4.15 feet, while a subject at two feet has a depth of field of less than half an inch. A long telephoto lens will also create shallow depth of field.

SECTION 3: INDOOR AND OUTDOOR DAY SETUP EXAMPLES FROM "FRAGMENTS"

Let's take a look at Joe Simon's "Fragments" and discuss how he shaped lighting for an indoor and outdoor shot. (See Figures 3.18–3.24, pp. 156–161.)

- Watch the film at www.vimeo.com/120850943.

Simon's company, The Delivery Men, based in Austin, Texas, was hired to create a short, "Fragments", to highlight the features of the Canon C100 Mark II. It tells the story of the memories of a young couple. (Analysis in the captions.)

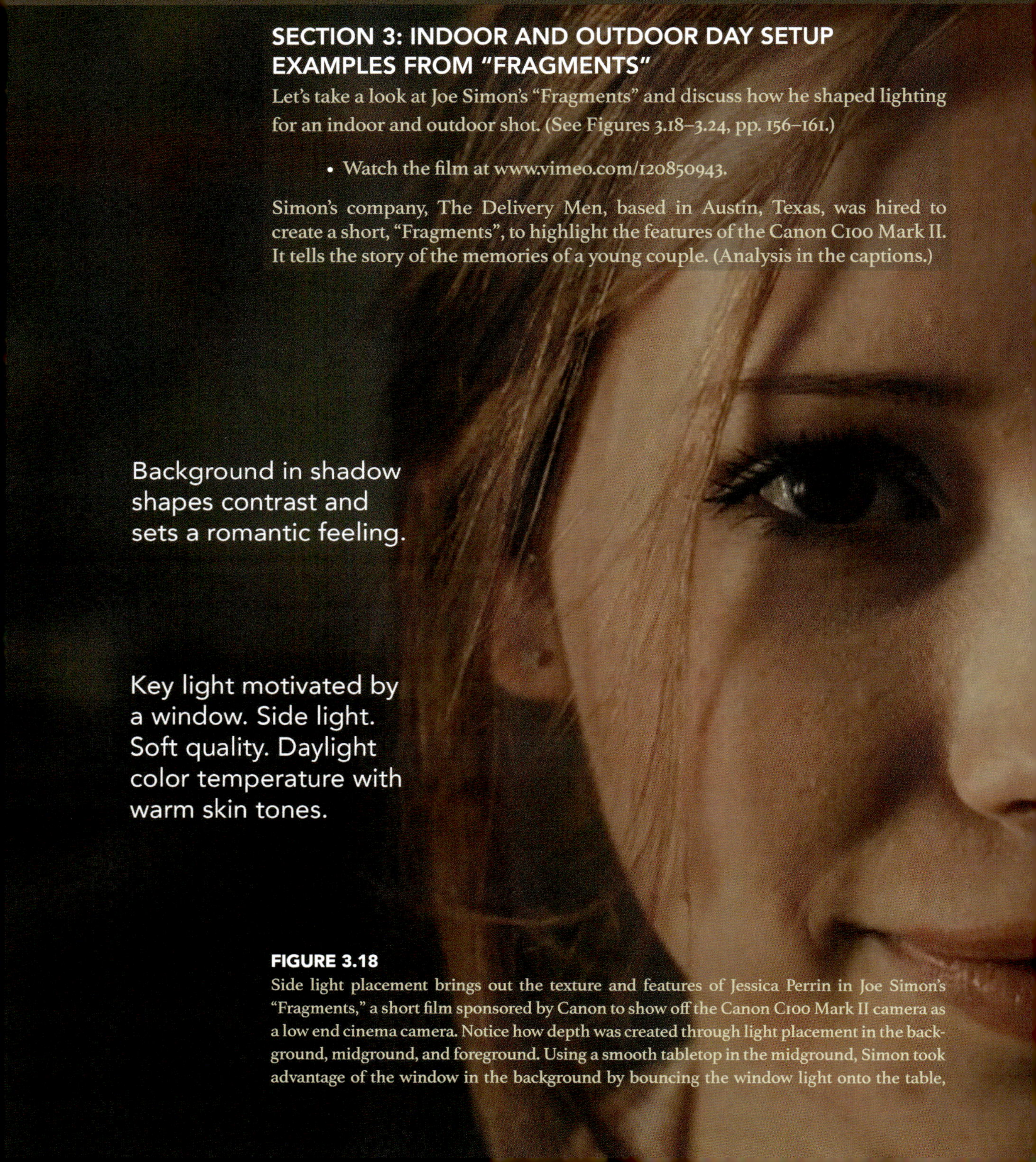

Background in shadow shapes contrast and sets a romantic feeling.

Key light motivated by a window. Side light. Soft quality. Daylight color temperature with warm skin tones.

FIGURE 3.18
Side light placement brings out the texture and features of Jessica Perrin in Joe Simon's "Fragments," a short film sponsored by Canon to show off the Canon C100 Mark II camera as a low end cinema camera. Notice how depth was created through light placement in the background, midground, and foreground. Using a smooth tabletop in the midground, Simon took advantage of the window in the background by bouncing the window light onto the table,

VISUAL STORYTELLING THROUGH LIGHTING   CHAPTER 3   157

Background light from window.

A soft quality fill light adds warmth to her face, but note how it is dimmer than the key light.

Shadow area beaks up the window light reflecting on the table, adding moody contrast.

providing depth to the shot. Furthermore, negative fill on the screen-left side background allows her face to stand out. This negative fill also defines this shot as high contrast, with a range of dark shadows to blown out highlights in the background window.
(Image ©2015 Canon USA, Inc. Used with permission.)

FIGURES 3.19–3.22
In the first image (top), we see a part of the setup of the shot found in Figure 3.18. A scrim is placed in front of a window to control light spilling into the scene. In the second, a light added, the scrim is used as a bounce, making the light quality soft. This is the primary light source in the scene and it is the key light. The use of the light and scrim allows the filmmakers to control the light over time. Otherwise the light direction and quality of the sun would change over the time it takes to shoot the scene.

VISUAL STORYTELLING THROUGH LIGHTING   CHAPTER 3   159

In the third image (top), a fill light is added. Notice the use of a scrim in front of the light source. This makes the light indirect, providing a soft light quality. The light also has a dimmer control so the cinematographer can determine the intensity of the light. In the fourth image, Joe Simon on camera sets up the shot. We can see the intensity of the window light falling onto Perrin's face, compared to the less intense natural light from the door windows in the background. In addition, the light above right provides a soft fill light falling onto her left cheek and shoulder.

(Images ©2015 Canon USA, Inc. Used with permission.)

FIGURE 3.23
Dietrich Schmidt chases Jessica Perrin in the yard during their courtship. By placing the actors and camera in the right position, Simon makes the most of the natural sunlight (as the key light)—it acts as a 3/4 kicker on Schmidt and Perrin, the hard light source of the sun rims their head and shoulders, defining their shapes and separating them from the background. (Image ©2015 Canon USA, Inc. Used with permission.)

Section Review

1. Take a shot from one of your favorite films or television dramas and examine how lighting and any modifiers may have been used.

2. Take this same shot and recreate it using lights and lighting modifiers to try to mimic the light quality in that shot.

FIGURE 3.24
The cinematographer must control the light. By using a white board, fill light bounces from the sun, lighting the actors' faces and preventing Perrin and Schmidt from being too dark on camera. With the sun so bright, the contrast ratio would be too high and we would lose details. By bouncing sunlight, it acts as a soft fill seen in Figure 3.23.

(Image by Brent Ramsey. ©2015 Canon USA, Inc. Used with permission.)

SECTION 4: OUTDOOR NIGHT CASE STUDY FROM *JESSICA JONES* WITH DP MANUEL BILLETER

Immediately you're struck by the cinematography in *Jessica Jones*, the Netflix series adapted from the comic book of the same name. Manuel Billeter, the DP, gained an education in film studies and not in film production, but he has embraced a strong stylized approach to the series. In one interview, he mentioned how has was influenced by Wong Kar Wai, David Fincher, Stanley Kubrick, and Federico Fellini (Chimera, n.d.). "Television today calls for an approach that isn't dumbed-down or fast-tracked," says Billeter. He continues:

> We came up with a clear vision that was off the beaten path and we stuck to it. That was our recipe for creative success. The noir atmos-phere was woven in from page one of the first script. The character is living somewhat in hiding, and she is often watching people. [Director] S.J. [Clarkson] and I thought it would be good to put a lot of layers between the camera and the actors—reflections, foreground obstruction, and visual occlusions. Combined with some unbalanced framing, it supports the story and creates an impression on the viewer. You have to dig deep and peel away those layers to get to the core of this character. (Chimera, n.d.)

The layers Billeter creates are not only utilized by the architectural elements in the found space, but also in the layers of lighting. In describing this opening sequence from *Jessica Jones* (Figure 3.25, pp. 164–165), Billeter explains in an interview with me, that "there is a little bit of an art to a bygone era of New York in terms of the location under the train trestle. There's something timeless about it, something nostalgic about it with the notion of trains being beneath it, and of course the steam—both create an atmosphere to set a stage that is a little bit stylized and evocative in terms of what the whole series should feel. It's some of my proudest work" (Lancaster, 2018).

As for the color scheme of the lighting, Billeter says that:

> we wanted to keep it very stark and simple. There are only three colors: there's black, and then there's this green (which is a gel I used), and then there's the dirty orangy-yellow backlight to emphasize the steel structure. I found that fascinating, because we created a certain visual rhythm within each composition; there's jagged edges, there's clear lines; there's perspective coming in; and then there's the round rivets in the steel structure. And what I think is an important element—and it can't be

overstated—all of this supports the narrative, the story, even the types of cars that were chosen, which are all old-fashioned and beater cars, more of the seventies. No modern cars. Even though we don't focus on the cars, it still influences the overall experience. (Lancaster, 2018)

> "We wanted to keep it very stark and simple. There's only three colors: there's black, and then there's this green (which is a gel I used), and then there's the dirty orangy-yellow backlight to emphasize the steel structure. I found that fascinating, because we created a certain visual rhythm within each composition; there's jagged edges, there's clear lines; there's perspective coming in; and then there's the round rivets in the steel structure. And what I think is an important element—and it can't be overstated—all of this supports the narrative."
>
> —Manuel Billeter, DP of *Jessica Jones*

In choosing the bluish-green turquoise color in the scene—most predominately seen as a diagonal line along an iron bar in the location (cuts 2, 4-6, 8)—Billeter wanted it to create tension through the contrast of color between the green and the yellow-orange lighting. "These two colors clash a little bit," he explains. "They're colors that don't match very well, even though you find them in nature all the time." The colors were chosen to "support the passion that is present in the scene. A little hint of something that is different than the rest of the colors help opens up" and reinforce the story, he explains (Lancaster, 2018).

When adding long lenses to this type of lighting, Billeter notes, these lit objects become "blurry shapes suspended in air, which is exactly what we wanted—to create layers. It demands some sort of an effort from the audience to interpret the images." Furthermore, they shifted the camera to the left and added the long lens to place the diagonal shape in the long shot, "an out of focus architecture element" (Lancaster, 2018). (See Figure 3.25, cuts 2, 4–6, 8, pp. 164–165.)

In cut 7, Billeter notes how the diagonal yellow-orange light was a "happy accident when shooting through the windshield of this car. The sodium vapor backlight was hitting it and created this crazy flare on the windshield itself. It creates a visual tension that I find interesting. It creates a lot of chaos in a way, which suits the scene when you see the embrace of legs and arms and contortions, which supports the scene of dark debauchery in hiding but still in plain view" (Lancaster, 2018).

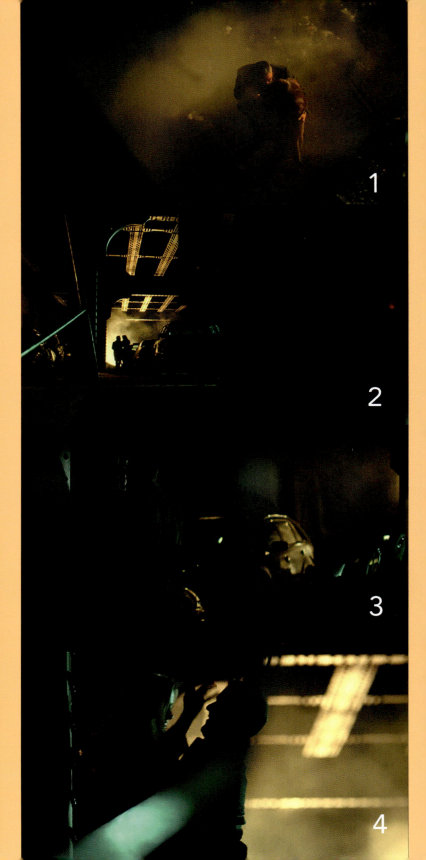

The colors chosen for this scene reinforce the negative connotations of the psychological uses of color:
- Teal: envy, femininity
- Yellow: irresponsible, unstable
- Black: death, evil, mystery

(See Figure 2.14, p. 77.)

Because this scene depicts the woman cheating on her husband, the sense of envy, irresponsibility, unstable behavior, evil, and mystery coming through the colors thematically reinforce the story points that Billeter wanted to make in the scene.

Section review

1. Explain the reasons behind some of the choices Billeter made in shooting this scene from *Jessica Jones*.

2. Take a scene from one of your favorite films or television dramas and analyze the lighting choices in detail. You may want to research any interviews with the cinematographer and discover the choices behind the lighting in the film or show. Describe how the choice of lenses, composition, and color help convey the story.

FIGURE 3.25
In this scene from first episode of *Jessica Jones* "AKA Ladies Night" (ep. 1.1), directed by S.J. Clarkson, we see *noir* style lighting with the colors of a Wong Kar-Wai film. DP: Manuel Billeter.
(©2015 Marvel Studios.)

SECTION 5: INDOOR NIGHT CASE STUDY FROM OZU'S *TOKYO TWILIGHT* CLASS PROJECT REINTERPRETATION

Don't just use light because it looks cool, but use it for the dramatic intention of the scene. Read scene 21 from Ozu's *Tokyo Twilight* (1957) (Figure 3.26, pages 167–169). As implied, the Girl has failed in her goal of getting help from the Boy, explored in the earlier scene in Chapter 1 (pages 32–33). She's now in despair and when he enters the scene, her pent up rage comes through.

Let's take a look at the script and discover the dramatic core of this scene. The blocking and camera notes on the script reflect my analysis of the characters' needs of the scene. The actors (Sean Young and Mikayla Khramov) worked out the blocking of the last slap at the table, rather than standing up, saving us another lighting setup.

1. *What does each character want?* The Girl wants to get drunk and wallow in her sorrows. The Boy wants to come across as the stand-up guy, who tried to find her, to help her. But it's too late. She's already made the decision to abort the baby.

2. *What do they do to get what they want?* The Girl finishes her first drink quickly, then orders another. The Boy makes excuses about his attempt to find her and how bad he's felt.

3. *What prevents them from getting what they want?* The bartender questions the Girl. The Girl will not take any excuses from the Boy and slaps him several times. She receives no comfort from her drink, because the Boy interrupts her.

See Figure 3.26 for an analysis of the script. The scene is full of drama, so dramatic lighting is needed. Flat lighting would not provide the tension needed. High contrast, the use of light and shadow, helps convey the emotions boiling beneath the surface of the Girl. Let's examine more closely the lighting plot (layout on paper, p. 169) in Figure 3.26. Arri Fresnels (650W) were used, along with a Westcott Scrim Jim kit, and the location practicals (The Museum Club in Flagstaff, Arizona). (See Figures 3.27–3.29, pp. 170–175.)

FIGURE 3.26 (pages 167–169)
The transcribed script from Ozu's *Tokyo Story* (scene transcribed by the author). Shot as a classroom exercise, we saved time by setting the Girl already sitting at the table and we picked up the scene beginning one-third down on page 2 to the bottom of the page without any shots covered on pages 1 and 3. Notes on the lighting setup are on the last page (to be examined below).

VISUAL STORYTELLING THROUGH LIGHTING   CHAPTER 3   167

EXT. STREET--EARLY EVENING

Ambient outdoor sounds. Shots of the street as a GIRL walks into a a bar.

Light may not be good enough for this shot. Perhaps try an exterior shot downtown.

INT. BAR--EARLY EVENING

24mm deep focus. Wide shot OTS, dirty. Back and forth between the girl and bartender.

The place is empty. The BARTENDER stands at the bar reading a newspaper. The girl walks in.

She looks down, despondent, not making eye contact. (She's had the abortion and has told no one, she feels cut-off from any support.)

                    BARTENDER
    Welcome.

The girl walks to a table and sits down, facing the door.

                    GIRL
    Give me some sake.

                    BARTENDER
    Huh. It's getting colder. Might snow.

Wide shot 24 or 35mm deep focus. Static, showing both men. We're just seeing the action, wide.

He gets up and prepares the drink. An OLDER PERSON sits by himself at the bar.

Does not look at the girl.

                    MAN
    I hear Mr. Kimra's going to move.
    He was here last night. Said he was
    looking around Kamata.

He continues to make the a drink.

                    BARTENDER
    Did he find an apartment?

The man nods. The bartender brings her the drink.

                    BARTENDER
    Here you are.

He sits back down with his newspaper.

                    BARTENDER
    They say apartments are scarce
    these days. And the newer ones are
    real expensive. You gotta hustle.

The girl gulps down her drink as she ignores the bartender's banter.

NOTE: With the above composition, we see the girl in the foreground--face towards the camera--with the two men in the background. In the reverse angle, she is in the distance back to camera (try 35mm).

                                        (CONTINUED)

CONTINUED: 2.

[35mm deep focus. Medium shot OTS, clean. Static shot. Back and forth between the girl and bartender.]

                    GIRL
          Bring me another.

The man looks at her closely.

                    BARTENDER
          Are you sure? That was a lot.

                    GIRL
          I'm fine.

She's clearly not fine.

                    BARTENDER
          If you insist.

He does not get the drink ready before the boy enters.

He prepares another drink. She sits alone at the table, holding back tears. Her BOY walks in. They look at each other.

[As the boy walks in, we push in on her slowly from a medium to a big close-up. 85mm, shallow depth of field.]

We hear him enter and see the reaction on her face, the bartender in the background, working. The boy walks past the camera as he pulls the chair out and sits down.

This movement occurs before he speaks.

                    BOY
          So this is where you've been.

He walks to her table and sits down.

                    BOY
          I looked all over. Couldn't find
          you anywhere.

Covering his ass. He's hoping she'll forgive him for just showing up.

She stares at him in disbelief.

[We then move to a 50mm, shallow, CU OTS, dirty, hand held, back and forth.]

                    BOY
          I knew you had no one to talk to. I
          couldn't sleep at night, thinking
          how worried you must be. It's true.
          Look how I'm wasting away.

He is trying to convince himself that this is true.

She glares at him, then slaps him hard against the face three times, fast. At the third strike he jumps up.

[Medium, 135, shallow, static.]

                    BOY
          What was that for? Stop it!

She leaps up and strikes him again, then runs out the door, leaving it open. The boy sits at her table in shame. The bartender comes over with her second drink.

                    BOY
          That sure startled me.

[Medium wide, 35mm, deep focus.]

                    BARTENDER
          What was that about? Made me spill
          the drink.

(CONTINUED)

CONTINUED: 3.

He sets the drink down next to the boy, then walks over to
close the door. He ~~sits back down~~ with his newspaper.

> Goes back to the bar.

                     BARTENDER
         Girls these days sure are
         hot-tempered. They'll walk all over
         you if you're not tough.

> His back is to door.

Push in on boy, 24mm from wide to a CU.

The boy just stares into space, contemplating his folly. We
hear the sound of a train, pulling its horn multiple times
as a warning, followed by breaks squealing.

                     BARTENDER
         Did something happen? I'm gonna
         see.

He hurries out the door.

Rack focus from his CU to bartender going to the door and opening it, going out, then rack back to boy's CU in focus.

                     BARTENDER (OS)
         Hey! What happened?

The boy just sits at the table and stares as we see a few
people outside run by the window. We see the boy breathing
deep as he tries to control his emotions.

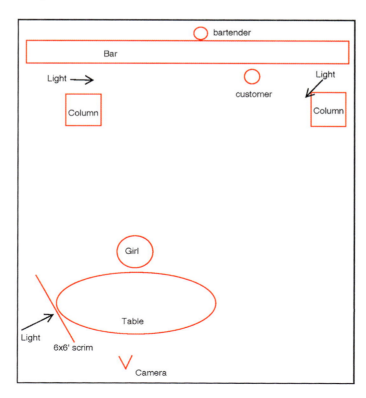

Practical lights include ceiling recess lamps and neon lights in the background and shapes the realism and mood of the space. Back side light from behind the pillar in shadow lights the characters at the bar and adds texture to the scene.

Soft 3/4 front fill light removes some of the shadows from her face.

Shadows, or negative fill, adds dramatic tension throughout the scene.

Light quality, intensity, direction, and texture: Soft fill on Girl (Mikayla Khramov), screen-left a lot less intense than the key; intense hard key screen-right with 3/4 rear kicker placed behind a column in the background; this light hits her hair, neck, arm, and leg helping to separate her from the background and provides intense dramatic contrast to the shadows and soft lights.

The key light also reflects from the surfaces of a couple of small tables, screen-right, helping to break up the blacks on this side of the screen. The background light is a hard side light hitting the bartender and customer from screen-left to screen-right (light hidden behind column in the background).

The side lighting helps shape the texture in the scene by allowing shadows to bring out details on faces and objects. (It is a bit

VISUAL STORYTELLING THROUGH LIGHTING   CHAPTER 3   171

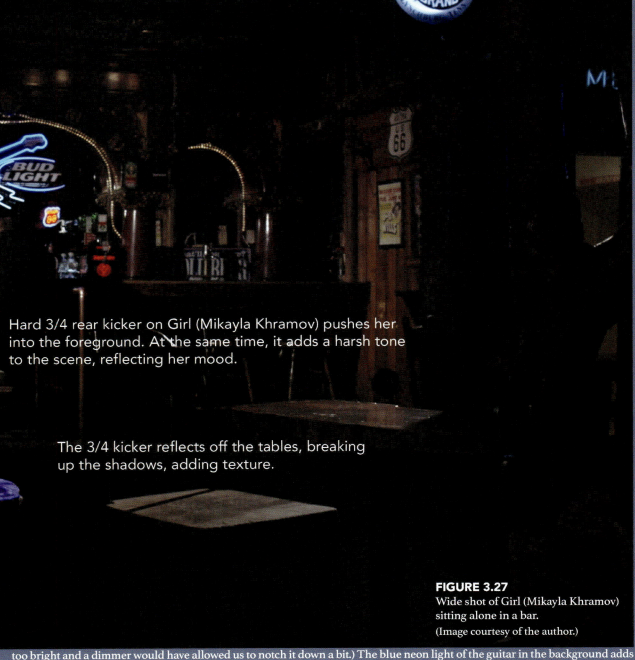

Hard 3/4 rear kicker on Girl (Mikayla Khramov) pushes her into the foreground. At the same time, it adds a harsh tone to the scene, reflecting her mood.

The 3/4 kicker reflects off the tables, breaking up the shadows, adding texture.

FIGURE 3.27
Wide shot of Girl (Mikayla Khramov) sitting alone in a bar.
(Image courtesy of the author.)

too bright and a dimmer would have allowed us to notch it down a bit.) The blue neon light of the guitar in the background adds atmosphere to the scene (and reflects nicely off the edge of Girl's table).

Contrast ratio: This is a high contrast scene with the hair (or rim light) from the 3/4 rear kicker creating the brightest area of the screen. Plenty of shadows from negative fill helps shape dramatic tension in the scene, expressing the Girl's dark emotions. These shadows were caused by closing the barn doors on the Fresnels so the light would spill out only on certain portions of the setting. A 6 × 6 ft scrim was placed in front of the fill light in order to soften and dim it.

Color temperature: Balanced for tungsten lights.

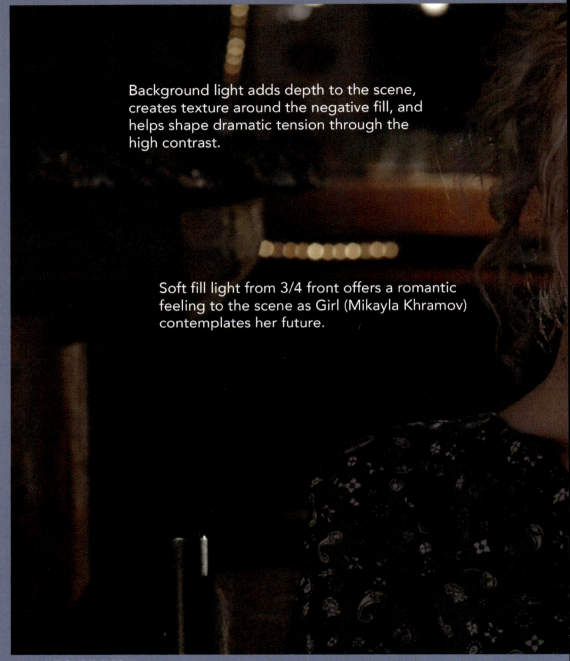

FIGURE 3.28
Push in from a medium CU to CU of the Girl. Same lighting setup as 3.27. Take note of the details in the texture and intensity of the lights. The long lens magnifies the image, including the background, adding a soft focus to it, and brining a sense of a compression of space. (Image courtesy of the author.)

VISUAL STORYTELLING THROUGH LIGHTING   CHAPTER 3   173

Hard 3/4 rear kicker pushes her into the foreground. The harsh light builds high contrast, a key element when creating a moody tone in a scene.

Background lighting from window provides a cool outdoor day color temperature, offering a complementary color to the warm tones of the faces.

Middle-ground lighting on extras in the background. Soft fill light on both performers. Notice how the soft fill light is downside to the camera.

Light quality, intensity, direction, and texture: Lights were essentially reversed, the former soft fill light on the girl, became the 3/4 rear kicker on Boy (Sean Young), and it is a bit too bright, but the intensity opposes his nonchalant attitude, giving the shot additional tension as he tries to make excuses for himself. The texture of his beard and hair come out along the edge of the kicker. Also, along the ceiling, the window light is angled from about a 3/4 rear direction, bringing out the wood beams as part of its texture. A scrim was placed in the former key light position, making it a soft fill. The background lighting shoots out from a daylight back window, causing blue light to hit the midground portion of the shot (especially along the ceiling).

Contrast ratio: This is a high contrast scene with the hair light from the 3/4 rear kicker creating the brightest area of the screen. Plenty of shadows from negative fill helps shape dramatic tension in the scene, expressing the Girl's dark emotions. These shadows were caused by closing the barn doors so the light would spill out only on certain portions of the setting. A 6 × 6 ft scrim was placed in front of the fill light in order to soften and dim it.

Color temperature: The key and fill lights were balanced for tungsten. The background lighting goes blue due to the outdoor lighting on the key and fill lights. The warm tone helps with the romantic intention in the scene. Also note another light was added screen-left midground, placing some light on extras in the background.

Hard 3/4 kicker on Boy (Sean Young). This key light up camera side strikingly contrasts with the negative fill, and shapes the texture of the scene. At the same time, it helps build tension, reflecting the emotions of the characters.

FIGURE 3.29
CU of the Boy (Sean Lang) as an over-the-shoulder, dirty, from the Girl.
(Image courtesy of the author.)

Section review
1. Using the scene you've been developing from Chapters 1 and 2, now add lighting choices based on your story analysis.
2. Set up lights for this scene and shoot it (even if you shoot stills with stand-ins).

SECTION 6: DOCUMENTARY LIGHTING CASE STUDY FROM *CHEF'S TABLE* WITH DP ADAM BRICKER

DP Adam Bricker, a cinematographer for Netflix's *Chef's Table*, recalls Executive Producer David Gelb's desire that the chefs be portrayed as "superheroes." As Bricker explains to me in an interview, "Our job is to tell the superhero origin story, and we want it to be naturalistically beautiful and cinematic to support that level of storytelling. The cinematography must have the appropriate gravitas and style."[1]

To achieve this, Bricker discusses how he creates a set of technical rules that help achieve a cinematic look under documentary circumstances. "We'll shoot at a pre-determined f-stop, use a particular focal length lens, and avoid a mixed color temperature," he says. "For example, most documentaries shoot *vérité* under pre-existing, found light conditions. On *Chef's Table*, we have a preset visual rule that all light must be of a uniform color temperature. Thus, at the start of each scene we pause and take a few minutes to think about preexisting lighting, turn-off or swap-out light bulbs, close window blinds, etc. A few deliberate choices, a set of rules to adhere to—that attention to detail means ultimately the final product is more cohesive and cinematic than it would have been." He adds:

> From a blocking and camera placement perspective, the goal is to keep the subject in between camera and the primary light source to achieve a cinematic far-side key light. [See cuts 1, 4, and 12, p. 179.] In a scripted project with a large crew, we'd typically add a key-light in this position. Since we're reliant on pre-existing lighting, the direction of our key-light is dependent on the relative position of the camera and subject to the source. Achieving cinematic lighting requires the director and cinematographer collaborating to make deliberate blocking choices. With this mindset, you can achieve cinematic results in a documentary scenario.

Bricker emphasizes how making informed choices elevates the quality of the cinematography and storytelling. *Chef's Table* employs three types of lighting and shooting styles based on the story content.

---

[1] All quotes from Bricker from a personal interview with the author in 2018, unless otherwise noted.

1. Documentary *vérité*

Bricker notes that "these shots are the documentary components and express a cinematic, heightened naturalism." He recommends using existing lights (with control based on camera placement, blocking, and neutralizing color temperature sources). The shooting style is a mix of handheld (stabilized with an EasyRig) and Steadicam.

"We're making creative choices that are strong, but to execute them well requires the whole team being on the same page," he says. For example, with the fig trees scene the intent of the light was to make the scene feel romantic, because as Bricker explains, "she's falling in love with the ingredients." Getting the right light for the scene meant shooting during the 45 minutes of magic hour—and required shifting the production schedule to accommodate.

But ultimately, it was worth it. As Bricker notes, "The sun is low and you are free to shoot almost any direction at that time of the day and it's going to have a beautiful, romantic feel." (See frames 1–12 in Figure 3.30, p. 179.)

"These visual rules should be implemented on an almost subconscious level and shouldn't interfere with your ability to be in the moment as an operator," Bricker explains. When you're rolling, it's important to be free to think from a story perspective. "I'm operating [the camera], but I'm thinking, what if we only use the scene as slow motion b-roll of the figs for the fig dish? What if the scene becomes about her and her relationship to the farmer? Or what if we cut out the farmer entirely and this scene is just slow motion b-roll of Dominique working as the sun sets?" Bricker questions.

> As you're operating, you're thinking more from a story perspective and less from a technical one. You're thinking about how you can make this scene as versatile as possible for editorial and get as many different looks and moods to make it a cohesive piece. That's the mindset you're in, much more so than thinking about her relationship to negative fill or light. You're in it from a storytelling perspective. You're thinking about camera angles and composition on one level, while trying to keep the operating elegant and spontaneous as you're following the subject.

The visual and technical choices with this type of *vérité* work must be thought through in advance.

Light quality, intensity, direction, and texture: Looking at the sequence in Figure 3.30 (p. 179), we can see that by choosing magic hour, cinematographer Adam Bricker embraced the soft quality of the light with a fairly low intensity in order to create an atmosphere of romance, because, as he explains, Crenn is "in love with the food." (See cuts 2, 3, 8, 9, 11, and 12.) The direction of the light wasn't a key factor since there is no hard light source, with the light scattered by the trees or when the sun was down, the dusk of the sky—all of which factored into an approach that reinforced the story.

Contrast ratio: With the sun low and with the exposure set for the subjects, the sky did not blow out. As can be seen with the shots of Peter Jacobsen and Crenn throughout this sequence, soft light bounces off faces and hands, the light wrapping around curves, bringing out textures through shadow as the ground reflects and adds a bit of fill, but not enough to remove shadows, providing a nice contrast ratio—but not one that's extreme. (See cuts 1–5, 8–12, and 19.) This textured lighting—taking advantage of a soft key from above and shadows from the sides and below, makes for beautiful natural light cinematography.

Color temperature: The early evening daylight temperature (2000–3500K)—with its soft blue hues—blends well with the green vegetation, providing color contrast and a sense of the evening air.

2. Interviews

Lights are added, designed to emphasize existing light in the space. "You want it to be cinematic," Bricker notes, "but you want it to be cohesive with the existing naturalistic documentary footage. The worst case scenario, from our point of view, would be to cut to this interview and suddenly have it look lit and out of place." He explains in detail on how it is important to achieve an integrated look:

> We do light those interviews to maintain a consistent contrast ratio and draw the viewer's eye. We put light in the subject's eyes so you're drawn to their story, and we pull the subject from the background. But we're doing all these things like you would in a narrative movie. The lighting and the subject placement and the camera placement are all designed to make it feel cohesive. You don't want it to look lit—so the lighting approach must be cohesive with the location. You don't want to notice the lighting. You want the lighting to be elegant and justified by the location. Then it plays well with the rest of the unlit documentary footage. [See 14, 16, 18, 20, and 22 in Figure 3.30.]

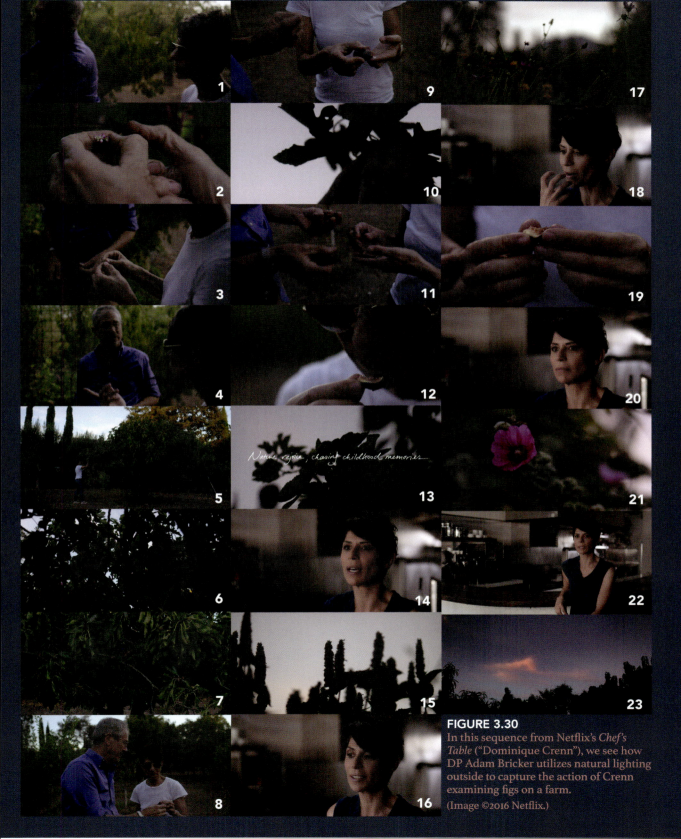

FIGURE 3.30
In this sequence from Netflix's *Chef's Table* ("Dominique Crenn"), we see how DP Adam Bricker utilizes natural lighting outside to capture the action of Crenn examining figs on a farm. (Image ©2016 Netflix.)

For example, Bricker explains, "Dominique Crenn is sitting and it feels like her key light is coming from a window and her hair light is motivated off of a window or a practical lamp in the background. It's essential that you have a backlight and a key light and that you have a contrast ratio, but those things must be justified in the practical space." (See Figure 3.31.)

Light quality, intensity, direction, and texture: The interview shot of Crenn uses lights, but in such a way that it melds into the setting. We don't notice that it is lit. The quality of the light on Crenn's face is from a soft key from the left, designed to look like window light. Eye lights draw us to her face. The shadows on the screen-right of her face fall off softly without any harshness. Hair light helps texture her dark hair and separates her from the background. The bright light in the background provides a motivated back light, giving the image depth, and it draws us to the right side of the screen where Crenn is placed. Notice how the placement of lights—soft background light screen-left, shadow in the center background, the hard bright light on the screen-right—are all designed to sculpt the space naturally with light and shadow.

Contrast ratio: The placement of shadow along with the mostly soft lighting textures the entire interview, providing a strong cinematic look with a high contrast ratio—from the black background directly behind Crenn and her dark hair to the middle tones of soft lighting on the left background wall to the bright light coming from the back screen-right—all is purposely designed to heighten naturalistic lighting in space. Flat lighting or conventional 3-point lighting would take away from the story and would conflict with the surrounding documentary footage.

Color temperature: The temperature is balanced to a naturalistic daylight look with the sense of window lights. Any other practical light, such as a fluorescent, would have been turned off by the crew so as to not add any mixed color temperature to the scene.

VISUAL STORYTELLING THROUGH LIGHTING   CHAPTER 3   181

FIGURE 3.31
CU of Dominique Crenn in *Chef's Table*. The key light is motivated to make it feel as if she's being lit by a window. The background light is usually motivated by a practical lamp or window. Note the eye light, designed to draw the audience to her face, the source of the story. The contrast ratio and texture of the space—along with a consistent color temperature—adds to the cinematic feel of the shot. "You can certainly be moody with the lighting," Bricker notes, "but it needs to be naturalistic and cohesive with the documentary footage."
(Image ©2016 Netflix.)

3. Food symphony

The beauty shots of the plated dishes are the "most expressionistic part of the episodes," Bricker says. It's the main food photography part of the shoot and with fewer narrative demands from each shot, there's greater room for outside-the-box creativity, he explains. With the Dominique episode, they focused on the poetry as the form of expression they would use for the food symphony section, because of the poetic stories she presents on cards with the food at her restaurant in San Francisco. Bricker adds, "We wanted the light to feel soft but moody. I don't like flat, overlit food. I like food to have shadow." (See Figure 3.32.)

Light quality, intensity, direction, and texture: In this sequence, we see a mix of interview shots (cuts 6, 9, 12, 14, and 17) intercut with food prep and the stages of food preparation (1–5, 7, 8, 10, 11, 13, 15, and 16). Slow motion is utilized in the food shots, as well as a strong use of light and shadow. Bricker explains that he does not like flat, overlit food, but wants to use shadows, which we can see shaped in the final food shot from this sequence (18, 20). And we can see how the low angle of light captures the top of the dish and food—allowing for shadows to fall off around the food that's inside the dish. A light placed directly over the food would have flattened the image and removed the texture of shadows provided by the side light, which also reinforces the texture and cinematic quality of the food itself. A archive photo provides historial context with Crenn as a child (19). Cuts 1–3 include Crenn's poetry that she displays with her food at her restaurant. (See close-up in Figure 3.33, p. 184–185.)

Contrast ratio: The contrast ratio remains high as we see shadows fall into the blacks, while the light glints across the food with some nice soft highlights. Interview shots clip at the back window.

Color temperature: The balanced temperature sculpts a cohesive look to the food. It's engages a white daylight balance, providing a stimulating environment.

FIGURE 3.32 (facing page)
One of the food symphony sequences from *Chef's Table* ("Dominique Crenn"). The lighting and their approach to shooting is expressionistic. DP Adam Bricker.
(Image ©2016 Netflix.)

VISUAL STORYTELLING THROUGH LIGHTING   CHAPTER 3   185

FIGURE 3.33
A final shot in one of the food symphony sequences from *Chef's Table* ("Dominique Crenn"). Take note of how side lighting provides texture through shadow placement. DP Adam Bricker. (Image ©2016 Netflix.)

FIGURE 3.34
In this shot from Netflix's *Chef's Table* ("Dominique Crenn"), we see how cinematographer Adam Bricker utilizes the sun as a back/rim light as Crenn inspects shrimp at Half Moon Bay. (Image ©2016 Netflix.)

Outdoor cinematography tip from DP Adam Bricker
It's important to make conscious choices to set yourself up for creative success in an outdoor shoot. Make storytelling choices about the time of day and the camera's positioning to the subject and the sun. Shooting documentary, you're trying to make as many creative choices as you can without getting in the way of the pace. There are no textbook right or wrong choices—but you want to be making and controlling decisions. Then you're telling a story, you're creating a mood, you're creating a tone. It becomes deliberate and cohesive.

Having the sun directly behind Dominique Crenn when she's walking in San Francisco feeling free, loving the city, and reflecting on her life—having the sun behind her flaring the lens supports that story. But you could also do the exact opposite of that and have the sun directly in her face. It could be aggressive or blinding and that could be a different choice—and that could help tell a different story. There's really no definitive way to do it. You just want to be thinking about what you're doing, making a conscious decision on how you're going to shoot. You could use a bounce board or a reflector and return a little light if that helps tell your story. You don't want to be using a reflector just to use it. Instead, make a conscious decision as to why you're doing that and you'll get a great deal more meaning from your efforts. (See Figure 3.34, background image on this page.)

Section review
1. Describe the three styles of lighting found in *Chef's Table*.
2. How do these lighting styles help shape the story?

This chapter provided an overview of lighting choices for fiction and nonfiction shoots. It was not intended as an exhaustive overview of the different types of lights that can be used. Once you understand how to use the six elements of lighting in support of the story, then you could, for example, use bright work lights from a hardware store, some black wrap to control light spill, and white and black bounce boards—to control the shape of the light you want (or use high-end lights). The types of lights are not nearly as important as understanding the dramatic elements of the scene and then making the right choices in placing light and shadow to visually bring out or enhance the emotions found in the story (which is tied to visual blocking and composition with the right lens choice).

We defined the terms needed for the role of light in a scene:

- Key
- Fill
- Back and rim
- Background

We also explored key terms of lighting from the perspective of receiving enough information to inform dramatic decisions in a workshop style approach:

- Light quality
- Intensity
- Direction
- Texture
- Contrast
- Color temperature

In addition, we looked at the concept of exposure and how we can control it, using a histograms and waveforms to monitor light levels. We also examined how scrims and lights were used in Joe Simon's "Fragments," allowing us to see how he set up these shots and what each shot looked like from the indoor and outside setups. This was also applied to an outdoor case study examination of a scene from *Jessica Jones*, along with the choices DP Manuel Billeter made.

We also took a section of a scene from Ozu's *Tokyo Twilight*, as reinterpreted by my students and me, giving a dramatic analysis of the scene. We then applied the dramatic understanding of the scene to the lighting setup and provided a lighting plot of one of the shots.

Lastly, we examined Adam Bricker's cinematography in an episode of *Chef's Table*, "Dominique Crenn," providing tips and thought processes behind a working cinematographer in one of the best lit documentaries produced in contemporary documentary filmmaking.

WORKS CITED

Chimera. "A Marvel DP: A Discussion on Cinematography with Manuel Billeter on Lighting *Jessica Jones* for Netflix." Chimera Chasing Light Blog. N.D. www.chimeralighting.com/marvel-dp-discussion-cinematography-manuel-billeter-lighting-jessica-jones-netflix

Fauer, Jon. *Cinematographer Style: The Complete Interviews, Vol. 1*. American Society of Cinematographers, 2008.

Knoop, Martine. "Dynamic Lighting for Well-Being in the Work Places: Addressing the Visual, Emotional, and Biological Aspects of Lighting Design." Proceedings of the Fifteenth International Symposium Lighting Engineering. Slovenija. 2006: 63–74. www.researchgate.net/publication/237105345_Dynamic_lighting_for_well-being_in_work_places_Addressing_the_visual_emotional_and_biological_aspects_of_lighting_design

Kyriacou, C.P. and Hastings, M.H. "Circadian clocks: Genes, sleep, and cognition." *Trends in Cognitive Science* 14 (2010): 259–267.

Lancaster, Kurt. "Manuel Billeter interview." 11 May 2018. Personal notes from a phone interview.

Netflix. "AKA Ladies Night." *Jessica Jones*. Marvel and ABC Studios, 2015. DP: Manuel Billeter. www.netflix.com/title/80002311

Netflix. "Dominique Crenn." *Chef's Table*. 2.4. Chef's Pictures One, 2015. www.netflix.com/title/80075152

Seymour, Mike. "Red Centre Podcast: Red Day & Shane Hurlbut." Fxguide.com. #56. 15 February 2010. https://fxguide.com/quicktakes/red-centre-podcast-out-red-day-shane-hurlbut

Tomassoni, R., Galetta, G., and Treglia, E. "Psychology of Light: How Light Influences the Health and Psyche." *Psychology* 6 (2015): 1216–1222. http://dx.doi.org/10.4236/psych.2015.610119 *and* http://file.scirp.org/pdf/PSYCH_2015080510351792.pdf

Viera, D. and Viera, M. *Lighting for Film and Digital Cinematography*. Wadsworth, 2005.

Behind the scenes photo from cinematography classroom exercise with a Canon C200 shooting in RAW. Performers: Kelcie Weber and Eric Carver.
(Image courtesy of the author.)

CHAPTER 4

VISUAL STORYTELLING WITH CAMERA LOG, RAW, AND LUTs

Filmmakers used to shoot on film, where the speed of a particular film stock was fixed (ISO), and lights had to be carefully measured with a light meter. Film was shipped off to labs, processed, and returned for dailies and editing. Color timers would adjust the exposure and color of the film. Although shooting on film is still an option for some, most have now shifted to digital filmmaking. Software tools placed inside cameras (as well as in editing and coloring software) allow shooters to help overcome the limitations of digital film acquisition, such as a lack of smooth roll-off in shadows and highlights, image artifacts caused by noise levels, the results of a limited dynamic range, and so forth.

In-camera software tools manipulate how an image and the corresponding color and luminosity values get compressed (allowing for more storage space on media), or not if the camera is recording uncompressed RAW. In either case, settings on the camera can determine how color gets seen, such as processing with a color range (or gamut) for high definition video (standardized as Rec. 709) or for 4K and 8K (Rec. 2020 for standard dynamic range and Rec. 2100 for high dynamic range).

Furthermore, these color gamut standards may be "baked" into the image as it's recorded or they may just be used as a reference that can be altered later in post. Some camera settings allow you to shoot flat in "log," where the linear signal of light is turned into logarithmic curve data in order to squeeze more dynamic range out of a camera's sensor. To overcome the flat look of the image while shooting, LUTs are used to compensate for this flat image so the cinematographer can see what the final image could look like in post.

Finally, RAW, whether compressed or uncompressed, simply takes the visual data off the sensor without using any type of baked in look, utilizing metadata that can be fully manipulated in post by adjusting color and exposure values.

Knowing what these different modes of shooting are and how they impact post means that we must understand what lies beneath the "hood" of a camera. This chapter examines the heart of a camera, then goes into the purposes behind shooting in log, RAW, and with LUTs—the advantages and disadvantages of each. Here's the topical outline of this chapter:

1. Overview of a dozen key camera features
2. Shooting in log
3. Shooting in RAW
4. Shooting with LUTs

Some cinematography books go into how to use specific cameras and provide an overview of their features and limitations, but since this type of material can be found in manuals and on the web, this book does not go into specific cameras. However, what is covered in Section 1 of this chapter can be applied to any camera, since it helps you to understand what the major features of cameras are. With that knowledge, you can intelligently understand what to look for in a camera.

Out of all of the chapters in this book, this is the most technical, but an understanding of how to use key tools in a camera is the foundation to understanding what camera you should choose in support of a story.

SECTION 1: AN OVERVIEW OF A DOZEN KEY CAMERA FEATURES

Instead of describing specific cameras, this section provides an overview of what to look for in any camera you get. Most professional cinematographers don't buy their own camera. They rent them based on the job, the needs of the client or production. But there are many low-budget filmmakers and many who work at client-based production houses that do purchase cameras. Whether renting or owning, with evolving camera technology—and manufacturers release new cameras or update older models nearly every year—it's important to understand what to look for in a camera, the key features, and core elements, which are similar across different camera manufacturers and models.

No matter what camera you decide to shoot on, the important elements include the sensor size, resolution, frame rate, type of shutter, dynamic range, compression codecs, lens mount, and audio quality—I'll describe what these mean, below. (If you're recording sound separately, the audio quality isn't as important.)

1. Lens mount

Different cameras come with different lens mounts based on the brands of cameras: Canon, Sony, Panasonic, Olympus, and so forth. Some companies use other manufactures' lenses. For example, Blackmagic Design release cameras with Canon's EF mounts and MFT (Micro Four-Thirds), as well as PL mounts, which are standard for professional cinema lenses. MFT mount cameras are used on smaller sensor cameras. In many ways your choice of lenses will determine the type of lens mount you need, and, perhaps, the camera you may end up using. Some manufacturers create mount adapters, so that, for example, you can even attach high-end PL-mount cinema lenses to some DSLRs.

2. Sensor type

CCD (Charged Coupled Device)

This contains a global shutter that captures the entire frame at the same moment. High-end cameras, scientific instruments, and even older model video cameras, used CCDs, but they're more expensive to make. Joe Rubinstein, who designed the Digital Bolex D16 camera, explains: "The pixels that are next to each other on CCD sensors effect each other. When one pixel overflows with energy it effects the pixels around it. The pixels work together as a unit, much the way chemicals on a film plane do. We believe this gives the sensor a more organic look" (personal interview). There is less light sensitivity with CCDs and, due to the expense, most camera manufacturers use CMOS sensors. (The CCD sensor for the Digital Bolex, for example, costs about $1000.)

CMOS (Complementary Metal Oxide Semiconductor)

These relatively inexpensive sensors are good in low light, and allow for high frame rate recording. The pixels are read linearly from top left to bottom right while the shutter is open. Due to this delay of the top to bottom scan, these sensors tend to express a rolling shutter, where parts of a fast moving object may appear to bend in the frame. Thus, under certain conditions, there may be issues of skewing, spatial aliasing, and temporal aliasing. In most cases cinematographers shooting under normal conditions will not be faced with these issues.

However, manufacturers are finding new ways to place global shutter options on their CMOS sensor cameras through evolving technology, so the entire image can be scanned, avoiding the limitation of the rolling shutter. For example, Sony states how their new sensor, announced in winter 2018, uses analog/digital converters underneath each pixel and they "instantly convert the analog signal from all the simultaneously exposed pixels in parallel to a digital signal to temporarily store it in digital memory"—preventing "the image distortion (focal plane distortion) specific to CMOS image sensors that read pixel signals row by row" (Sony, 2018).

3. Sensor size

The sensor size is measured in millimeters, while the resolution of the sensor represents how many pixels are being used. In some cameras, such as Blackmagic's Ursa Mini, you can set the resolution on their super 35mm (S35mm) sensor to 4.6K, 4K, 2K, full HD, or even less, while the Digital Bolex, shoots 2K and full HD on a 16mm size sensor. The sensor size affects how the focal length of lenses determine the field of view. In the cinema world, the S35mm is the standard by which other sensors get measured. (See Figure 4.1, next page.)

See www.abelcine.com/fov/ for a visual reference guide where you can determine different cameras' fields of views based on the focal length of the lens.

Full frame
This frame is the size of old school 35mm photography film (but not 35mm cinema film). Some manufacturers released the full frame sensor on certain cinema cameras, such as the Canon C700 FF and the ARRI ALEXA LF, for example. Due to the larger sensor, filmmakers can get really shallow depth of field when shooting wide open apertures. You don't need a full frame sensor camera if you're going for a standard S35mm cinema look.

Cropped frame
In the photography world, this refers to a sensor size different than the full frame 35mm, such as the APS-C sensor, which results in a 1.6× change in focal length when compared to a full frame sensor (a 50mm lens on a full frame sensor will appear to be 80mm on a cropped sensor). Most DSLRs, including the Canon 70D and 80D, and so forth, utilize cropped frame sensors, but these are actually close in size to the S35mm sensor.

S35mm
This is the cinema standard, found in the Alexa cameras, Canon's Cinema EOS line (such as the C200 and C300), Blackmagic Design's URSA mini, among others. Cinematographers consider this to be the standard frame size.

Micro Four-Thirds (MFT)
A smaller format found on many mirrorless cameras (such as Panasonic's GH5 and Blackmagic Design's Pocket Cinema Camera 4K). Because it is a smaller sensor, the shallow depth of field is less.

Super 16mm
The 16mm sensor mimics the look of 16mm film, a size used in many portable film cameras found in documentary work in the 1960s and 1970s. This is the sensor size found on the Digital Bolex D16 and the original Blackmagic Pocket Cinema Camera.

SENSOR SIZES &

Measurements are in m
"D" = Diagonal in mm of sensor or film area (same
Number of Pixels on horizintal axis repr

2/3" video
8.8 x 6.6
D - 11
HD

Super 16mm Film & Blackmagic Pocket
12.5 x 7
D - 14.33
HD

Blackmagic 2.5K
15.8 x 8.8
D - 18.09
2.5K

Panasonic GH5 Micro Four Thirds
17.3 x 13
D - 21.64
4K

RED RAVE
23.04 x 10
D - 25.45
4.5K

Sony NEX
23.5 x 15.6
D - 28.21
4K

Panasonic VariCam 35 & VariCam LT
24.5 x 12.9
D - 27.78
4K

Canon C100, C200, C300, C500
24.6 x 13.8
D - 28.21
HD / 4K

Brackmagic U Mini Pro 4.6
25.34 x 14.2
D - 29.07
4.6K

RED Helium 8K FF
29.90 x 15.77
D - 33.80
8K

RED Dragon 6K FF
30.7 x 15.8
D - 34.53
6K

Full Frame 35mm Film, Sony Venice, ARRI Alexa LF Sony a7SII, Canon 5D MK IV
36 x 24
D - 43.27

6K - Sony Venice
4.4K - ARRI Alexa LF
4K - Sony a7S II
4K - Canon 5D MKIV
4K - Nikon D850

FORMATS

...dth × height
...ameter of image circle needed to cover it)
...ed in Ks (HD = 1920 × 1080)

Canon 7D Mark II
22.4 × 15
D - 26.8
5.5K Stills / HD Video

Sony FS5, FS7, F5, F55
24 × 12.7
D - 27.15
4K

ARRI ALEXA 16x9
23.76 × 13.37
D - 27.26
2.8K

ARRI ALEXA 4:3 mode
23.76 × 17.82
D - 29.70
2.8K

Super 35mm Film 4 Perf (4:3)
24.89 × 18.66
D - 31.10
FILM

ARRI ALEXA Open Gate mode
28.17 × 18.13
D - 33.52
3.4K

RED MONSTRO VV 8K FF / RED WEAPON VV 8K FF Panavision DXL
40.96 × 21.6
D - 47.19
8K

ARRI ALEXA 65
54.12 × 25.59
D - 59.87
6.5K

FIGURE 4.1
This chart provides an overview of comparable sensor sizes and resolutions across a variety of popular cameras. Note that the sensor size does not determine resolution, since manufacturers squeeze more pixels into the same area to increase resolution. (Typos in original.)
(LaFleur, 2018.)
(Chart ©2018 Mark LaFleur. Used with permission.)

4. Resolution: Full HD, 2K, 4K, 8K

The number of pixels used to record. The higher the number the higher the resolution. Full HD is 1920×1080 and is the current standard for Blu-ray DVDs and broadcast television. 2K is cinema quality for projection. 4K is starting to become the new standard and more televisions are being made with 4K. (See Figure 4.1, p. 196-197.)

There are several benefits to shooting in 4K:

1. Future proof. Store your film or project in 4K so it's ready when there's a larger market for it.

2. Cropping a shot. The editor, producer, or director may want to crop an image and if you have a large area of resolution (such as 4K or higher), then the image can be cropped or recomposed for an HD or 2K projection without losing any data, which can cause aliasing. As 4K becomes the standard, this will, perhaps, be the *only* advantage for shooting above 4K resolution.

3. Fixing unwanted jerky motion in a shot. Editing software can smooth out wobbly shots. If you're shooting in full HD or 2K (or higher than 4K for a 4K image output), the stabilization software shares and grabs data around the frame of the problem shot in order to stabilize it. If there's no space around the shot, then the image will lose some resolution, but if there's a lot of space around it, then it can pull data from the larger resolution without impacting the output resolution.

4. For virtual reality (VR) work or projecting onto large immersive screens, high resolutions (4K and above) will be a benefit.

Notice that I didn't list "more cinematic" as a reason to shoot in 4K! Increased resolution does not make an image more cinematic. Indeed, most people will not notice the difference between 2K and 4K. According to Steve Yedlin, ASC, the eye itself cannot really distinguish these resolution differences under normal viewing conditions. Yedlin argues that what *looks* like higher resolution is increased image sharpening. He notes:

> The reality is that the normal, non-superhuman eye really can't see the difference between 2K and 4K at any comfortable Screen-Size-to-Viewing-Distance ratio (I mean, MAYBE you can see the difference if you sit in the very front row of a theater, which is such a poor film-going experience anyway that everyone avoids it—but for any normal, comfortable viewing in theater or at home, it makes no difference).

Almost all 4k images are mastered with artificial sharpening (sometimes in-camera, sometimes in-post, sometimes in-monitor, and sometimes a combination of all three)—that's because the merchants making the 4k stuff want to trumpet that 4k makes it better so they can sell TVs and projectors and disk players and stuff, but when they see that it literally doesn't actually look any different than 2k (to the human eye), they realize they can't sell it and so have to do something to it to make it stand out and make the consumer say 'wow.'

So, they add artificial sharpening. Which is ironic since 4k is supposed to be 'better quality' or 'more fidelity,' and artificial sharpening is itself a degradation of quality and fidelity—and it's also something that could just as easily be added to HD or 2k content. But I believe that this artificial sharpening and not true resolution is the biggest difference that's actually visible in most cases (I'm not saying whether or not the actual resolution exists, just that it's not what's visible to a viewer). (Yedlin, n.d.)

His argument about camera resolution is worth the read. (See Yedlin, 2016 and Haine, 2017.)

5. Dynamic range

The ability of a sensor to record in a range of dark to bright without losing information in the extreme ranges. If a camera has a dynamic range of 12 stops, it means that it can capture a range of detail from dark to light within this 12 stop range. If the scene is beyond a 12 stop range, then the values above these 12 stops will not be recorded. The darks will either go black (crushed) or the brights will go all white (blown-out or clipped), depending on which side you expose the image.

Typically, you'll want to expose for the highlights, since data can be recovered in the dark regions—while impossible with clipped shots. Some cameras can record images in a "flat" log mode. Using mathematical processes, log modes spread equal levels of image data along the full dynamic range, making the image appear flat or washed out onscreen. It's designed for postproduction work by which you pull this data out in the highlights and the shadows, recovering a larger dynamic range and allowing for greater color grading. As noted in the previous chapter on lighting, you can read general exposure data if you use false color, histogram, or waveform, which shows the intensity of darks to lights on a scale on a camera's monitor. This allows you to adjust the exposure if you're clipping values in the whites or crushing the blacks. (If you crush blacks and recover the data, it'll be noisy, but if you clip the highlights, they're gone forever.)

6. Frame rate

The film standard is 24fps (frames per second); NTSC Television is 30fps and PAL television is 25fps (these are based on the electrical current rates of 60Hz and 50Hz cycles, depending on what country you shoot in). High frame rates allow you to create slow motion shots, since you're getting more data and conforming it to 24fps: putting more images into the same space slows them and vice versa (shooting at 16 fps, will cause a faster rate). The higher the frame rate, the slower the playback of motion. A 60fps rate will give you a pleasant, smooth slow motion. For certain scenes and shots, this is an important tool for filmmakers. Frame rates that show 23.97 or 29.97 refer to the space needed for a television broadcast to carry an audio signal.

7. Shutter angle/speed

A standard look to your footage will be a shutter angle of 180 degrees or 1/48th per second shutter speed (with a 24fps frame rate). This is half of a circle standard in a film camera as the shutter rotates, letting in half the light in a single rotation. The smaller the angle, such as 90 or 45 degrees (or the higher the shutter speed, such as 1/500th), the more staccato the look with minimum motion blur; the larger the angle, such as 270 degrees (or the lower the shutter speed, such as 1/24th), the smoother the look with increased motion blur.

Shane Hurlbut, ASC, describes the shutter angle this way:

> Imagine a pie, and that pie has 24 pieces. If the film plane or digital sensor in your camera were to always to see the lens, this would be shutterless. Nothing is obstructing its view with a 360-degree shutter. To the best of my knowledge, this can only be done on digital cameras, unless you pull the shutter physically out of a film camera. At 360 degrees, you will have a lot of motion blur in your action because as an actor moves his arm or his drumstick you are seeing it on all 24 pieces of the pie. If you were to use a 180-degree shutter, which has become the industry standard at 24fps, you would see motion blur that we have all come accustomed to in the theater. At 180 degrees, the film plane or digital sensor at 1/50 or more exacting 1/48 sec of a second would be seeing the drumstick on 12 out of the 24 pieces. (Hurlbut, n.d.)

8. Color space and color gamut

Although not technically a feature of a camera, the cinematographer should be aware of the what the camera does within the limits of the color space it records. Human eyes see a large range of colors, but cameras do not record as much information as the eyes take in, so certain standards have been applied to how color is reproduced and represented in cameras (as well as in print, television sets, and for computer monitors, among other forms of technology). Each of these uses a different color model, such as RGB for monitors and CMYK for print.

A color gamut limits the range of colors calibrated within a color space. Examples include: Rec. 709, Rec. 2010, and DCI-P3. (See Figure 4.2.) The target color gamut uses a color model (such as RGB, which is a "convention for encoding and recording color information") (Simple DCP, 2016).

The Rec. 709 color gamut, for example, is one of these standards designed for standard high definition television (1080p). It contains a range of color within the RGB color model (usually the Adobe RGB color space); the specific footprint of colors within the RGB color space—defined as three specific points of red, green, and blue, along with a defined white point (the mapping of the colors), known as the color gamut. Rec. 2020 is the standard developed for ultra high definition in 4K, while DCI-P3 expresses the 2K color gamut for cinema projectors.

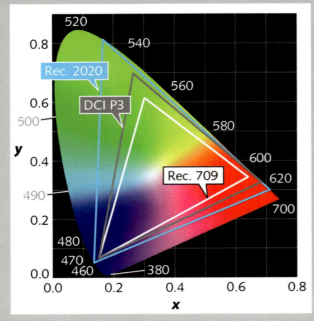

FIGURE 4.2
A chromaticity diagram showing the full range of colors that the average human eye can see, along with the range of colors mapped and defined as the Rec. 2020 color gamut (for 4K ultra high definition), Rec. 709 (for standard high definition, 1080p), and DCI-P3 (2K) for digital film projection in cinemas. The D65 point refers to a standard white point (measured at 6500K), found at the white convergence point at the center of the chart.

(Image courtesy of W. Conard Holton. ©2017 Laser Focus World. Used with permission.)

9. Compression and bit depth

Every consumer camera and DSLRs in video mode records in 8-bit H.264 codec (compression/decompression algorithm). The term 8-bit means there are 256 points of data per pixel, and H.264 is a compression standard engineers created to make the image look great with a small file size—which means the image is compressed. (The H.265 compression scheme is the standard for compressed 4K options.) It looks good in a small file size, because it is a finishing codec designed for online streaming and with Blu-ray DVDs. Manufacturers use these in consumer and lower end cinema cameras so a lot more data can be recorded onto memory cards. But they're not good for editing, since data is being shared across images. When you import these compressed files into your video editing software, they're typically decompressed for editing, increasing the file size into Apple's ProRes or equivalent codec (4:2:2—a note about this on p. 203). This isn't really a big issue if you get the look of the shot in camera accurate (proper color balance and exposure, for example). If your color and exposure are inaccurate, you can tweak the image a bit in post to correct some issues, but the images quickly fall apart if you push or pull exposure too far or alter the colors too much, because there's not enough data within the compressed image to recover details.

Treat 8-bit like negative reversal film stock (if you're old school). High-end professional cameras, and some of the cheaper cinema cameras, such as Blackmagic Design's cameras, can shoot in ProRes at different compression rates. An 8-bit compression contains 256 points of info (4:2:0 and 4:2:2), 10-bits contain 1024 pieces of data (4:2:2), and 12-bits (4:4:4) is uncompressed containing 4096 bits of data per pixel. The less the compression, the more data you get and more headroom you'll have in post to make corrections and adjust the look and feel of your project during color grading. Other cameras use uncompressed and compressed forms of RAW, providing the best quality image, but requiring a lot of recording and storage space (2K recording at uncompressed RAW will click in at about 500GB for about 90 minutes of recording).

The higher the bit depth the deeper the colors and wider the exposure latitude. There's a certain thickness to the image when shooting in 12-bits, making it comparable in some ways to the feel of analog film.

10. Chroma subsampling

The eye perceives the nuance of brightness more than color. To take advantage of this, chroma (or color) subsampling compresses color information to save space. In this type of compression, there's one piece of information for luminance (brightness) and two for color (chrominance). The numbers represent the one brightness sample rate (given as a 4) and two color sample rates among a group of pixels (given as a 0: no sample; 2: half sample; or 4: full sample, no compression). All pixels get full brightness or luma values, thus these sequences always begin as 4. (When there's a fourth number 4, that represents the chroma channel for those doing green screen work.)

4:4:4

All light and colors are sampled at the same rate. There is no subsampling, so this provides the strongest or deepest color sample for postproduction work.

4:2:2

In a four pixel sample, all the luma values are used (4), but only half the color data (2:2) are used. The image is considered very good and nearly indistinguishable from 4:4:4—except when you need to do heavy post work, when the image will fall apart into blocky, noisy artifacts, and banding across colors.

4:2:0

Same level of luminance, but now half the color data of 4:2:2. The image will fall apart quickly in post if you have to make changes to the image—so the importance of getting the image correct in camera.

11. Audio quality

Don't skimp on audio. Poorly recorded audio is the number one killer of a project. For this reason, you must be able to see levels on a meter and listen to the audio being recorded on headphones. Either you're doing this yourself or you're hiring a sound recordist to do this. There are no shortcuts to good audio. Some settings to keep in mind:

- 24-bit audio should be the standard (as opposed to many cameras still using 16-bit)—more data gives you better headroom in post. It doesn't matter if it's 48kHz or 96kHz, just as long as you have the higher bit rate for increased headroom.

- XLR inputs are a must, giving low interference, and low impedance. It's the professional standard. If your camera doesn't have an XLR connector, then you'll want a field mixer and/or recorder with XLR connections, resulting in the recording of audio separate from audio in camera. The 1/8 inch inputs found on many DSLRs, the C100 with the top handle removed, and the original Blackmagic Pocket Cinema Camera are high impedance (which can pick up noise) and are not used by professionals. It's ok to use such mics for reference audio.

If your camera doesn't have good audio recording, use an external audio recorder to get strong and clean audio. It's best to have a dedicated sound recordist, but, when you can't, dedicated audio recorders will give you better audio than the camera.

12. Other

Other pro features on cameras include a built-in waveform monitor, the ability to sync time code, taps for professional battery connections, focus assist, autofocus features (for tracking focus on a moving subject, which is important for some documentary filmmakers), and so forth. Most of these are not necessary in creating a strong cinematic image, since good exposure, color balance, and lighting are the most important features for controlling the look of a project. These other elements become convenient extras. A cinematographer who understands visual storytelling will shoot a better-looking film on an 8-bit DSLR than a newbie with an ARRI ALEXA recording in 12-bit RAW, because the fundamental skills of storytelling and how to use the basic tools, as noted throughout this book, provides the foundation for creating strong cinematic storytelling, whether it's a commercial, a client based promotional film, a documentary, or a feature narrative film.

Section review
1. What key features should you look for in a camera? Define each (there are at least 11).
2. What is bit depth and why is it important in cinematography?
3. Which is more important, high camera resolution or high bit depth? Defend your position.
4. How should you prepare and shoot on an 8-bit camera?

SECTION 2: SHOOTING IN LOG
What is it?

Light affects digital sensors in a linear way—twice the light gets twice the data—to get something 4 times brighter, it'll need 16 times the amount of light, for example. This is what f-stops do—each stop range is a halving or doubling of the amount of light, depending if you're opening the aperture or closing it. In an 8-bit recording, cinematographer Phil Rhodes notes, the linear data would translate values of black at 2 through to whites at 256 bits of information (2–4–8–16–32–64–128–256) (Rhodes, 2017). Black is only getting 2 pieces of digital data, while white is getting 128 or half the data. Most of the data that are being recorded from the sensor fall in the highlights.

Neither film nor our eyes react to light intensity in a linear way. Double the light and our eyes (and film) don't perceive this change as *twice* as much light, but only as a fraction—we're receiving the information on a logarithmic scale. When applied to cameras, the data spreads out evenly so the blacks contain the same amount of data as the whites. On an 8-bit camera, there would be 32 pieces of data, while on a 10-bit camera there would be 64. (See Figure 4.3.)

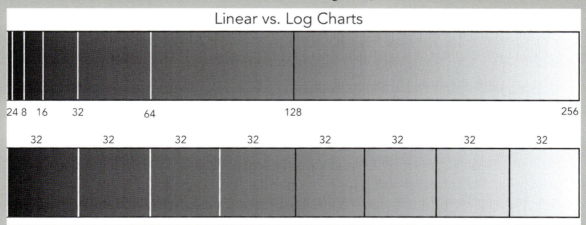

FIGURE 4.3
In an 8-bit linear scale, *top*, each f-stop doubles (or halves) the amount of light, providing linear data values of 2, 4, 8, 16, 32, 64, 128, 256. That's 2 pieces of information for the blacks, while the brightest value gets 128 pieces of the data, or half the pie. With little data in the blacks, where the eye perceives the most nuance, there's not much data to play with; there's a lot of data in the whites, where the eye perceives little nuance.

The log scale, *bottom*, fixes this issue, so that in an 8-bit system, there are 32 pieces of information spread evenly throughout the range (256/8 = 32). (Rhodes, 2017)

(Graph created by the author, inspired by Rhodes, 2017.)

By spreading out the data evenly, the linear data becomes a log curve. (See Figure 4.4.)

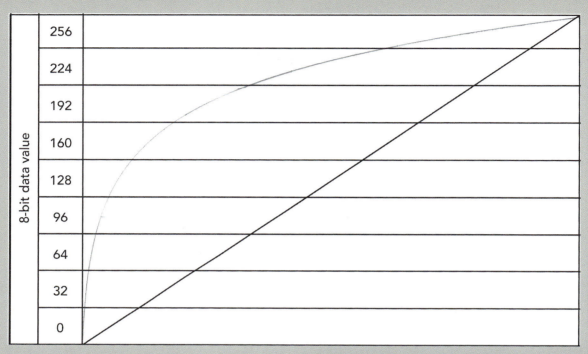

FIGURE 4.4
Here are the same data placed on a graph for an 8-bit linear vs. log scale with black on the left and white on the right. Rhodes notes how the log curve "version rushes quickly up through the shadow detail, ensuring dimmer picture information represented with a reasonable number of code values, then flattens in the highlights, reducing the number of values used to represent them. The same number of values are used per stop. It's also intuitive to see here why log images look so low in contrast: blacks are massively lifted" (Rhodes, 2017). This is why contrast needs to be added to log footage during post.

(Graph created by author, inspired by Rhodes, 2017.)

Rhodes explains:

> Converting the data such that each f-stop occupies the same range of values is straightforward, a base-2 logarithm, such that doubling the light falling on an object exposed at (say) value 32 moves it to value 64, and doubling it again moves it to value 96. In this graph, we can see the output of a notional linear 8-bit camera (let's say there are 12 stops of dynamic range between "black" and "white"), […], and the effect logarithmic processing has on the data, […]. (Rhodes, 2017)

However, the resulting recorded image looks flat, perceived as a milky, washed-out look. The image needs to be processed (with a LUT, or look-up table, on an external monitor) in order to see the intended result while shooting. Contrast needs to be applied in post as part of the color correction process. Film, when processed, results in a characteristic curve, which includes the gamma—the angle of the slope of the straight part of the curve—which determines the contrast of the image. The shoulder indicates the point where the highlights roll off into white and the toe reveals the point where the shadows roll off into black. The straight part of the slope also indicates the film's latitude (or dynamic range). (See Figure 4.5.)

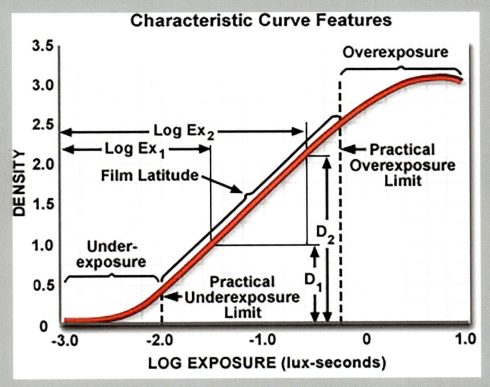

FIGURE 4.5
The characteristic curve of film—the measure of light and the density of the film after processing, revealing the film's overall latitude on the straight part of the slope (known as the gamma), as well as where the exposure rolls off into the shadows (toe) and highlights (shoulder) (Abramowitz and Davidson, 2000).

(Graph by ©Molecular Expressions at Florida State University. Used with permission.)

Expose to avoid shadow noise in log

Because the shadows lift when shooting in log, the shadows deepen when adding a contrast curve in post, there tends to be more noise. To solve this problem, expose more of the highlights, but be careful not to overexpose! When the contrast curve is added and you're pulling the shadows in post, the noise will be less (see Hardy, 2015). By opening the f-stop of the camera by one or two stops this increases the amount of recorded digital data—f/16, for example, lets in 32 times less light than an aperture set to f/2.8, therefore it's using less data. So if you have room in your exposure range to overexpose a stop or two (without, again, blowing out the highlights), then you have more data or headroom in post; therefore, a metered reading of f/16 might be recorded at f/11 or f/8, for example. "Essentially, by exposing a stop or two brighter [...], then pulling down the exposure in post, you can ensure that your image will have much cleaner shadows" (Hardy, 2015).

See Figure 4.6 (p. 209) for an example of log footage and the postprocess footage by Italian cinematographer, Matteo Bertoli. Here, Bertoli's log footage allows details to be pulled out of the highlights and shadows. He believes that, for those who are learning how to use log, the $15 FiLMiC Pro app for smartphones is a good tool. He adds, "From a colorist point of view this is huge and will also allow beginner filmmakers or cinematographers to experiment in postproduction without spending a fortune for a camera" (Bertoli, 2017).

You'll need to do research when shooting log on different cameras, since each one expresses a different response. For example, Canon provides three different log curves in some of their cameras (such as the C200 and C300). Canon Log, for example, is an 8-bit curve providing 13.5 stops of dynamic range, while Canon Log 2 is a 10-bit curve giving a 15 stop range. Canon Log 3 is designed for minimum grading, providing a 14 stop range.

When to shoot log

Shoot with a log curve under high contrast conditions, especially when you need the extra dynamic range—or latitude—for your scene. This will eke out additional latitude on the sensor (spreading the data over 14 stops, for example), but it will require you to add a contrast curve to the footage in post, creating a film-like characteristic curve. If you do not add contrast your end result will be a milky-white wash on your image, so be sure to add that step into your post workflow!

VISUAL STORYTELLING WITH CAMERA LOG, RAW, AND LUTs   CHAPTER 4   209

FIGURE 4.6
The top image shows the log footage where the image is flat (and the background looks blown out). The bottom shot reveals the image after contrast was added. Take note how the highlights were recovered, allowing us to see details and texture in most of the clouds. This was shot on an iPhone 7 Plus using FiLMiC Pro app. Stats: 24fps, 100mb, 2.59 aspect ratio, log mode. Graded in DaVinci Resolve with FilmConvert (a plugin tool for software that emulates film stock).
(Images ©2017 Matteo Bertoli Visuals. Used with permission.)

When not to shoot log

If you're shooting in a limited dynamic range, such as when it is dark and the contrast ratio is low, then shoot normally, since the low dynamic range is not going to give you any advantage in log mode and will actually make the footage noisier. If your environment is controlled and you've set the levels of your lights properly, setting up a 6-stop dynamic range, for example, then you should not shoot in log. Cinematographer and Digital Imaging Technician (DIT) Alister Chapman explains that in low contrast situations:

> If you can expose correctly with a 14 stop recording bucket like log you are only using a little over 35% of the available data and that's a terrible waste. You won't have much data to help you separate out any noise from the desired picture information in postproduction and because your recorded signal is small any compression noise will be relatively big in comparison to the picture information.
>
> This is when it's time to abandon log and go back to a conventional gamma curve. You don't need log when the scene only has a limited dynamic range. If you use Rec-709, which has a 6-stop range (without any knee) instead of log, at the same ISO, then now, instead of recording using only 35% of the available data, you will be using almost 85% of the available data, and that's going to give you much more real picture information to work with in postproduction. You will get a much better end result by not using log. (Chapman, 2015; quote edited for syntax)

The reason for this? Chapman notes how you lose data along each step of a large dynamic range. For example, if you have a 14-stop dynamic range when shooting in log, then there will be less overall data than when shooting in a lower dynamic range, because you're still dealing with a certain number of bits (256 in 8-bit compression and 1024 in a 10-bit compression). Spread 1024 among 14 stops and you have 73.14 pieces of data (per pixel), which could be used for the shades of color and exposure in post. Using a 10-stop range, you're working with 102.4 bits of data, over 70 percent more than using a 14-stop range (Chapman, 2015).

When to shoot Rec. 709 and Rec. 2020

If your postproduction time is limited, such as same day news footage, then you may not have any time to do additional post work, other than editing and doing primary color correction (if any at all), then shoot in Rec. 709. In low light conditions, in a controlled environment, or when shooting in low-contrast scenes within 5 to 6 stops, then shoot Rec. 709. (Rec. 2020 will become the standard in the future as it records a wide color gamut and becomes a 4K standard.)

Section review
1. What is the difference between linear shooting and log shooting?
2. When should you shoot in log and under what conditions? Why?
3. How should you expose a log image if you want to avoid noise?
4. When should you avoid shooting in log? Why?

SECTION 3: SHOOTING IN RAW
What is it?

When shooting Rec. 709 video format—from 8-bit H.264 to 10-bit ProRes at 4:2:2 (or any of these formats in log)—the image becomes compressed and filtered, and the sensor data processed. Typically, the filter uses a Bayer pattern, where red and green are filtered on one row, then blue and green on the next, alternating along each row of pixels. The color information is shared, so less of the color data is used with the Bayer pattern, saving space (around two-thirds), while still maintaining accuracy. Processing the image after it comes off the sensor and through the Bayer color filter array (and other versions of it), is called demosaicing.

In RAW the data is typically uncompressed and the data unprocessed (although still typically going through a Bayer pattern color filter), recorded as metadata that can then be manipulated (after demosaicing) in post. You can alter the color and exposure without the limits of image compression—which tends to fall apart in compressed formats when pushed too far, due to the "thinness" of the color depth. (See Figure 4.7.)

FIGURE 4.7
The Bayer pattern found on color filter arrays of single sensor cameras. The green also includes luminosity data, while the red and blue fall on alternate lines, saving data space. Each different color reflects the other colors away, while absorbing the intended color.
(Image courtesy Sean McHugh. ©2018 CambridgeInColour.com. Used with permission.)

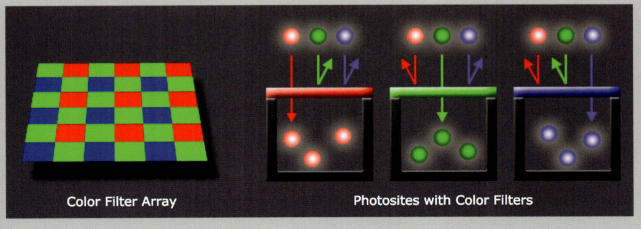

Color Filter Array   Photosites with Color Filters

The Bayer pattern is already a format that subsamples the image, so by placing a Bayer pattern over a RAW sensor, technically it converts it to a 2:1:1 image. As Ben Allen, ACS (Australian Cinematographers Society), explains in a personal email:

> Even though the subsampling is happening in the structure of the image sensor itself, the fact that Bayer is in reality a subsampled format means that there is potential for errors to occur by recording it to a different subsampling structure such as 4:2:2.

> I think this is why the difference between 4:2:2 and 4:4:4 ProRes has become more significant with single sensor cameras. It's not because there's that big a difference between 4:2:2 and 4:4:4 in real world recordings but that the conversion from Bayer to RGB to 4:2:2 has the potential to create errors.

At the same time, Allen notes, "the interpolation from the Bayer pixels to full RGB pixels is fantastic and it's why RAW and single chip cameras work so well."

Richard Butler, writing in *Digital Photography Review*, explains how "Raw files are linear, not logarithmic," and the "bit depth is primarily about how much of your camera's captured dynamic range can be *retained*," allowing for "having enough RAW values left to encode shadow detail" (Butler, 2017). At the same time, Butler contends that "you only get the camera's full DR [dynamic range] at base ISO. As soon as you increase the ISO setting, you'll amplify the brightest stop of captured data beyond clipping, such that you very quickly get to the stage where you're losing 1EV [exposure value] of DR for every 1EV increase in ISO" (2017). He admits that compressed RAW files are "a different story" (2017).

In my sense, the use of the RAW image is the closest you can get to shooting on film in the digital domain. As I wrote in one of my previous books, *Cinema RAW*:

> To shoot RAW means to thicken the color of your images, making them more dense—a lot more data provides more headroom to push and pull footage in post, to correct errors made during shooting, as well as to shape the look and feel of your film. (Lancaster, 2014)

Because of compression in-camera there's not as much headroom in post when shooting in 8-bit cameras; while 10-bit offers more, it's still not nearly as much as a 12-bit recording. Cinematographer Allen, writing for Newsshooter.com, notes that RAW is a fairly simple process:

> Remember, there's nothing magical about RAW. It's just a really efficient way of taking the data off a Bayer pattern sensor with minimal processing and recording [...] to be able to apply the digital processing that's otherwise done in-camera to be done at the equivalent quality in post-production. (Allen, 2018)

Therefore, Allen notes, you can alter the color, such as color correction and exposure (ISO), as if you're doing it in-camera before you shoot—but now you can do it in post.

In Apple's white paper about their ProRes RAW codec, they describe the difference between normal shooting and RAW as:

> At playback time, an application needs only to decode the conventional video file to produce RGB images that can be edited and displayed. The demosaicing and processing have already been performed by the camera at capture time and are "burned in."
>
> In contrast, ProRes RAW directly encodes the Bayer pattern image. Demosaicing and processing are deferred to the time of playback and are performed by application software. [...]
>
> Using ProRes RAW lets you defer the choice of demosaicing algorithm until postproduction and allows you to take advantage of raw processing enhancements and demosaicing algorithm improvements in future software. (Apple, 2018)

At this time, I see the process of shooting RAW in an uncompressed 12-bit 4:4:4 format as the closest filmmakers will get to shooting on film stock—and in some ways it's better than analogue film, since you can shape it into nearly any color you want without the image falling apart. The thickness of the color depth and deeper exposure levels make shooting in RAW special. With cameras that shoot in log mode, you can shoot RAW in log, which will increase the dynamic range of the camera. RAW files can also be converted to a log file in post.

In late 2018, Blackmagic Design released their RAW format, Blackmagic RAW, designed to take advantage of the camera and the camera's sensor. Grant Petty, the founder of Blackmagic Design, explains how their goal is to "bypass the 4:2:2 video filtering, because that video filtering is quite damaging. It's quite bad. It kills half the color detail" (Petty, 2018).

He adds that their form of RAW conveys a small file size due to a form of compressed RAW that's lossless. This works, he adds, because "the compression [occurs] before the RAW conversion [resulting in] higher compression without degrading image quality." At the same time, he states, "You're not compressing final imagery. You're actually compressing RAW data before it turns into imagery, so it's much easier to decode without image artifacts." Petty claims that beta testers shooting tests at a 12:1 compression ratio "haven't been able to see any artifacts, which is really quite incredible" (Petty, 2018). He beleives that Blackmagic RAW should replace all video codecs and other forms of RAW.

When to shoot in RAW

If you have the option, it's better to shoot in RAW, than not. But, because it takes time to process data, only shoot in RAW when you have the time to process the footage. Use RAW when shooting a feature film, or a short narrative or documentary where the highest quality image is important. And shoot in RAW when you want to shape the look and feel of your project in post. Different cameras utilize different workflows for RAW. In most cases, when shooting RAW, the image must be "developed."

If you're shooting with a Canon C200, for example, Canon recommends using Canon's RAW Development Software in order to "unpack" the compressed RAW data (which essentially records data across shared frames). With the RAW data unpacked, it can then be set in a variety of color spaces, such as Canon's Cinema Gamut, or placed into a log file. Canon recommends, for example, that you set the C200 to Canon Log 2 and to Cinema Gamut in order to get the full 15-stop dynamic range of the sensor, as well as the "widest range of encoded colors" (Canon, 2017).

In either case, whatever software you use, the footage needs to be developed and placed in a color gamut (DaVinci Resolve is standard free software for doing this processing, color correcting, and color grading; see www.blackmagicdesign.com/products/davinciresolve). (See Figures 4.8 and 4.9, pp. 215–217.)

When not to shoot in RAW

RAW shooting eats up a lot of data. The internal 500GB SSD drive in my Digital Bolex D16 (which shoots uncompressed 12-bit CinemaDNG RAW) can hold about 2 hours of footage in full HD mode, while the 2K mode records just over 90 minutes. But hard drives are cheap. At the time of this writing (January 2019), you can purchase a G-Technology 10GB external hard drive with a USB 3.0 connection for $370 (a USB-C drive is around $550). CFast 2.0 cards can become pricey and need to be worked into your camera budget: a 256GB card ranges from $300 to $700. Some cameras contain USB-C ports and you can connect an SSD drive to the camera through such ports, thus saving money.

When you need a quick turnaround time, such as when working in television news or if you're lacking the budget for extra hard drives or CFast 2.0 cards, you may want to shoot in a compressed format (ones that deliver Rec. 709, for example). On the other hand, if Blackmagic RAW holds to its promises, then you'll be able to shoot compressed RAW without eating up a lot of data.

FIGURE 4.8
A Canon Log 2 image applied to RAW footage. The image appears flat, with data ready to be unpacked for color grading in post. Scene from cinematography class exercise. See Chapter 5 (pp. 254–255) for post application to this image. Performer, Eric Carver.
(Image courtesy of the author.)

Section review
1. What is RAW?
2. What are the advantages and disadvantages of shooting in RAW?
3. When should you shoot in RAW?
4. When should you avoid shooting in RAW?

SECTION 4: SHOOTING WITH LUTS

When shooting in log or RAW, the use of look-up tables (LUTs) allows you to see the intended result of an image on a camera monitor and/or external monitor. Otherwise, you'll be looking at the flat, milky white wash in log; RAW needs to be debayered and processed to be seen. Producers and clients do *not* want to see log mode footage! LUTs are usually applied in post to help create the final look of a film, but they can also be used in some cameras and external monitors: either to see what the image *could* look like in post after contrast is added to the log footage, along with a manipulation of color; or to provide a look for a RAW image. Since LUTs contain a set of number values that can be applied uniformly across shots, these numbers or values can be manipulated into certain looks, including looks that emulate, in some ways particular analog film stocks.

Rec. 709, the standard HD LUT, simply converts or normalizes the flat log image or RAW into a standard high definition color space providing a fairly accurate representation of what the final image could look like in post—creating a standardized look. There are many different kinds of LUTs that engage creative ways of producing the image, for example film emulation LUTs. LUTs tend to work better when images are properly exposed and color balanced. In RAW, you can certainly recover data by pushing and/or pulling the exposure of the image—which should be done before applying the LUT. If images are wildly different in color and exposure, then applying creative LUTs may not produce the same results across different shots. They're really designed for properly exposed and color corrected images.

Most cinema cameras allow you to add LUTs internally, so you can view them on the camera's monitor. Most external monitors also allow you to add LUTs, which is useful if your camera doesn't contain that feature. See Chapter 5 "Workflow and Tools for the Beginning Cinematographer" for the use of LUTs in postproduction.

VISUAL STORYTELLING WITH CAMERA LOG, RAW, AND LUTs CHAPTER 4 217

FIGURE 4.9
Wide dynamic range with Canon C200 in RAW in this rehearsal scene from a cinematography class exercise at Northern Arizona University. The LUT is applied for video village monitoring. Performers: Eric Carver and Kelcie Weber. (Image courtesy of the author.)

Section review
1. What is a LUT and what does it stand for?
2. What is the relationship of a LUT to shooting in log?
3. Why should you use a LUT when shooting in-camera?

This chapter provided ways to think about what's under the hood of a camera so that you don't get caught up in marketing hype. Choose the camera that best suites your need by considering the kind of compression it uses, and remember, for example, that resolution is not as important as color bit depth. It also provided tools to think about when shooting in log or RAW, as well as the application of LUTs into your shoots.

WORKS CITED

Abramowitz, Mortimer and Michael W. Davidson. "Fundamentals of Film Exposure." 10 June 2000. National High Magnetic Field Laboratory, The Florida State University. www.micro.magnet.fsu.edu/primer/photomicrography/filmexposure.html

Allen, Ben. "Understanding ProRes RAW—Is it ProRes or is it RAW?" News-shooter.com. 7 May 2018. www.newsshooter.com/2018/05/07/understanding-prores-raw-is-it-prores-or-is-it-raw

—— Personal email. 2018.

Apple, Inc. "Apple ProRes RAW." White Paper. April 2018. www.apple.com/final-cut-pro/docs/Apple_ProRes_RAW_White_Paper.pdf

Bertoli, Matteo. "Shooting 4K Log on the iPhone with Filmic Pro." Petapixel.com. 16 January 2017. www.petapixel.com/2017/01/16/shooting-4k-log-iphone-filmic-pro

Butler, Richard. "RAW bit depth is about dynamic range, not the number of colors you get to capture." dpreview.com. 1 September 2017. www.dpreview.com/articles/4653441881/bit-depth-is-about-dynamic-range-not-the-number-of-colors-you-get-to-capture

Canon. "Post-Production Brief with the EOS C200." 31 May 2017. www.learn.usa.canon.com/resources/articles/2017/eos-c200-post-production-brief.shtml

Chapman, Alister. "If Shooting in Low Light Don't Use Log!" Xdcam-user.com. 2 October 2015. www.xdcam-user.com/2015/10/if-shooting-in-low-light-dont-use-log

Haine, Charles. "Yedlin Blows the Lid Off Camera Resolution Myths." 10 August 2017. www.nofilmschool.com/2017/08/yedlin-camera-resolution-myths

Hardy, Robert. "A Beginner's Guide to Shooting & Grading Log Footage." Nofilmschool.com. 15 November 2015. www.nofilmschool.com/2015/11/beginners-guide-shooting-grading-log-footage

Hurlbut, Shane, ASC. "Creating a Level of Intensity with Internal Camera Settings." TheHurlBlog.com. No date. www.thehurlblog.com/cinematography-intensity-with-internal-camera-settings

LaFleur, Mark. "A Filmmaker's Guide to Sensor Sizes and Lens Formats." SharedGrid Blog. 15 January 2018. www.blog.sharegrid.com/blog/a-filmmakers-guide-to-sensor-sizes-and-lens-formats

Lancaster, Kurt. *Cinema Raw*. Focal Press, 2014.

McHugh, Sean. "Digital Camera Sensors." CambridgeInColour.com. No date. www.cambridgeincolour.com/tutorials/camera-sensors.htm

Petty, Grant. "Blackmagic RAW." Video. Blackmagic Design. 2018. www.blackmagicdesign.com/products/blackmagicursaminipro/blackmagicraw

Rhodes, Phil. "Log Recording Standards?" RedSharkNews.com. 10 December 2017. www.redsharknews.com/technology/item/1975-how-to-understand-log-or-cine-style-recordings

Simple DCP. "Color in Digital Cinema." 28 August 2016. www.simpledcp.com/digital-cinema-color

Sony. "Sony Develops a Back-Illuminated CMOS Image Sensor with Pixel-Parallel A/D Converter That Enables Global Shutter Function." 13 February 2018. www.sony.net/SonyInfo/News/Press/201802/18-018E/index.html

Withers, Steve. "What is Wide Colour Gamut (WCG)? Rec. 709, DCI-P3 and Rec. 2020, What Do they All Mean? AV Forums. 20 August 2016. www.avforums.com/article/what-is-wide-colour-gamut-wcg.12811

Yedlin, Steve, ASC. "On Color Science for Filmmakers." 20 June 2016. www.yedlin.net/OnColorScience

— Personal letter to unknown recipient. No date. www.yedlin.net/150421_01.html

Still from cinematography class exercise at Northern Arizona University. Eric Carver and Kelcie Weber, performers.
(Image courtesy of the author.)

CHAPTER 5

Workflow and Tools for the Beginning Cinematographer

In this final chapter, I provide workflow concepts for the beginning cinematographer—as well as tools, worksheets, checklists, and forms to help plan shoots. Definitions, examples, and the theoretical framework were covered in the previous chapters. This chapter explores some of the steps and tools for planning projects during preproduction, tools to help with the planning, and what to look for in the postproduction color correction and color grading process. Since this is mainly a review chapter, I do not provide section reviews. I also don't go into the production process, since classes, video tutorials, and direct shooting experience offer the strongest ways to learn production as a cinematographer.

SECTION 1. PREPRODUCTION FOR CINEMATOGRAPHERS

Script analysis

The most important aspect of the preproduction process involves a script analysis, as detailed in Chapter 1. This is the point where filmmakers translate the emotional motivations of characters into physical things that can be shot, including elements of blocking and body language. Although the cinematographer does not engage in blocking—since that's clearly the director's job—she must still express a clear understanding of the potential visual story in the script and engage in a keen understanding of it in order to interpret the director's vision into compositional and lighting elements rendered onscreen.

I've created a Dramatic analysis chart where you can take note of the point of view character. For this chart, write down each character and their needs and wants: what motivates them—the film objective. (If the character only exists in one scene, then only write down their scene objective.) Then write down their objective in each scene. Include a description of actions—the sub-objectives—they take in their attempt to attain their scene objective. Also, take note of what prevents them from attaining their objective in the conflict column. Write down any notes on how to make the scene visual, everything from blocking ideas, body language, composition, lens choices, and lighting—whatever inspires you to translate that scene into physical things an audience can see.

In an interview with *Filmmaker* magazine, Shane Hurlbut, ASC, put the workflow with the director in this way:

> The director sits down and we design the whole look of the movie. He tells me what the emotional content feels like, what the characters are going through. Reading the script, I create what we call an emotional breakdown where I break down the emotions of each character throughout the film, and then I texture the lighting and the camera emotion to accent and amplify those emotions. […] So it's taking the notes from the director, and systematically putting it in to a look and a feel and a mood and a tone. (Murie, 2014)

Conceiving the story and finding ways to visualize it is the most important job of the cinematographer and director team. The script analysis chart below is an outline to get you started in that analysis.

Dramatic Analysis Chart				
Title:				
Scene:				
Character (POV)	Needs and wants (film objective)	Scene objective and sub-objectives (what they want and the actions they take)	Conflict (what gets in their way)	Visual notes (make these elements physical)

Composition, lenses, shot list

As examined in Chapter 2, the composition—defined by the boundaries of the aspect ratio—includes at least ten elements:

1. Shot size and lens
2. Camera height and angle
3. Camera motion
4. Focal depth of field
5. Light and dark
6. Line and linear perspective
7. Layers
8. Weight
9. Color
10. Texture

Use these compositional tools to reinforce, amplify, and otherwise support the unfolding story. Determine (and make choices about) the use of lines and linear perspective as it relates to the story, for example.

What will be the focal depth of field? Why is there more compositional weight to the image, here, but not there? When should the camera move? Should it be slow, fast, medium, smooth, or shaky? What are the foreground, midground, and background layers in the scene? How high should the camera be? What should the color scheme be? Where should light and shadows be placed? What is the texture of the scene?

Use the Scene composition chart for every scene, taking note of how the scene begins (the normal emotional state) and the point where the emotional stakes shift. Make some kind of change to the composition (change up how the tools are being used) when the scene changes emotionally—most likely at a climax, perhaps when a character realizes something and/or must make a decision, the point where the original state or intent of scene changes.

Maybe you add camera movement, or go to a shallow depth of field (where before there was deep focus), or cut to a close-up (where before there were medium and wide shots), or change the linear perspective, and so forth. Several combinations of these could be used (changing all of them would be overkill). These decisions involve choosing the point-of-view character, which goes back to the dramatic analysis.

All of these answers become clear as you weigh them against the needs of the story, referring to the psychological impact of shot sizes, camera height, camera movement, color, all of the elements referenced in the charts below (recreated here from Chapter 2, except for the color chart on p. 77).

The Scene composition chart will help you to define the normal state of the character's world, the emotional state of the point-of-view character as we begin the scene, followed by a place to note the change in composition at the moment the scene shifts. The emotions either go up or down and so change the composition by changing at least one of the ten tools. This will allow you to shift into the right gear in supporting the change in story.

As for the lens, you may change the focal length and shot sizes over the course of the scene, but save any significant changes for the scene shift. Take note of how and when you're using different types of shots in order to convey the best choice for the story. For psychological impact of camera motion, lens, and shot size, refer to the tables on pages 225–229. It's recommended that you create a storyboard or a detailed prose shot list that best describes your choices and how they're impacting the changing emotions in a scene. You should be able to defend your choices based on your story analysis.

	Scene Composition Chart	
Title and aspect ratio:		
Scene:		
	Setup (normal state of affairs)	Scene shift (change of emotion)
Shot size (and lens)		
Camera height and angle		
Camera motion		
Focal depth of field		
Light and dark		
Line and linear perspective		
Layers		

Weight		
Color		
Texture		

Emotional Distance and Intimacy in Shot Sizes	
Wide	Captures and sets the characters' locations in a scene. *Psychologically, it offers the least intimacy between characters.* It's similar to having a conversation between two people standing against opposite walls in a room.
Medium	Normal conversational distance between people. *Psychologically equivalent to people having a conversation at a comfortable distance without invading personal space.*
Close	Distance of intimacy. *We're now in someone's personal and emotional space.* This usually occurs in real life when people are in love or in a fight.

Psychological Impact of Lenses		
Shot type and lens size	Depth of field	Uses and psychological impact
Super wide fisheye or convex lens 6–12mm	Deep focus	The image curves along the edge of the shot and causes the image to become distorted. • *Provides a sense of expansiveness in wide shots.* • *May add comedic effect; or where distortion and confusion is needed when brought close to a subject.* • *Could be used to show a security camera's view, bug eyes, or even an alien..*
Wide 12–18mm	Deep focus	Provides expansive clarity, a view showing details from foreground to background. Places character(s) within a heightened sense of space. A tight close-up on subjects may lead to visual distortion. (You can place the lens close to a subject in the foreground and have the background focus fall off.) • *Use to ground a character in geometric space and location in wide shots.* • *Use to provide an expansive view of a scene.* • *Use to express instability or zaniness in tight shots.* • *Use to show discomfort between characters, since the world becomes distorted.*

Normal wide 18–34mm	Deep focus Open aperture to get shallow depth of field	A step below a "normal" field of view, the standard wide angle view provides a sense of geometric space, because it not only picks up details from foreground to background through deep focus (under normal aperture), but it also covers the area around the edge of the subject when setting wide shots. A tight close-up on subjects may lead to visual distortion in lower focal lengths. (You can place the lens close to a subject in the foreground and have the background focus fall off.) • *Places characters within a heightened sense of space.* • *Use to provide a sense of grounding in space and location in wider shots.* • *Offers a bit of instability or zaniness in tight shots when brought close to the subject, especially in the lower focal lengths.* • *Makes you feel like you're participating in the action.* • *May also allow for a sense of discomfort between characters, since the world becomes a bit distorted compared to the normal view of the world.*
Normal view 35–55mm	Deep focus at high aperture Shallow focus at low aperture	Psychologically for viewers, this is the normal field of view for the human eye (one eye)—normal lenses do not capture peripheral vision. There's no distortion on the edge of the frame. • *Use when offering a sense of "normality" to a scene and equal balance of power.* • *Normal lenses offer intimacy when the camera is level, because the balance of power is equal.*
Fairly tight 60–100mm	Image becomes magnified and may start feeling compressed at the proper camera-subject distance. Provides shallow depth of field.	Depending on the tightness of a shot, it can provide a decent reach to get a character in a tight close-up with a shallow depth of field. The image starts getting compressed and shallow in narrow fields of view as the lenses get longer, magnifying the shot. • *Use to provide focus on a single character or cutaway shot.* • *Use to provide a sense of distance in an intimate scene.* • *Brings beauty to a character (a good "portrait" lens would fall in the 85–135mm range).*
Tight 100–400mm (or longer)	Magnified shot with shallow depth of field at normal aperture. Compression occurs with the lens far enough away from the subject (with proper camera–subject distance).	For reaching close when the camera is farther away from a subject—magnifies the background and foreground providing a sense of compression when the camera is properly placed at the right distance. • *Use when you need to get close to a subject when the camera is farther away.* • *May enhance an objective view due to a distancing of intimacy in a scene.* • *Brings a heightened sense of beauty to a character.*

Tilt shift lens (variety of focal lengths)	Shallow to deep depending on the focal length and aperture of the lens.	Allows you to adjust focus within a specific field of view within the shot, providing a highly stylized shot. • Can provide a sense of miniaturization to a scene. • Use to stylize the subject or scene, such as in a dream state or drug-induced altered viewpoint, or even an alien landscape.

Emotional Impact of Camera Height and Angle	
High angle	The camera's point of view is from on high looking down onto the subject, causing the subject to look up towards the camera. This height can be just slightly higher than the eyeline or higher. *It tends to result in a sense of subservience and weakness. There is no intimacy in this type of shot, due to the balance of power being uneven.*
Low angle	The camera's point of view is low, looking up at the subject, so the subject must look down towards the camera. The height can be just slightly below the eyeline or lower. *It typically gives the character dominance, authority, superiority, and strength. There is no intimacy in this type of shot, due to the balance of power being uneven.*
Level	Camera's lens is at eye level to the subject. Use a level shot with a normal lens to provide intimacy in a close-up, due to the perceived equal power relationship. *It often provides a sense of evenness of power since no one is looking down or up at someone, and allows for intimacy.*
Dutch angle	Camera tilted unevenly from the horizon line. *Tends to induce a sense of disarrangement or confusion on the part of the subject.*
Front	**When on axis and level,** *provides the strongest intimacy since the full face is exposed.*
Side	Sees action from the side. *It pulls us away from intimacy since we're not seeing the full face where emotion is most fully expressed.*
Rear	The furthest emotional distance from a character, since we do not see their face. *We feel tension because we don't know what the character is feeling, doing, or looking at.*

Psychological Impact of Camera Movement			
Type of camera motion	Tool	Motion type	Uses of motion and psychological impact
Pan	Tripod	Absolute	Covers space from left of screen to right and vice versa on a static axis (tripod). • Use to cover subject movement, moving from one subject to another to show the relationship between them in space. • Use to cover the reaction of someone. Following the eyes, the energy of one person looking at another—we pan to see what the character looking sees. • Use to cover a person drawing attention to an object and following it, used in some ways as the continuation of a physical action. • Psychologically, an audience wants to see what another character is looking at, so the pan releases this tension as we want to follow the gaze.
Tilt	Tripod	Absolute	Covers space from bottom to top of screen and vice versa on a static axis. Similar to the pan, but pointing vertically up and down rather than horizontally left and right. • Use to cover the reaction of someone. Following the eyes, the energy of one person looking up or down at another, we tilt to see what the character looking sees. • Use to cover a person drawing attention to an object and following it up or down, used in some ways as the continuation of a physical action. • Potential to reveal importance of grandeur or majesty of an object or subject, by tilting up to reveal a towering figure or object. May be menacing to the subject if shot from a low angle. • Changes the power relationship in a scene when height of the angle is changed from low to high and high to low.
Zoom	Lens	Absolute	Change focal length within a shot (quick zooms are referred to as snap zooms). • We're conscious that a camera is being used (to create the effect of newsreel footage, like a live event—someone with a camera covering an event, providing a subjective look). • Use to move close or farther away from the subject while maintaining absolute motion, so only use if the subjective view is needed. • Effective as a snap zoom to push the audience quickly and abruptly into an emotional moment, causing them to feel off balance (such as in battle scenes or some other intense physical activity), providing a subjective sense that the action is unfolding by the moment and the camera is there to cover it as it happens.

Push in (dolly)	Track, slider, steadicam, gimbal, jib	Relative	Camera physically moves closer to the subject or object. • *Use to intensify or heighten emotion in a scene as the audience enters the intimate space of a subject.* • *Move slowly to make the shift in emotion subtle.* • *Move quickly for obvious impact and/or rushed feeling.*
Pull out (dolly)	Track, slider, steadicam, gimbal, jib	Relative	Camera physically moves away from the subject or object. • *Use to diminish emotion in a scene as the audience moves out of the intimate space of a subject making them feel isolated or lonely.* • *Move slowly to make the shift in emotion subtle.* • *Move quickly for obvious impact and/or rushed feeling.*
Parallel (or lateral) tracking	Track, slider, steadicam, gimbal	Relative	Camera physically follows the action of a character in parallel to the subject's movement. Or it reveals different action in a shot, even passing time. • *Tracking away from a character creates distance from the subject and may reveal loneliness or disconnectedness from the world.* • *Tracking towards a character allows us to enter the emotion of a character from a distance.* • *Tracking with the character in a profile shot is far less intimate, but puts the audience into the scene as if they are with the character.*
Jib (crane)	Jib, gimbal	Relative	Camera can physically move up and down in space, as well as allowing it to push in and/or pull out of space within the same shot. (The up or down and push or pull may be done simultaneously.) • *Use to reach deep into space (of the location or set) where it may be difficult to get a shot otherwise (such as when trying to set tracks in a tight space).* • *Use to pull back and leave a scene, departing from a character and leaving them in a landscape—good way to exit a specific type of scene, causing a de-establishing shot.* • *Use to swoop into a scene and look around a space that could not be shot with another type of move.* • *When starting low and moving up, reveals an expanse of scenery and distances us from the emotional point of view of characters.* • *Looking down from above provides an omniscient view of landscape and action.* • *When starting high and moving low, provides a shift from omniscient POV to a personal intimacy as we enter the emotional space of the characters.*
Handheld	Hands, gimbal, steadicam	Relative	The handheld look, when done smoothly, offers a way for the visual movement to float through space. • *Use to provide a sense of floating and peace.* • *When using choppy quick movement, then use to convey a sense of frenetic, out-of-control behavior.*

Camera test

Any camera you choose to work with should be tested through the entire production workflow in low light, normal light, and intense light—the entire dynamic range from darks to highlights—in order to see how the camera responds to normal and extreme working conditions. You want to see how the camera performs within low- and high-contrast situations in order to determine its limits, so that you can stay within certain lighting parameters.

Shane Hurlbut, ASC, says that cameras contain different types of sensors, and that, in the digital age, that's similar to working with film emulsion in the analog age:

> Treat your new digital camera like a new film emulsion that needs testing. Why? Because every sensor is different. They have unique qualities, different latitudes, color spaces, log files, bit depth. How it rolls off with over and underexposure. If it has aliasing, or moiré, just to name a few. (Hurlbut, n.d.)

Take the camera through its paces, setting up lights or using outdoor natural light, create an environment that will be similar to your actual working environment during the shoot—and especially determine *what* your normal working conditions should be. This is not a scientific test in a lab. It needs to be a real-world test. After choosing your camera, take it through the production and post-production workflow, examining several things:

1. Exposure and dynamic range
   a. *Low light and low contrast.* As explained in the previous chapter, most cameras record and "see" in Rec. 709 color gamut, but when shooting in log or RAW, the Rec. 709 is used for perceived accuracy of the image.

   Record images for an in-camera look (the burned-in image of "what you see is what you get"), log, or RAW. Test them all if the camera contains all of these capabilities. Balance your turnaround time with the best tool you want to use. Try in camera LUTs, if you want to get a sense of what the final image may look like after color grading in post. How do each of these handle low light and low contrast situations?

   If you're using a middle gray card (representing the value of skin tones), then you can measure the levels with a meter, waveform monitor, or false color scale. On the waveform monitor, the middle gray card should read just above 40% towards 55%. Using a white card or any white reflectance value at 90%, the waveform IRE setting should be around 100%.

    i. In-camera "burned in" look ("what you see is what you get")
    ii. LUT or simple Rec. 709 (or Rec. 2020)
    iii. Log
    iv. RAW

b. *High contrast—test for extremes.* Using the gray card and white card, along with a waveform monitor; you can map your contrast range (seeing where your blacks gets crushed and your whites clip). If you don't have a waveform in-camera, then use a light meter to do the same thing. Point at the brightest and darkest areas so you'll know the contrast range using your f-stop readings (along with your set ISO and shutter speed/angle). If your values clip or get crushed, then adjust the intensity of the light (diffuse the highlights and/or add more light in the shadows). Test using what you have available for the camera:

    i. In-camera "burned in" look ("what you see is what you get)
    ii. LUT or simple Rec. 709 (or Rec. 2020 for 4K)
    iii. Log
    iv. RAW

2. *Set/location color test*

If you're shooting in different conditions, such as outdoor night and day and/or indoor night and day, or green screen, then test the camera in all of these conditions. As noted in the psychology of color section in Chapter 2 (pp. 76–78), color comes from the color temperature of lights, costumes, sets, and props. If you're shooting fiction, you should be able to control most of these, however in documentary work, you will be more limited. As part of the cinematographer's tools (with the director's input), create a "look book" that expresses the look and feel of the film, including colors. In either case, see how your camera performs with the colors you'll be facing in your shoot. Work with these colors in your test, as you see how each of these modes of shooting impact the color:

a. In-camera "burned-in" look ("what you see is what you get")

b. LUT or simple Rec. 709 (or Rec. 2020)
c. Log
d. RAW

You will need to take this test into postproduction in order to see how the camera handles color in context with accurate skin tones. See Section 3, Postproduction for Cinematographers, p. 236.

3. *Postproduction*

This will be explored more fully, below, but the basic camera test needs to include the following steps in order to discover how the camera handles dynamic range, low light, high contrast, and color.

a. If shot in log, add contrast curve.
b. Primary color correction—adjust exposure and even out colors shot to shot.
c. Secondary color correction—not really needed for the test, but you can drill down and isolate specific elements in the composition, adjusting the exposure, color, and saturation to see how colors hold up.
d. LUT—apply different LUTs to see how the camera handles certain ones. Will they help deliver the final look you're trying to achieve?

Ultimately, if you're shooting in RAW, it doesn't really matter what camera you're shooting with, since you can adjust color and exposure as needed (as long you haven't crushed the image too far or clipped your highlights).

Technical scout form

If you're shooting on location, you need to take note of, for example, the electrical grid, natural light through windows—all of the elements that you will face in that location so you can plan accordingly.

Technical Scout Location Form

Title:		
Scene:		
Address and contact info:		
Time of day	INT. or EXT. Day	INT. or EXT. Night
Existing light	Color temp:	Mis:
Existing light quality	Hard	Soft
Existing light color temperature	Practical lights (tungsten, fluorescent)	Daylight
Electrical grid	Circuit breaker and number of circuits and type of circuits (15, 20, 30 amps)	Location of outlets Grounded outlets?
Existing practical and window lighting	How will these lights be used (or not)?	
Floor plan (take note of outlets, circuit breaker, windows, practical lights, and potential lighting setups)		

App tools

The following apps will help you plan your shoots:

- **Magic ViewFinder** (free) both iOS and Android—for Canon, Sony, Blackmagic, and other cameras (choose the app for the camera company you're using). This director's viewfinder includes a scrolling focal length wheel, along with the ability to choose color balance, depth of field, auto focus or manual focus, LUTs, and so forth. This is my go-to app, which is great for scouting and setting up shots.
www.dev.kadru.net/

- **Artemis Director's Viewfinder** (~$30)—it replicates the viewfinder field of a variety of cameras and lenses so you can check your composition without using the camera. Good for field-testing shots and checking compositions on-set.
www.chemicalwedding.tv/

- **Sun Surveyor**—an app that maps the location of the sun based on your location and time.
www.sunsurveyor.com/

- **Shot Designer**—an app that allows you to set up shots and camera placement within a floor plan.
www.hollywoodcamerawork.com/shot-designer.html

- **Cine Meter II** (~$25)—an app that includes such tools as waveform monitor and false color to help set your exposure. You can set the white balance, ISO, shutter speed, and aperture, as well as using spot metering. An important tool, especially if your camera is missing these features. You can set the ISO, shutter speed, and aperture.
www.adamwilt.com/cinemeterii/

- **AJA DataCalc**—calculates the amount of data recorded based on the bit rate settings for both storage space size and recording time.
www.aja.com/family/software#datacalc

- **Digital Cinema Pocket Guides**—essentially, a series of trimmed down guides on camera operation and settings. They also include research from multiple sources, so they visually offer information not found in manuals.
www.theblackandblue.com/pocket-guides/

- **DSLR Slate**—if you don't have a slate and need to record not only the slate data (scene, take #, frame rate, and director), but it can also record the settings on your camera (especially useful in post), such as ISO, shutter speed, white balance, and so forth.
  www.lastshotapps.com/LastShotApps/Apps/Entries/2010/5/19_DSLR_Slate.html

- **pCAM Film+Digital**—includes 24 different tools for cinematography, including a depth of field calculator, field of view, comparing relative size based on different sensors, focal length matching for lenses, and so forth.
  www.pcam.app/Pro/pCAM_Pro.html

SECTION 2: PRODUCTION FOR CINEMATOGRAPHERS

The cinematographer leads the camera, light, and grip departments. I'm not going to discuss the day-to-day responsibilities of each member of a camera crew, since these can be found online quite easily, but here's an overview of a typical crew for a film; there will be a lot fewer people on low-budget and student films, where people tend to take on multiple responsibilities.

Camera department—the camera and everything associated with it. The camera crew includes:

- **Camera Operator**—operates the camera, framing shots, angles, and camera movement. (In student productions and small low budget productions the cinematographer may also operate the camera.)

- **1st Assistant Camera (1st AC)**—runs the camera department; tests the gear before the shoot; gets the camera ready for the shoot, builds up the camera and its accessories; makes sure the crew and equipment are ready to go during production; changes lenses for the Camera Operator and also pulls focus.

- **2nd Assistant Camera (2nd AC)**—assists the 1st AC in prepping the camera gear; fills out the camera log, writing down the f-stop settings, the focal length of the lens (especially important for reshoots)

- **Digital Imaging Technician (DIT)**—works with the cinematographer in achieving the look of the film through digital means, often using LUTs to help set up what the final look will be like in post, so they are running the computer and helping to shape what the image will look like in post (using the computer for this while on-set); they manage the data on set; they may be expected to understand the intricacies of camera settings, since they will be the one called upon to troubleshoot issues with the camera, computers, hard drives—anything to do with the recording and display of the image; may also be the loader and the person in charge of organizing the media files, metadata, and backing up all recorded files from the camera.

- **Loader**—in charge of the recording media of the camera, offloading the cards, and backing them up on hard drives; works with the digital imaging technician to keep files organized and in the proper format.

Light department—the crew in charge of the lights and electricity for the set. The gaffer is the head electrician; the best boy is the foreman in charge of the lighting crew. The lighting technician is the person in charge of the electricity for lights—they set up the lights and lamps; and are aware of safety procedures.

Grip department—the crew comprising the key grip, best boy grip, a regular grip, and dolly grip; in charge of equipment for lights (such as flags, silks, and scrims); in addition, they're in charge of the gear that makes the cameras move, from dollies to cranes.

SECTION 3: POSTPRODUCTION FOR CINEMATOGRAPHERS

The final look and feel of a film are created in post, so it is here where cinematographers can lose control of their images shot on set. Writing in a 2010 publication of *Screen*, Richard Misek, presciently notes:

> A film's 'look' is now no longer set during production. Primary colour grading is now carried out digitally, and as a result can be used to adjust colour balance without the restrictions inherent in photochemical colour timing. Red, green, and blue can be adjusted in any combination without causing reduced exposure. Conversely, exposure can be changed without affecting colour balance; and this is only the beginning of what can now be done with colour. (Misek, 2010: 405)

In 2007, the Technology Committee of the American Society of Cinematographers (ASC) attempted to control the post process to some degree by developing a color decision list (CDL), a metadata tag found on digital shots providing the intended on-set color values and exposure data for postproduction colorists.

On many digitally acquired shoots, a digital imaging technician (DIT) works with the director and cinematographer to deliver files that attain intended looks. But, as Misek notes, the CDL only applies to the primary color correction process, "notably RGB values, saturation, contrast, and brightness," not to the secondary process (where parts of the screen can be targeted for color and exposure changes) (Misek, 2010: 408).

Writing in *American Cinematographer* magazine, Benjamin B, quoting Joshua Pines, vice president of Technicolor Digital Intermediates and who sits on the Digital Intermediate (DI) subcommittee of American Society of Cinematographers' (ASC) Technology Committee, explains how the CDL is "a way of giving creative control back to the cinematographer. Just like the director has first cut, the cinematographer should have first look." Furthermore, Lou Levinson, the chair of the DI subcommittee and a colorist at Post Logic Studios, notes how, "At its core, the ASC CDL was designed to move a very simple set of color corrections across platforms" (Benjamin B, 2008).

> Levinson emphasizes that in order for the CDL to work, a production must decide on the project's monitoring and color space. There are two main choices: 1) film emulation, a look-up table (LUT) used to simulate a film print on a video monitor, and 2) Rec 709, standard color space for a hi-def video signal. (Benjamin B, 2008)

World-renowned colorist Peter Doyle (*The Lord of the Rings*, *Harry Potter* films, *The Darkest Hour*, among others), speaking at a conference on High Dynamic Range (HDR) sponsored by the French Society of Cinematographers, describes four "voices" that now help shape the look of a film in Hollywood cinema (quoted in Benjamin B, 2018):

1. Production (producer, director, DP, etc.)
2. Studio
3. Marketing
4. Manufacturers

The management of color among various stakeholders is so strong that contracts need to state who "gets to do the grade," Doyle says (Benjamin B, 2018).

Despite potential conflict in the final look of the film among these various entities, cinematographers are the strongest stakeholders in shaping the look of the film, since they guide the director's vision through the lens and lighting. Italian cinematographer Matteo Bertoli believes that "cinematography and color grading are extremely connected." In this sense he thinks cinematographers should know how to do basic color grading using Resolve—especially if they're on a low budget production. "I think every cinematographer should have basic knowledge of DaVinci Resolve," he explains in an interview, "so they know where they can push the footage, what they can and cannot do." Furthermore, it will give them the opportunity to "play around with the clips and send colorist/producers some samples/ideas of what they are trying to achieve" (Bertoli, 2018).

Indeed, the DP of *Jessica Jones*, Manuel Billeter, discusses how he would take screen grabs from every setup "so the lab could match the dailies to my suggestions" (Stuart 2016, 45).

With big budget productions, hiring a professional colorist, is a good thing. When working with a colorist, Bertoli wants to see stills from the colorist in order to see the look before it's finalized. He feels "pretty comfortable using Resolve and I am totally happy with what I am getting." He does not like making extreme changes in the color process and tries to "achieve the look in camera," using the color tools to "boost the colors and do minor adjustments."

Bertoli thinks that high level cinematographers may just shoot their project, then move on to another project without worrying about the coloring phase, so most of the time they just "see the final product." But that could become a problem if there are extreme changes during post, he adds, "since my name is on that project and if the look of the film changes completely, that's not good."

The following information is offered in the spirit of Bertoli's advice. Rather than an examination of how to use these color-grading tools, step by step, I provide an overview of some of them in order to help inform the cinematographer. With that awareness the cinematographer will be able to either use tutorials so they can grade their own footage, or they will at least gain an awareness of how the tools are used so you can communicate better with a professional colorist.

Color correction and grading tools

Colorists typically do their work in two phases: color correction and color grading. Color correction is simply the application of color and exposure tools to unify exposure in a scene (changing a mistakenly underexposed shot to proper exposure, for example), or to unify color in a scene (correcting a tungsten-balanced shot to an outdoor color temperature, for example). Color correction fixes the invariable mistakes that occur on a busy, fast-moving shoot. It is also the step where the colorist applies contrast to the flat look of a log shot, making it look natural—which may be done with a LUT, such as with Rec. 709, for example. The colorist can use the values within the CDL to fix these mistakes while staying within the cinematographer's parameters.

The tools used for color correction involve setting the color temperature, tint, color wheels, color curves, and the exposure levels of shadows, midtones, and highlights.

The second job of the colorist involves color grading, the process of finalizing the look and feel of the film, and these changes may be subtle. This is where film-look LUTs are applied, as well as where certain parts of a screen are adjusted using secondary color correction tools—although sometimes these are used to fix color and exposure issues occurring in just a part of the screen (such as adjusting the skin tone color on a person's face).

Tools of the colorist
This is not a tutorial on how to use these tools, since there are plenty of web tutorials that teach people how to use this software (filmsimplified.com is a good one I've used to gain a certain mastery of the major tools of DaVinci Resolve, for example). Rather, I examine what these tools look like and what they do, so you gain a fundamental understanding how images can be manipulated in post.

Scopes
To read the color and exposure of shots in post, several scopes have been developed to help (some of these also appear in camera and monitor displays for fieldwork).

Waveform monitor—measures exposure from black to white, reading data across the image from left to right. The data on the far left matches the image on the far left, for example. Skin tones (if exposed in a standard way) tend to fall in between 55-70% on a waveform monitor. (See Figures 5.1a and 5.1b, pp. 240–241.)

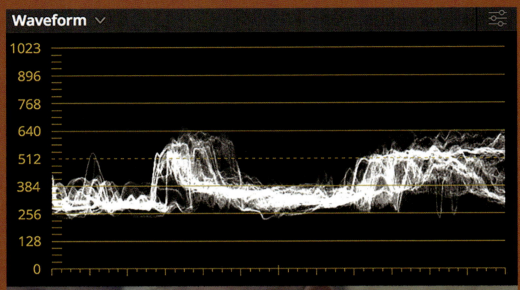

FIGURE 5.1a
Images one and two (*above*) shows a flat image revealing a low dynamic range as the image becomes flat in log mode. The washed out flat image can be read on the waveform monitor scale (*top*) revealing a fairly flat reading on the scope. Notice how the scope rises from 256-640 on the left third, matching the man's face on the left third. The scope's luminance data lines up precisely with the image.

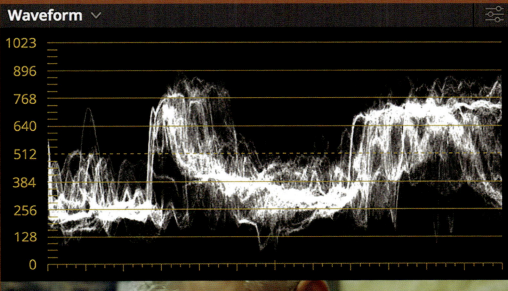

FIGURE 5.1b
In thse images (*above*), we now see the image after contrast has been applied, correcting the log mode into a more natural image. The waveform monitor scale (*top*) now reveals a stronger contrast (the color has also been adjusted).

(Images courtesy of the author.)

RGB Parade—similar to the waveform monitor, but with separate red, green, and blue color channels. Useful for reading specific elements of color that are off balance. You can adjust these within the shadows, midtones, and/or highlights (the lift, gamma, and gain in the primaries wheel section of Resolve).
(See Figure 5.2.)

FIGURE 5.2
The RGB Parade sequence reveals how to balance colors using the Primaries bars in Resolve, while observing the RGB Parade scope (3 and 5).

We can see the first uncorrected image (1) as it appears out of the camera (12-bit RAW on a Digital Bolex D16).

The second image (2) shows the color correction, with the RGB Parade of the corrected image in 3.

By making small adjustments of colors by using the Primaries Bars in Resolve (4), we can see the corresponding changes in the RGB Parade (5).

The final result (6), shows a properly adjusted image.

(Images courtesy of the author.)

WORKFLOW AND TOOLS FOR THE BEGINNING CINEMATOGRAPHER   CHAPTER 5   243

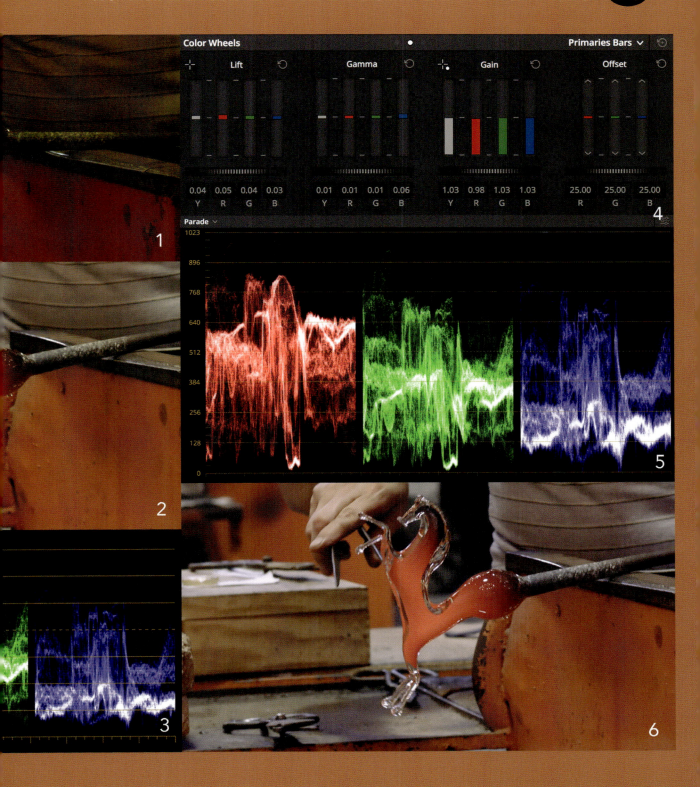

Vectorscope—reads color intensity on a color wheel and includes a skin tone line to determine the accuracy of skin colors. (See Figure 5.3.)

FIGURE 5.3

The Vectorscope in Resolve. This sequence reveals an image with some color correction added (1). Image 2 represents the position of colors and their intensity on the Vectorscope. The colors of the color wheel are not shown, but, instead, it uses letters: R = red, M = magenta, B = blue, C = cyan, G = green, Y = yellow. The more the values reach out to the edge of the circle, the more saturated the colors.

We can see in this scope (2) that image 1, overall, edges towards yellow, with some elements of green (in the fluorescent lights, not yet corrected), and some red (the face of the man).

By choosing the Qualifier tool (3), I click on the man's face (4), selecting it (the scale in 3 shows the hue, saturation, and luminance values; the HSL tool), a process of secondary color correction. I isolate the material around the man's face (4) so that when I make changes on the color wheels (not shown), the changes occur mostly on his face.

By masking out the other parts of the image, we can focus on adjusting just the man's skin tones.

We can see that the Vectorscope (5) now shows color landing on the skin tone line (around the 10 o'clock position). The final corrected result (6) shows how the man's face has been accurately adjusted because the scope tells us this with the color values falling on the skin tone line.
(Images courtesy of the author.)

Workflow and Tools for the Beginning Cinematographer   Chapter 5

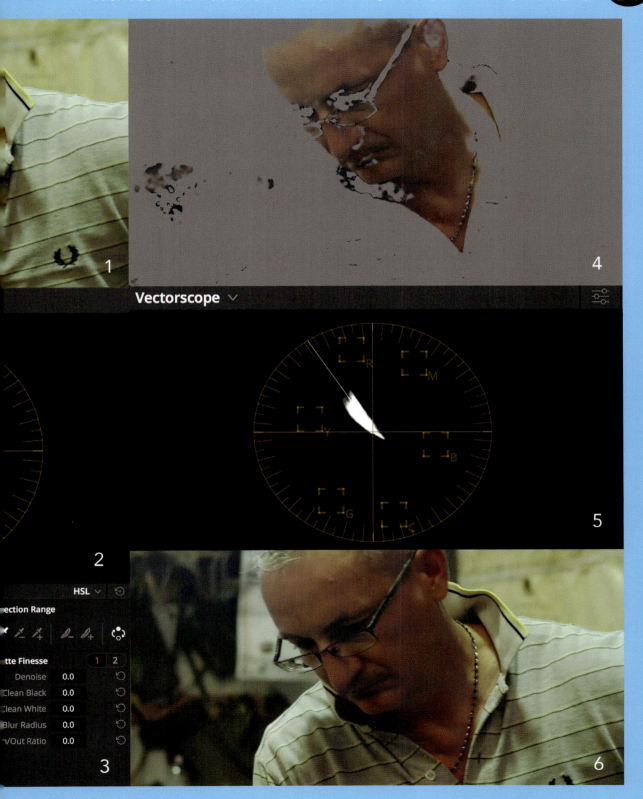

Histogram—measures exposure intensity for the overall image, ranging in values from black to white (left to right,). While the waveform monitor represents the luminosity values in the image going left to right, the histogram simply provides an overall value of intensity on a 0 to 100 scale. Both the histogram and waveform monitors are regularly found in camera monitors, so they can be used while shooting.

In postproduction, the histogram allows you to make a quick check of the contrast range of the darks to brights, as well as looking at the overall average exposure. A wide value would, of course, represent high contrast, while low values will quickly reveal if the image is dark overall, in the middle, or in the highlights. It also reveals low contrast elements—which may not need much adjustment, since that may be the look of the film. Some scopes show the luminosity value of red, green, and blue (RGB) channels. (See Figure 5.4.)

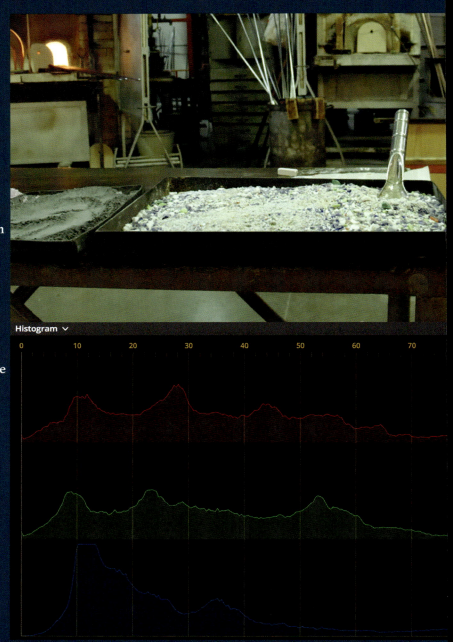

FIGURE 5.4a
The histogram reveals the luminosity of the RGB channels. The uncorrected image (*top*), reveals green from the fluorescent lights, which we can see in the second image, the histogram (*bottom*), showing green spread out through the shadows, midtones, and highlights.

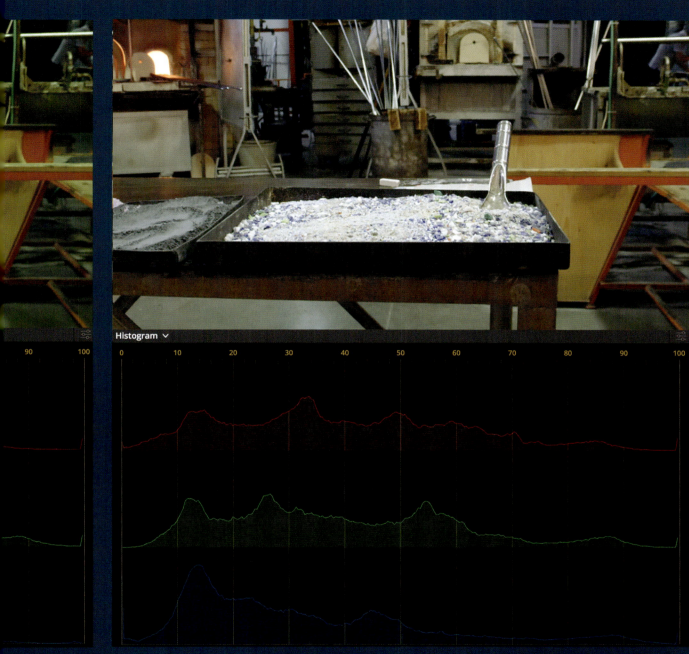

FIGURE 5.4b
By adjusting the color through Resolve's Primaries Bars (not shown), we can add blue to the shadows so that the shadows of red, green, and blue are aligned (*bottom*) and, therefore, balanced, and the image begins to even out (*top*). In addition, by adjusting the highlights of green (taking some of the green away and adding blue, as well as adjusting some of the midtones in the Primaries Bars) the image becomes more balanced (*top*).
(Images courtesy of the author.)

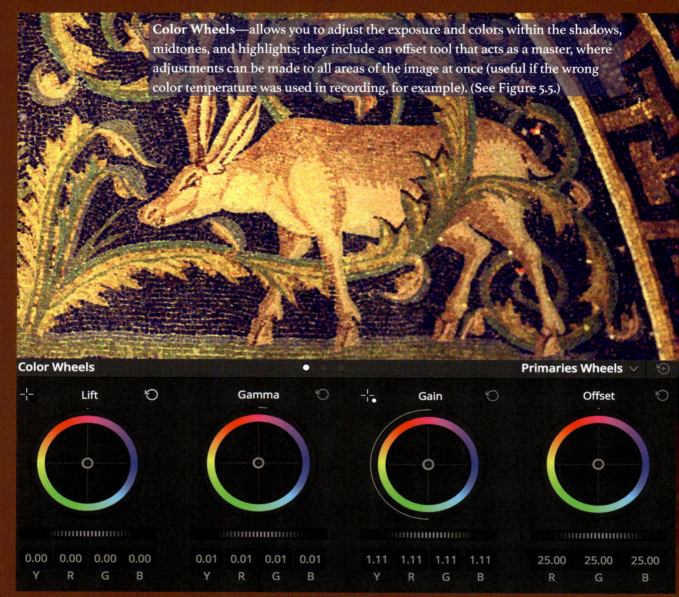

Color Wheels—allows you to adjust the exposure and colors within the shadows, midtones, and highlights; they include an offset tool that acts as a master, where adjustments can be made to all areas of the image at once (useful if the wrong color temperature was used in recording, for example). (See Figure 5.5.)

FIGURE 5.5a
Color Wheels in DaVinci Resolve (*bottom*). All color wheels reference the placement of color on a circle. Adjustments are made by dragging the center point towards the color you want. The farther you drag it to the edge of the circle, the more saturated the color becomes. Values can be adjusted in the shadows, midtones, and highlights (Lift, Gamma, Gain). The wheels express primary and secondary colors, the opposite points of the circle representing the complementary color. The top image shows too much blue. We can move the center point towards red, the complementary color opposite of blue on the wheel, to fix this problem.

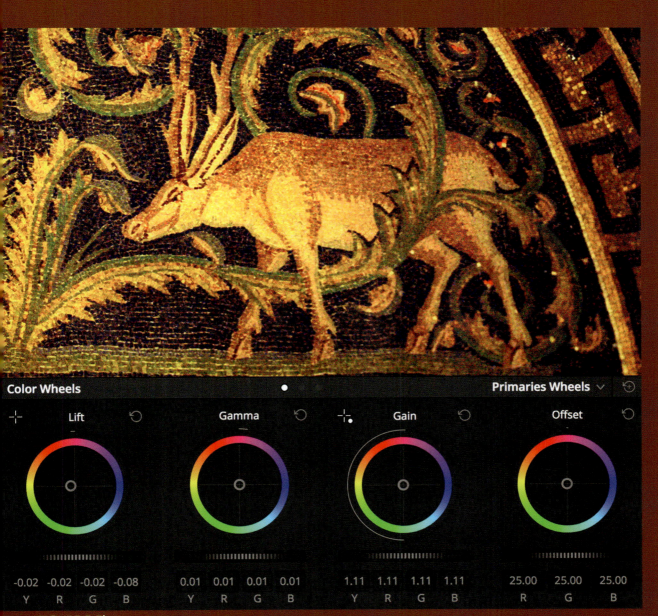

FIGURE 5.5b
As shown in 5a, top, there's too much blue in the shadows, so by dragging the Lift point towards red (*bottom*), the image (*top*) begins to balance out. Notice that minute changes go a long way. The wheel dials below the color wheels allow you to adjust luminance values, so you can make the shadows, midtones, and highlights brighter or darker. In this case, I lift the shadows. Numerical values are below the wheels, the Y represents the luminosity levels, and RGB for the red, green, and blue values. Shot of ancient mosaics from Revenna, Italy.
(Images courtesy of the author.)

Curves—allows you to adjust luminance values, shaping a linear line to a contrast curve, for example. You can also adjust specific colors by clicking on the curve to create a point and dragging it up or down. In this example, I pull down green in order to take out some green in the image.
(See Figure 5.6.)

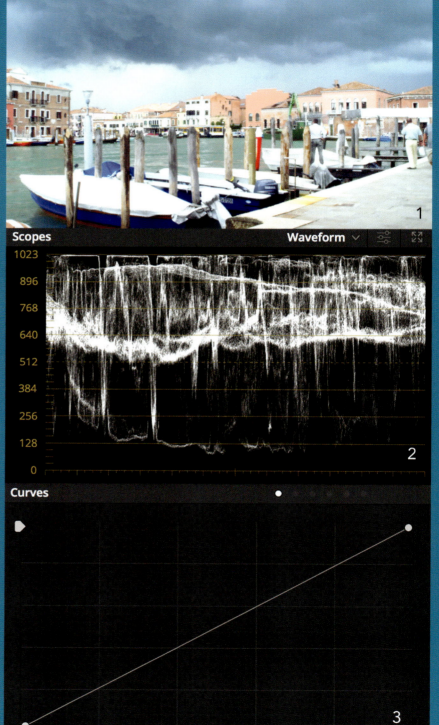

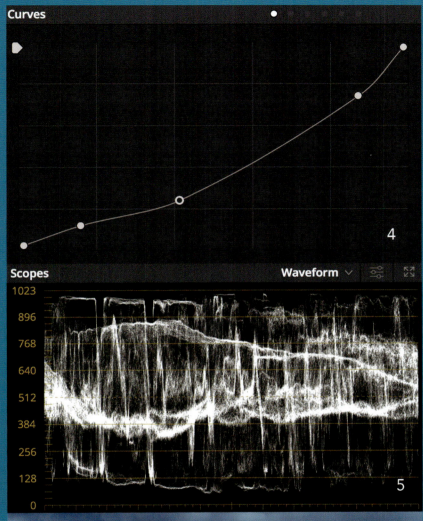

FIGURE 5.6
Here, we see an image that is a little over-exposed in the highlights (1). We can see the overexposure of the image in the highlights in the waveform monitor (2). A linear slope reveals no changes to the contrast curve (3). By adjusting the curve, adding contrast to the highlights and midtones (4), we see increased contrast (5), making the image much more dynamic (6). Shot in Murano, Italy.
(Images courtesy of the author.)

Red, green, and blue channels can also be isolated with curves, allowing you to pull down (or add) elements of these colors. (See Figure 5.7.)

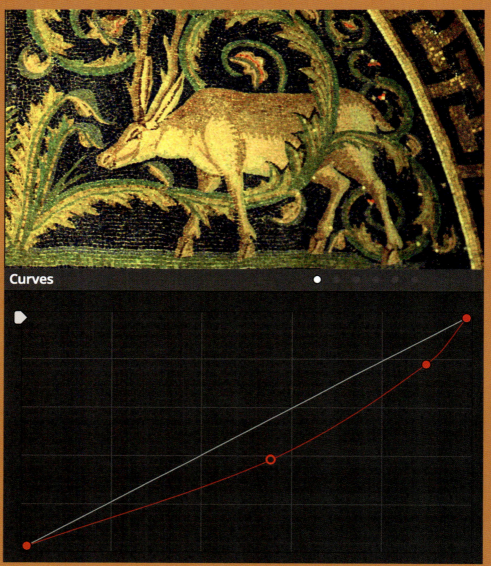

FIGURE 5.7
You can also use RGB curves and isolate one color, such as red and take out red highlights, if needed (*bottom*). Compare the image (*top*) to Figure 5.5 (p. 248) where it takes on a more reddish hue, while this image contains more green due to the red being pulled out of it.
(Images courtesy of the author.)

- **HSL Qualifier** (Hue, Saturation, Luminance)—using a picker, you can adjust specific elements of an image based on the color (hue), adjusting the saturation level of it (increasing or decreasing it), as well as the brightness values. This is an advanced secondary color tool, meaning you can target specific elements of the image to adjust. (See Figure 5.3, p. 245, for an example of a part of this in action.)

- **Windows and Tracker** (not shown)—another advanced secondary color tool that allows you to shape an area of the image and make adjustments either inside or outside of that shape. The trick involves images that move. The tracker tool maps the movement of the image, allowing the changes you've made to lock onto a moving image.

There are many more tools in Resolve and other color grading software. The intent of this section has been to provide an overview of how some of these tools can help shape the final look of an image. Each tool contains many more nuances and abilities that may be utilized to shape the look of a film. It is recommended that you learn how to use each of these tools so you can make grades to your own projects if you're working on a low-budget film. Otherwise, gain enough knowledge so that you can communicate effectively with a colorist. As can be seen in the example of Figures 5.5 (p. 248) and 5.7 (p. 252), most of these tools can be used in conjunction with each other, the color wheels taking the blue out of the image in 5.5, then isolating a red curve further allows a colorist to take out the reds from the midtones and highlights, resulting in the image in Figure 5.7.

LUTs

LUTs in post are often used as one of the final touches in color grading an image, shaping it in a creative way. Goran Ljubuncic, a filmmaker from Israel, discusses the LUT workflow on his blog site, Lutify.me. He advises filmmakers to follow these steps:

1. Normalize your footage as the very first step.
2. Once your footage is normalized, it's time to color correct it and balance it.
3. Applying a creative LUT is to be done only after we normalized our image and color corrected it
4. Last step would be secondary corrections (Ljubuncic, 2016)

Through this process, Ljubuncic feels that the best approach to utilizing a LUT involves making sure your footage is normalized first (such as putting it into a Rec. 709 LUT). Then once it's normalized, you can make the color and exposure accurate. At this point it'll be ready for a creative LUT, followed by secondary color correction adjustments, where you can target specific parts of the image in order to deliver the look you want. (See Figures 5.8–5.10, pp. 254–257.)

FIGURE 5.8
An image from a classroom exercise for night shooting with a C200 in RAW cinema mode with Canon Log 2 applied. Eric Carver, performer.
(Image courtesy of the author.)

WORKFLOW AND TOOLS FOR THE BEGINNING CINEMATOGRAPHER CHAPTER 5 255

FIGURE 5.9
This is the image after color correction. It looks great with the flat, milky wash removed, and a choice could be made that this is good to go with any LUT needed. On-set, the cinematography team approved this image as the look they were trying to get. What happens when the image is altered in post? (See the image on the next page.)
(Image courtesy of the author.)

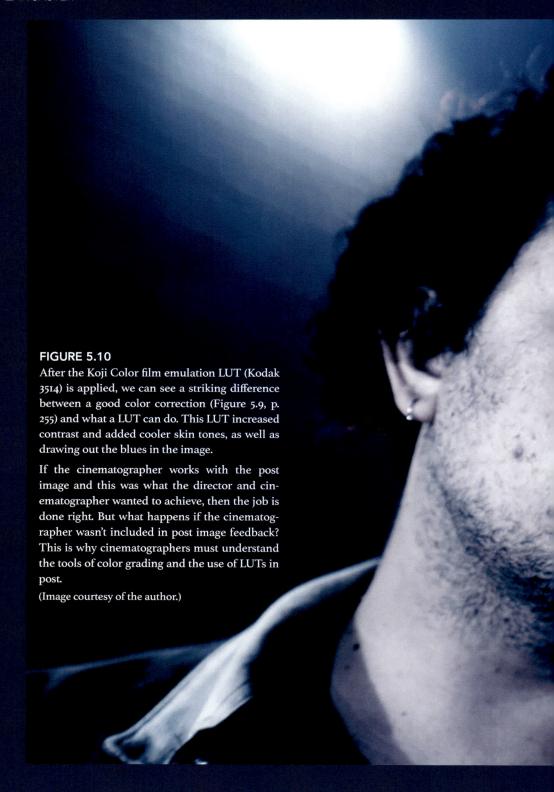

FIGURE 5.10
After the Koji Color film emulation LUT (Kodak 3514) is applied, we can see a striking difference between a good color correction (Figure 5.9, p. 255) and what a LUT can do. This LUT increased contrast and added cooler skin tones, as well as drawing out the blues in the image.

If the cinematographer works with the post image and this was what the director and cinematographer wanted to achieve, then the job is done right. But what happens if the cinematographer wasn't included in post image feedback? This is why cinematographers must understand the tools of color grading and the use of LUTs in post.

(Image courtesy of the author.)

Below, I provide a Color and Exposure Data Table to take notes during the shoot. This has nothing to do with ASC's CDL, but it will give beginning filmmakers the discipline to log their shots and use the log as a reference in post. Remember, once the ISO, f-stop, and shutter angle are set, they should remain the same throughout the scene—this will ensure exposure integrity across all the shots in the scene and save a lot of work in post correcting them. When a camera moves, the values of the scopes will change throughout a shot, of course, but a shot of the scope will provide a good reference during postproduction. Color space refers to the in-camera choice of recording in Rec. 709, Blackmagic Design Film, Canon Cinema Gamut, etc. The LUT refers to the monitor reference (such as Rec. 709 applied to a flat color space choice).

Color and Exposure Data Table							
Title:						Cinematographer:	
Scene/Shot #	ISO	f-stop	Shutter angle or speed	Color space	LUT	Exposure reference scope (waveform monitor, false color, or histogram image from camera)	

WORKS CITED

Benjamin B. "Colorist Peter Doyle—HDR, Vintage Workflows, Etiquette." Video. 31 March 2018. the film book. www.ascmag.com/blog/the-film-book/colorist-peter-doyle-video-about-hdr-film

—— "An Overview of the ASC CDL." *American Cinematographer*. Oct. 2008. www.theasc.com/ac_magazine/October2008/PostFocus/page1.html

Bertoli, Matteo. Personal interview with author. 2018.

Hurlbut, Shane, ASC. "The Importance of Camera Tests." Hurlbut Visuals. No date. www.thehurlblog.com/film-education-online-the-importance-of-camera-tests/

Ljubuncic, Goran. "Using LUTs? Here is What You Need to Know." Lutify.me. 2016. www.lutify.me/essential-steps-in-color-grading-when-using-luts

Misek, Richard. "The 'Look' and How to Keep It: Cinematography, Post-Oroduction and Digital Colour." *Screen*. 51.4. 2010: 404–409.

Murie, Michael. "Cinematographer Shane Hurlbut on The Illumination Experience and the Keys to the City." *Filmmaker*. 17 September 2014. www.filmmakermagazine.com/87575-cinematographer-shane-hurlbut-on-the-illumination-experience-and-the-keys-to-the-city

Stuart, Sophia. "Tough as Nails" *AGC Magazine*. January 2016: 38–48.

Still from Murano, Italy. courtesy of the author. Digital Bolex D16, 12-bit RAW.

Conclusion

I hope this book will take your filmmaking to the next level, advancing your career. That's why I wrote it. I wish I'd owned a book like this when I took my first filmmaking class. While I was earning my PhD at New York University, I took a 16mm immersive film course during six weeks in the summer. We used light meters, shot in black and white on Arriflex S cameras with 100 feet of 16mm film. And we had to make our shots and cut the film on a Steenbeck flatbed, delivering a story on two minutes of film. There was no time to tell an audience how to think or telegraph inner thoughts through surface dialogue.

You had to *show* the story with brevity and focus. The visual story had to be delivered in the shot and through the body language of the performers. I used storyboards, which forced me to make sure I got the shots needed to build the story. It was my first taste of visual storytelling. It's how I learned filmmaking and it contained the seed that would work its way into this book years later.

In many ways *Basic Cinematography* is designed to make better filmmakers—not just learning what it takes to be a cinematographer, but what it takes to be a good filmmaker, whether you're a director, producer, editor, sound designer, or cinematographer. The team effort revolves around good visual (and aural) storytelling. The underlying story forces found in a script—embedded as conceptual ideas—need to be turned into physical material in a frame that we can see and hear.

I've always tried to

eat food with respect,

An interview with Fabio Bascialla, creator of the restaurant, Altro? in Bologna, Italy. The cinematography was inspired by *Chef's Table*.

Documentary by Haydon Hoffman, Daniel Brown Muñoz, Kassandra Kraus, and Alejandrin Zubia. (Image courtesy of the author.)

This often requires a rethink. We are so saturated by media we assume we know how it works and how it gets made. But, as most of my film students can attest, it's a lot harder than it looks! And this is true whether you're making a documentary or a work of fiction. There's a reason film schools exist. You don't become a chemist or an astronomer through osmosis, just because you think it'll be cool to pick up a camera. You must take foundation classes, learn the basics, and advance to more complicated courses later on. Learning film may seem to be easy, but it takes the same level of dedication as mastering the sciences, or becoming a good artist, a musician, an engineer, architect, or a novelist. You must read, wrestle with ideas, and practice. Get feedback from those you trust (usually not from friends and family). Make your next work stronger.

How do you make better work? I see too many students flounder in filmmaking, because they've started with the camera rather than with the story. Or they've written a mediocre script derivative of bad Hollywood movies and then shot them in a mediocre way. Even worse, some who think they know what they're doing use dialogue to tell their story, thinking that's what makes a film. The way of the amateur. The easy path.

The harder path requires you to reach deep into your painful and beautiful experiences in life, and translate them into images that you can rewrite with your camera—into compelling images shaped by light and shadow, composition and lenses, capturing the natural behavior and subtext of people.

It's how the real magic happens. This book should supplement your technical knowledge and allow you to take the stories you want to tell—and make them in new and creative ways. Whether you place a wide angle lens on a close-up in order to make your audience feel a bit uncomfortable, because that's how the characters are feeling, or you put on a long lens from far away to capture a beautiful close-up that defines a storytelling moment, as the camera begins to move in order to reinforce, psychologically, that moment.

Film and television dramas are becoming more sophisticated in their use of visual language in revealing stories. Films that *tell* rather than *show* weaken and bore us, because there is no work left for our own imagination and we become insulted by the spoon-feeding. We want to *work* for the story. It makes us more intelligent, more sophisticated—and isn't that what we, too, want to be doing as filmmakers?

CONCLUSION

Use this book to remind yourself that you can go back to the roots of filmmaking and make intelligent, elegant films. Cameras have become more sophisticated, but have we as filmmakers? Are we staging and shooting at a level that reveals the inner motivations of characters, or are we just trying to make cool looking shots? Take a look at the work of Bruno Delbonnel, whose sophisticated work in *Amélie* (2001) and *The Darkest Hour* (2017) are master classes in cinematography, psychology of lenses, and staging. Look at how Manuel Billeter adapted the noir feel for *Jessica Jones* and added color and texture to create an atmosphere of a New York City that's never existed, but is always present as a visual mythology. If you want to master documentary cinematography in a contemporary way, examine closely the work of Adam Bricker, Will Basanta, Matthew Chavez, and Chloe Weaver on Netflix's *Chef's Table*. They write with a documentary camera like no one else I've seen.

I took a group of students to Bologna, Italy, for a couple of weeks in June, 2018. We studied *Chef's Table* and practiced shooting in their three styles (action, interview, and food preparation). For practice, the class shot me making cookies, then I had them shoot two exercises on their own. (These are experienced students having gone through two production classes and on post course, so they're not newbies.) I supervised their one-day shoots in Italy.

Although not perfect, they infused their work with the sensitivity of the cinematography from *Chef's Table*, utilizing elements of composition, lenses, lighting, color, and texture to tell their story at a fairly sophisticated level. The projects include:

- *Cremeria Santo Stefano* by Josh Feygin and Mari Elias: www.vimeo.com/288046655
- *Altro?* by Haydon Hoffman, Kassandra Kraus, Daniel Brown Muñoz, Alexi Parks, and Alejandrin Zubia: www.vimeo.com/290566387
- *Sfoglia Rina* by Ali Parks, Daniel Brown, and Kassandra Kraus: www.vimeo.com/309802475
- *Botanica Lab* by David Niehaus, Brian Kibbee, and Kyle Bagdonas. www.vimeo.com/288044012 https://vimeo.com/309802475

See stills from the Botanica Lab shoot over the next few pages. (Figures C.1–C.3, pp. 264–269.)

CONCLUSION 265

seeing my mother cook.

FIGURE C.1
An interview with Alejo Núñez Fernández, a chef from Botanica Lab in Bologna, Italy. The cinematography was inspired by *Chef's Table*.

Natural window light supplemented by a Dracast 160 LED and a reflector.

Documentary by David Niehaus, Brian Kibbee, and Kyle Bagdonas.

(Image courtesy of the author.)

FIGURE C.2
Action shot from Botanica Lab in Bologna, Italy. The cinematography was inspired by *Chef's Table*. Overhead natural light.
Shot on a Canon 5D Mark III Documentary by David Niehaus, Brian Kibbee, and Kyle Bagdonas.
(Image courtesy of the author.)

CONCLUSION 267

FIGURE C.3
Food shot from Botanica Lab in Bologna, Italy. The cinematography was inspired by *Chef's Table*. Overhead natural light supplemented by a Dracast 160 LED. Shot on a Canon 5D Mark III. Documentary by David Niehaus, Brian Kibbee, and Kyle Bagdonas.
(Image courtesy of the author.)

This is the type of work that can be produced when the principles of visual storytelling take priority in filmmaking. The language of cinematography is the same whether you're shooting fiction or documentary. Below are a few shots from a class exercise at Northern Arizona University. We don't have a sound stage, so we train our students to shoot on location.

In this location, outside a boiler plant on NAU's campus at night, we the instructors, myself and Anka Malatynska, set an adapted scene from *Blade Runner*. My goal was to help students understand how blocking conveys the visual story. Below was the segment of the script we used, altering it a bit to set it outdoors for the exercise (script by Hampton Fancher and David Peoples). (See Figure c.4.)

```
INT. APARTMENT--NIGHT

They come in, scared and exhausted. He goes to bar, pours
two drinks, hands her one. She watches him closely, does
what he does, clinging to him.

                    DECKARD
          Fuckin' skin job almost tore my
          head off.

She looks at him strangely. Skin job? Something occurs to
him.

                    DECKARD
          Where'd you learn to shoot like
          that?

                    RACHAEL
          Skin job?

He blanches.

                    DECKARD
          Ah ... replicant. It's a ...
          slang..term.

Offended, she turns as if to leave.

                    DECKARD
          It's safer in here. C'mon--whyn't
          you give me your coat?

He takes his off, and his gun, knife, etc., to show her it's
OK. She turns, lets him take her coat off.

                    DECKARD
          Got the shakes huh? I get those.
          Part of the business.

He walks her over to the sofa and sets her down.

                    RACHAEL
          I'm not in "the business." I am the
          business.

He goes to the bar, takes his shirt off, examines massive
bruise on his ribs.

                    RACHAEL
          If I ran away ... went up north.
          Would you come hunting?

He takes an ice pack from the freezer. Takes a couple
aspirin. Pokes around at his face, checks for loose teeth.

                    DECKARD
          No. Guess I owe you. But someone
          would.
```

FIGURE C.4 Original script segment from Blade Runner by Hampton Fancher and David Peoples. (Courtesy of the author.)

CONCLUSION

Student director, Kassandra Kraus, worked with Kelcie Weber and Eric Carver in blocking the scene. My stipulation entailed movement with intention. They're running and trying to hide. Rachael wants comfort, but she doesn't trust Deckard. He, however, wants to keep her safe. We were not trying to recreate the film, but to put our own interpretation on it, using the location. (The original is set indoors and we adapted it for outdoors for the sake of learning outdoor night shooting. A few lines were changed to make this adjustment.)

The next few images reveal how color temperature, blocking, lights, fog, and some hair were used as a creative tools in reinforcing the emotions of the scene. The scene was shot on a Canon C200 in RAW, wide dynamic range cinema mode. (See Figures C5–C8.)

FIGURE C.5
Behind the scenes photo of Deckard (Eric Carver) grabbing Rachael (Kelcie Weber) in rehearsal, showing the rehearsal process. The lighting and fog is accurate in the photograph, but the cinema shot with LUT and color applied is radically different, as seen on the next page. (Image courtesy of the author.)

FIGURE C.6
Screen grab of the shot as seen through the adjusted image from the Canon C200. We see the blocking, but now we see the Arri tungsten lights set on C-stands in the background (under the direction of the cinematography instructor, Anka Malatynska). The color balance is dialed in at 5200K, changing the look of the scene. Notice the blocking, as Deckard (Eric Carver)

CONCLUSION 273

pulls Rachael (Kelcie Weber) back to safety. As described in Chapter 1, actors do not stand around and talk. They must translate the subtext into actions based on a strong interpretive stance by the director. The lights, color, and fog reinforce the emotions of the story. (Image courtesy of the author.)

FIGURE C.7
Caillean Schmoll drops her hair in front of the lens of the Canon C200, as guided by cinematography instructor Anka Malatynska is in the foreground, out of focus. Jessica Duarte pulls focus as Ava Liu operates. The hair effect adds texture against the stabbing lights in the background of the shot.
(Image courtesy of the author.)

The choices in cinematography, here, reflects our interpretation of the story. The first step involved interpreting the script for this exercise, then working with the actors with the blocking. The blocking reflected Rachael's desire to pull away from Deckard due to her distrust of him, taking us to the end of the scene where she gains trust.

While rehearsal occurred, Malatynska worked with the camera and lighting crew to set up the first shot, a wide master as seen in Figure C.6 (p. 272–273). The lights stabbing through the fog in the background, along with the rotating red light, reflect the omnipresent eyes of the state and the harshness of the environment.

CONCLUSION

FIGURE C.8
Behind the scenes photo of Wuqiu "Eric" Fu on an Arri 650 with a red gel, used as a live rotating light during the scene. (Arri 650s in the background.) Performers Eric Carver and Kelcie Weber.
(Image courtesy of the author.)

The scene, missing a few shots, can be found at: www.vimeo.com/299739867.

Although not perfect, exercises like this and the documentary shorts described above, reveal how powerful cinematography can be carried out on a low budget. Similar scenes to those described here can be shot on inexpensive cameras using cheap hardware store lighting (along with some black wrap). High-end gear does not, on its own, make a good film.

By showing these student examples and class exercise, I want to prove that good cinematography, good filmmaking, involve the principles of visual storytelling. Which is what I hope this book has helped you to understand.

INDEX

Symbols

180 degree rule 84–5, 92
The 400 Blows 14–20

A

absolute camera motion 64
AJA DataCalc 274
Anima Abakr 42–3
Allen, Ben 212–13
Altro? 261–2
Amélie 263
American Zoetrope 140
aperture and ISO 144, 152–3
apps for filmmakers 234–5
    AJA DataCalc 234
    Artemis Director's Viewfinder 234
    Cine Meter II 234
    Digital Cinema Pocket Guides 234
    DSLR Slate 235
    Magic ViewFinder 234
    pCAM Film+Digital 235
    Shot Designer 234
    Sun Surveyor 234
Aristotle xiv
    Poetics 26–7
Arri lights 275
aspect ratio 56–7
Artemis Director's Viewfinder 234
audio quality 203–4

B

Bagdonas, Kyle 263–9
Basanta, Will 263
Bascialla, Fabio 261
Bayer pattern 211–12
Berkeley Media 92
Bertoli, Matteo 208–9, 238–9
Billeter, Manuel 95–8, 162–5, 263
Blackmagic RAW 214–15
Blade Runner 118, 124–5, 130–5, 138–9, 142, 148–9, 270–5
Blade Runner 2049 126, 127, 150–1
blocking
    classroom exercise example from Ozu's *Tokyo Twilight* 31–9
    definition of 1
    Stanislavski examples from *The Seagull* 8–13
body language 2–3, 5, 11, 13
    ex. *Girl with a Pearl Earring* 20–6
    in documentary 40–6
    Ozu's *Tokyo Twilight* 31–9
Botanica Lab 263–9
Bricker, Adam 98–101, 176–87, 263
Brown, Blain xv

Brown Muñoz, Daniel 261, 263
Butler, Richard 212

C

camera features 193
    lens mount 193
    Micro Four-Thirds (MFT) 195
    S35mm 195
    sensor size 194–7
        chart 197
        cropped frame 195
        full frame 194–5
    sensor type 193–4
    super 16mm 195
camera height and angle, emotional impact of 63, 227
camera motion, psychological impact of 64–6, 228–9
    hand-held 66
    jib 66
    pan 64
    parallel 65
    pull out (dolly) 65
    push in (dolly) 65
    tilt 65
    zoom 65
camera test 230
    exposure and dynamic range 230–1
    high contrast, test for extremes 231
    low light and low contrast 230
    postproduction 232
    set/location color test 231–2
Canon 5D Mark II 152–3
Canon 5D Mark III 267
Canon C100 Mark II 156–61
Canon C200 190, 271–5
Carver, Eric 215, 217, 271–3, 275
Casablanca 136–7
Chapman, Alister 210
Chavez, Matthew 263
Chef's Table 176–87, 261, 263–9
    case study in documentary lighting 176–87
    case study in lenses and composition 98–101
    "Dominique Crenn" episode 98–101
    "Francis Mallmann" episode 44–6, 48–9
Chekhov, Anton 5–12
characteristic curve features 207
chiaroscuro 70
chroma subsampling (4:4:4, 4:2:2, 4:2:0) 203

Cinematography: Theory and Practice xv
Cine Meter II 234
cinema vérité lighting 176–9
circadian rhythms
close-up shot 59
color 76–8
    colors convey emotions chart 77
    color gamut chart 201
color and exposure data table 258
color correction and grading tools 238–9
    color and exposure data table 258
    color wheels 248–9
    curves 250–2
    histogram 246–7
    HSL qualifier 253
    Look-up tables (LUTs) 253–8
    RGB parade 242–3
    vectorscope 244–5
    waveform monitor 239–41
    windows and tracker 253
Color Filter Arrays diagram 211
color temperature 123, 141–3
color wheels 248–9
Colors Convey Emotion chart 77
composition
    definition of 51; camera height and angle 61–3; Dutch angle 62; emotional impact of 63–5; front shot 62; high angle 61; level 62; low angle 62; rear shot 63; side or profile shot 62–3
    camera motion 64–6; absolute 64; motivated 64; relative 64; shaky 64
    color 76–8; Colors Conveys Emotion chart 77
    focal depth of field 66–9; deep focus 67; rack focus 67; shallow focus 67
    layers, in composition 73–4
    light and dark (chiaroscuro) 70
    lines and linear perspective 70–3
        psychological impact of 73
    shot sizes and lenses 56–61; close 59; medium 59; normal 58; objective 58; psychological impact of 225; subjective 58; wide 59
    texture 78–82; sharp 80; soft (*sfumato*) 79, 82
    weight 74–5
composition, lenses, shot list 223–9
compression and bit depth 202
contrast 123, 136-40
coverage 83

INDEX

Crazy/Beautiful 3
Cremeria Santo Stefano 263
Crenn, Dominique 98–101, 178–89
Crisis in Darfur Expands: Testimonials 42–3
The Crown 88–9
curves, color 250–2
cutaways 84

D

The Darkest Hour 263
da Vinci, Leonardo 79
DaVinci Resolve 214, 239–52
deep focus 67
Delbonnel, Bruno 263
Digital Cinema Pocket Guides 234
Dill, Bill 51, 88
documentary, lighting 176–87
dolly 65
dramatic action 26–31
Dramatic Analysis Chart 222
DSLR Slate 235
Duarte, Jessica 274
Dutch angle 62
dynamic range 199

E

edit, shooting for
    180 degree rule 85
    coverage 83
    cutaways 84
    eye lines 83
    jump cuts 86
    Kuleshov Effect 88–92
    point of view 84
Elias, Mari 263
emotional distance in shot sizes 225
emotional impact of camera height and angle 227
eye lines 83
exposure 144–155
    aperture and ISO 144, 152–3; Preston example 152–3
    histogram 144, 148–9; *Blade Runner* example 148–9
    lighting modifiers 144, 155–61; *Fragments* example 156–61
    ND filters 144, 154
    shutter angle and frame rate 144, 154–5
    waveform 144, 150–1; ex. *Blade Runner 2049* 150–1; ex. *Blade Runner* 150–1
    zone system 144–7; ex. *Tokyo Twilight* 146–7

F

Fancher, Hampton 270
Feygin, Josh 263
focal depth of field 66–9
Fox, Travis 42–3
Fragments 156–61
frame rate 200
Frank, Scott 54
front shot 62
Fu, Wuqiu (Eric) 275

G

Gelb, David 176–87
Girl with a Pearl Earring 20–6
    "pure cinema" 20
Godless 54–63, 67–82
Grimshaw, Anna and Ravetz, Amanda 43–4

H

hand-held shot 66
"hard" lighting 123–5
high angle 61
histogram 246–7
Hitchcock, Alfred 2
    rules of "pure cinema" film-making 14–20
Hoffman, Haydon 261, 263
HSL qualifier 253
Hurlbut, Shane 3, 4, 200, 222, 230
    definition of blocking 4

J

Jessica Jones 83–4, 87, 263
    case study in lenses and composition 95–8
    outdoor night lighting case study 162–5
jib 66
Joe Simon 156–61
Johnson, Kirsten 40
Jules and Jim 14
jump cuts 86

K

Khramov, Mikayla 104–15
Kibbee, Brian 263–9
Kodak 257
Koji Color 257
Kraus, Kassandra 261, 263, 271
Kuleshov effect 88–92
Kuleshov, Lev 88

L

Lang, Fritz 6
Lang, Sean 104–15
Late Spring 84
layers, in composition 73–4
Left Bank Pictures 89
lens mount 193
lenses and composition
    examples
        Chef's Table "Dominique Crenn" 98–101
        Jessica Jones 95–7
        Tokyo Twilight 102–15; script analysis 102–3
lenses, psychological impact of 58–61
level shot 62
light and dark (chiaroscuro) 70
lighting 191–205
    color temperature 123, 141–3
    contrast, definition and uses (high contrast) 123, 136; ex. *Blade Runner* 138–39; ex. *Casablanca* 136–37
    contrast, definition and uses (low contrast) 123, 140; ex. *THX 1138* 140
    direction; definition and uses 122, 128–9; back 128; ex. *Blade Runner* 125; background 128; ex. *Blade Runner* 126; front 128; ex. *Blade Runner* 130–31; height 129; side 128; ex. *Blade Runner* 125
    documentary lighting 176–87
    examples of lighting: *Chef's Table* "Adrienne Crenn"; blocking and camera placement 176–7; food symphony (product lighting) 182–5; interview lighting 178–81; outdoor cinematography tip, DP Adam Bricker 187; *vérité* lighting 176–9; visual rules 176–7; "Fragments" indoor and outdoor day 156–61; *Jessica Jones* outdoor night 162–5; *Tokyo Twilight* indoor night 166–75; script analysis 166–9; lighting analysis 170–5
    intensity (low and high) 122, 126–7
        definition and uses 126
        ex. *Blade Runner 2049* 126–7
    modifiers 144, 155–61
    placement: back and rim light 122; background light 122; fill light 122; key light 122

INDEX 279

psychology of 120
quality: definition and uses 122–5; ex. *Blade Runner* (hard) 124; ex. *Blade Runner* (soft) 125
ratios 141
texture 123, 129–35; definition and uses 129; ex. *Blade Runner* 130–5
white balance 143
linear vs. log charts 205–6
lines and linear perspective 70–3
Liu, Ava 274
Log, shooting in 205–11
    characteristic curve features 207
    expose to avoid shadow noise 208
    linear vs. log charts 205–6
    what is it? 205–7
    when not to shoot log 210
    when to shoot log 208
    when to shoot Rec. 709 and Rec. 2020 210–211
Look-up tables (LUTs), shooting with 216–18
low angle 62

M

MacDougall, David 41–2, 44, 90–3
Mackendrick, Alexander 15, 17, 18, 25, 27, 35
Magic ViewFinder 234
Malatynska, Anka 270, 272, 274
Mallmann, Francis xii–xxv, 44–9
Marvel Studios 83–4, 87, 95–8
Massachusetts Institute of Technology (MIT) xiv–xv
Matteo Bertoli Visuals 209
McHugh, Sean 211
medium shot 59
Meizler, Steven 54
Metropolis 6
A Midsummer Night's Dream xiv–xv
Mikotowicz, Tom xiv
Misek, Richard 76, 236
Micro Four-Thirds (MFT) 195
modifiers, lighting 144, 155–61
Mona Lisa 79
motivated camera motion 64

N

naturalistic acting 2
ND filters 144, 154
Netflix 44–9, 54, 57, 67–75, 80, 82–4, 87–8, 95–101, 162–5, 176–87
New York University xiv
Niehaus, David 263–9

normal shot 58
Northern Arizona University xiv
Núñez Fernández, Alejo 265

O

objective shot 58
observational cinema 41
Ozu, Yasujiro 28, 84, 102, 166

P

pan 64
Parks, Ali 263
pCam Film+Digital 235
Peoples, David 270
Poetics xiv, 26–7
point of view 84
postproduction for cinematographers
    role of the cinematographer 236–8
preproduction planning for cinematographers
    composition, lenses, shot list 223–9
    emotional distance in shot sizes 225
    emotional impact of camera height and angle 227
    psychological impact of camera movement 228–9
    psychological impact of lenses 225–7
    scene composition 224–5
    script analysis 221–2
production for cinematographers 235–6
profile shot 62–3
ProRes RAW 213
psychological impact of camera movement 64–6, 228–9
psychological impact of lenses 60–1, 225–7
psychology of lenses 60–1, 225–7
pull out (dolly) 65
pure cinema 2, 14–20
push in (dolly) 65

R

rack focus 67
RAW, shooting in 211–15
    Blackmagic RAW 214–15
    Color Filter Arrays diagram 211
    ProRes RAW 213
    what is it? 211–14
    when not to shoot in RAW 215
    when to shoot in RAW 214

REC. 709 191, 201, 210, 211, 215, 216
rear shot 63
relative camera motion 64
resolution 198–9
RGB parade 242–3
Rhodes, Phil 205–6

S

S35mm 195
Schechner, Richard xiv
scene composition 224–5
Schmoll, Caillean 274
The Seagull 5–6, 8–13
sensor
    chart 197
    size 194–7
    type 193–4
Sfoglia Rina 263
sfumato (soft texture) 79, 82
Shakespeare xiv–xv
shaky camera motion 64
shallow focus (depth of field) 67
sharp texture 80
Shot Designer 234
shot sizes and emotional distance 59, 225
shot sizes and lenses 56–61
shutter angle and frame rate 144, 154–5, 200
side or profile shot 62–3
soft lighting 123–4
soft texture (sfumato) 79, 82
Stanislavski, Konstantin 1–2, 5–6, 8–13, 34
Stockwell, John 3
Strangers on a Train 2, 16
subjective shot 58
subtext
    definition of 1, 15, 41–2
    examples
        The 400 Blows 18–19
        documentary work 40–6
        Girl with a Pearl Earring 20–6
        The Seagull 8–13
        Strangers on a Train 16–17
        Tokyo Twilight 31–9
Sun Surveyor 234
super 16mm 195

T

Tarkovsky, Andre 11, 13, 18, 35
technical scout form 232–3
ten tools of composition 53
texture, in composition 78–82
texture, in lighting 129–35
THX 1138 140

INDEX

tilt shot 65
Tokyo Twilight 28–40, 102–16
    case study in lenses and composition 102–16
    dramatic action 26–31
    indoor night lighting, class project 166–75
    subtext through blocking and body language 31–40
To Live with Herds 92–3
Truffaut, François 14–20, 27, 35, 42, 43, 46

U

University of Maine xiv

V

vectorscope 244–5

Vérité lighting 176–9

weight, compositional 74–5
wide shot 59
Warner Bros. 16, 118, 124-27, 131, 133, 135–40, 149–51
waveform monitor 144, 150–1
Weaver, Chloe 263
Weber, Kelcie 217, 271–3, 275
weight 74–5
windows and tracker 253

Z

Zeiss 152–3
Zsigmond, Vilmos 120
zone system 144–7
zoom shot 65
Zubia, Alejandrin 261, 263